Key Concepts in
Leadership

Recent volumes include:

Key Concepts in Sport and Exercise Research Methods
Michael Atkinson

Key Concepts in Media and Communications
Paul Jones and David Holmes

Key Concepts in Sport Psychology
John M. D. Kremer, Aidan Moran, Graham Walker, and Cathy Craig

Key Concepts in Tourist Studies
Melanie Smith, Nicola Macleod and Margaret Hart Robinson

Key Concepts in Leisure Studies
David Harris

Key Concepts in Mental Health (Second Edition)
David Pilgrim

The SAGE Key Concepts series provides students with accessible and authoritative knowledge of the essential topics in a variety of disciplines. Cross-referenced throughout, the format encourages critical evaluation through understanding. Written by experienced and respected academics, the books are indispensable study aids and guides to comprehension.

Key Concepts in
Leadership

JONATHAN GOSLING, STEPHANIE JONES
AND IAN SUTHERLAND with JOOST DIJKSTRA

Los Angeles | London | New Delhi
Singapore | Washington DC

Los Angeles | London | New Delhi
Singapore | Washington DC

SAGE Publications Ltd
1 Oliver's Yard
55 City Road
London EC1Y 1SP

SAGE Publications Inc.
2455 Teller Road
Thousand Oaks, California 91320

SAGE Publications India Pvt Ltd
B 1/I 1 Mohan Cooperative Industrial Area
Mathura Road
New Delhi 110 044

SAGE Publications Asia-Pacific Pte Ltd
3 Church Street
#10-04 Samsung Hub
Singapore 049483

Editor: Chris Rojek
Editorial assistant: Martine Jonsrud
Production editor: Katherine Haw
Copyeditor: Neil Dowden
Proofreader: Audrey Scriven
Indexer: Bill Farrington
Marketing manager: Alison Borg
Cover design: Wendy Scott
Typeset by: C&M Digitals (P) Ltd, Chennai, India
Printed by: CPI Group (UK) Ltd,
Croydon, CR0 4YY

Library of Congress Control Number: 2012932162

British Library Cataloguing in Publication data

A catalogue record for this book is available from
the British Library

ISBN 978-1-84920-588-7
ISBN 978-1-84920-589-4 (pbk)

Jonathan Gosling – to SJ, with thanks and admiration

Stephanie Jones – to CCW, with love

Ian Sutherland – to JK, with thanks and understanding

Joost Dijkstra – to Margot, for a better understanding of her business life

contents

contents

key concepts in
leadership

tables

tables

about the authors

Jonathan Gosling is Professor for Leadership at the Centre for Leadership Studies, University of Exeter, UK. He teaches and consults world-wide, and his many articles and books have been influential in both the study and practice of leadership. He is currently attempting to radically improve the management pipeline by launching the One Planet MBA.

Stephanie Jones, PhD, is Associate Professor of Organizational Behaviour at Maastricht School of Management, the Netherlands. She teaches leadership on the MSM MBA programme in Africa, China, Vietnam, Kazakhstan, Peru and many other locations. She is also a prolific author in the field, and is particularly interested in researching leadership in emerging markets – an area of the world where it would appear to be in great demand.

Ian Sutherland, PhD, is an Assistant Professor and Director of PhD Studies at the IEDC-Bled School of Management, Slovenia. Originally from Newfoundland, Canada, he is a cultural sociologist whose research, publications and teaching focus on creative processes, cultural leadership, and the arts in leadership development and practice.

Joost Dijkstra is CEO, World Trade Centre Aachen and a partner at NASH Consulting in Maastricht, The Netherlands, where his core activity is in creating value for mid-sized privately owned businesses. He is also a guest lecturer at Maastricht School of Management in Leadership, Change Management and Organizational Design. Before this, he was a General Manager of Intersport Netherlands and Director of International Marketing and Managing Director of the private-equity-owned packaging firm Ranpak.

acknowledgements

Parts of the chapter on leadership definitions and theories are based on an extract from J. Remme, S. Jones, B. van der Heijden and S. de Bono (2007) *Leadership, Change and Responsibility*. Oxford: Meyer & Meyer. This material is included here with permission from the publishers.

Parts of the introduction to entries 1, 4 and 12 are based on an extract from S. de Bono, S. Jones and B. van der Heijden (2008) *Managing Cultural Diversity*. Oxford: Meyer & Meyer. This material is included here with permission from the publishers.

Parts of entries 17, 19 and 25 are based on extracts from S. Jones (2010) *Psychological Testing*. Petersfield: Harriman House. This material is included here with permission from the publishers.

Different versions of some material (on Quiet Leadership and Toxic Leadership) have appeared in *Leadership Matters*, a regular publication of the Centre for Leadership Studies, University of Exeter, UK.

Parts of entries 3, 5, 8, 18, 22, 23, 27 and 31 include many references to S. Jones and J. Gosling (2005) *Nelson's Way: leadership lessons from the great commander*. London: Nicholas Brealey. Readers are referred to this book for further insights.

Parts of entries 2, 7, 21, 26 and 29 include many references to J. Gosling and H. Minzberg (2003) 'The Five Minds of the Manager', *Harvard Business Review*, November. Readers are referred to this article for further insights.

how to use this book

This book is designed to help you, the reader, to identify and consider the range of leadership styles, approaches and situations you might use to describe yourself and others. It explores the potential strengths and weaknesses associated with each leadership mode or preference, presented in a uniquely didactic way. The evolution and development of the field of leadership styles is outlined in the detailed introduction which follows.

Have you ever been accused of being authoritative, opportunistic or toxic as a leader? Is this bad? What does this really mean, and what are the implications? How about if you are praised for being purposive, ethical and reflective? Is this good? Again, what do these terms mean? To a certain extent these are explained by studying the history of leadership terms, but we need practical examples to help bring them to life.

Imagine you are being recruited for a leadership role. You are asked to describe the kind of leader you think you are, and the strengths and weaknesses of your approach. You may be reflecting on this very issue as you prepare for a new job or promotion interview. Is your leadership approach helping or hindering your career? Or, you are reporting to your boss, trying to describe your colleagues and management team in an accurate and detailed way. You are asked what kind of leaders you need for the future, given changing situations and tasks. These leaders might be recruited from outside or developed from within, but a leadership 'specification' with a detailed list of competencies and preferences is needed. Meanwhile, after this meeting with the big boss, you are trying to explain to your team what kind of leader you report to, and his or her priorities. Or you might be advising a client. Or you are discussing the attributes of a new political leader with friends in a social setting.

Whatever the scenario, you need words, definitions – a leadership vocabulary. So, you hunt through the index and the alphabetical listing of the entries in this book for ideas and inspiration, and check through the definitions and examples to either accept or reject the chosen terminology and descriptors, using the cross-referencing provided. Armed with more insights, you can feel more informed and confident.

The entries in this book look at a variety of leadership constructs, each with a balance or continuum of alternatives inviting debate and comparison, but not judging any as intrinsically 'good' or 'bad'. Each approach may be appropriate for different circumstances, jobs, tasks and organizational cultures. It's a question of 'horses for courses'. These descriptions of leadership can be used to help clarify the situations when different approaches may be appropriate. None are totally negative or totally positive – they all have their uses.

These leadership options can be expressed as extremes or sometimes as a continuum, and depend on personality, behaviour preferences, competencies and contexts. They can be intentional or involuntary, permanent or temporary.

Each entry defines a leadership concept and explains the balances, debates and options involved, considering leadership as a range of action possibilities. The entries provide detailed practical examples of leaders exhibiting these behaviours, considering the impact and implications, with reflective conclusions. The reader can easily identify his or her own style and approach, especially with feedback from colleagues, and select leadership approaches to which he or she might aspire or avoid. The entries can also be used to identify the leadership characteristics of others, especially in terms of those desired or to be avoided.

The criterion for inclusion of an entry was the existence of a distinct leadership approach with a clear opposite, both of which could be appropriate for a leadership situation. This dialectical approach adds value by going beyond claims that there is 'one best way to lead', recognizing instead the special mix that suits each situation.

While describing a way of leading, each entry also implies different ways of dealing with people and objectives. It provides models for describing leadership as an aspect of organizational cultures as well as an accurate, defined terminology for leader recruitment and development. We help you to frame answers to questions such as: What kind of leadership is going on here? Does this fit the situation or could it be more appropriate? When reading the descriptors listed here, remember they are not mutually exclusive, and it may be helpful to apply several to your analysis of an individual leader, organization or project.

The format for each entry includes a definition, an assessment of the value of the approach when applied to specific situations and an introduction to the 'voices', the practical examples of both sides of the particular leadership dialectic, with concluding remarks and suggestions for further reading.

We have chosen to list the concepts in alphabetical order to avoid bias – one approach is *not* inherently better than another. We value personal authenticity, integrity and situational sensitivity in leadership above any leadership panacea.

The 'voices' used in many of the examples (where not quoted from secondary sources) are based on the long and varied experiences of the four authors in teaching, training, consulting and leading, totalling over a hundred years combined – and their contacts and associates. The geographical spread of their experience includes North America, the United Kingdom, Europe, North Africa, Western Asia, South Asia and the Pacific Rim, and a variety of emerging markets.

introduction

Before we start looking at the 'Key Concepts' below, we discuss the origins and definitions of leadership theories and philosophies, and suggest that leadership theory also needs to take into account leadership practice. This is where the leadership debates – or dilemmas as we have posed them in this volume – come in. And we think that these debates, dilemmas and questions will open the study of leadership to an appreciation of the countervailing forces that give rise to so much diversity in the practice and experience of leadership.

As we will see in our entries discussing the key concepts of leadership, there is no one-dimensional view of leadership. We have approached the subject as a series of ongoing dialogues, continuing discussions, and sharing of impressions and insights – which we have tried to show here, with reflections by observers and practitioners. We have tried not to make judgements about 'good' or 'bad' practice, but have emphasized the diversity of styles, approaches and views found in everyday leadership scenarios in many different situations.

How can we analyse and synthesize these wide-ranging leadership perspectives? We could look at them first in *leadership motives*, *styles* and *attitudes*: why an individual might want to be a leader in the first place. A leader may pride himself or herself on expert knowledge of a particular sector, field or discipline of leadership, different from being a generalist leader, able to lead in any context. And there's the leader who is always visible, out in front, clearly seen by all, rather than behind the scenes. There is also the leader who balances his or her job and private life, keeping the latter very private and enjoying both public and private identities, compared with being extremely focused and passionate. Other leaders encourage others to participate, compared with one who favours the more authoritative approach of taking the lead in a more singular way and making individual decisions. There are also the debates about being predominantly a leader or a manager – whatever those differences mean in a particular context; and being inspirational, or pedestrian and ordinary. For many, it is OK just to focus on trying to do the job of a leader now, rather than thinking about leadership legacies.

How about analysing leadership in terms of the leader's *mindsets*? The way a leader thinks about and tackles the predicaments he or she faces include being reflective, thinking through why they might do their work in a certain way, and what they might do to keep on improving. But many operate in a knee-jerk way, doing what needs to be done and worrying about it later. Others analyse everything in detail, seeking explanations of structures and systems. Some operate in a much more unstructured way, focusing on maximizing the benefits of immediate opportunities. As business becomes more global, some leaders pride themselves on their worldly perspectives, seeking an understanding of the range of differences wherever they go. Other leaders look for commonalities and convergence. They see similar needs and demands by customers and business partners the world over.

Many leaders build relationships with their staff members, collaborating and sharing, whereas others are more distant and aloof. Their mindset might be that 'these people work for me – so I need to get value out of them!' Many leaders focus on action and continual change; others are more comfortable with continuity and preserving the benefits accrued in an organization's history.

Another, further way of considering leadership dilemmas is through reactions to *conflict*. What happens if a leader is highly competitive, or, by contrast, accommodating? How about compromising compared with more collaborative or co-operative behaviours? Leaders can also be high or low on taking a stance on avoiding – they will try to minimize stirring up trouble and also empower people, or they will get involved in everything.

Further leadership options may be determined by *leader personality* and *behaviour* differences. A leader may place a higher priority on the importance of emotional quotient (EQ), or might be more disposed towards the expert knowledge and intelligence quotient (IQ) in himself or herself and others. Some leaders behave as Shapers, with associated preferences for being Coordinators, Monitor-Evaluators and Resource Investigators. By contrast, other leaders see the Implementer preference as their main determinant of behaviour, and might also be Specialists and Completer-Finishers. Other leaders – less typically – prefer to operate as Teamworkers, keeping everyone happy, or as Plants, supplying creative and innovative ideas. A leader might also exhibit an extrovert personality, but many are introverted by nature. These factors can have an impact on leadership choices.

Leaders can also vary in the choices they make in terms of the approach to *leadership development* that they may have experienced – or the leader development strategies they are themselves implementing. Mentoring processes and being coached as a leader are popular among some – but many leaders believe that a more directive and getting-on-with-it, being-told-what-to-do style of leadership training can be just as effective. Some leaders are developed and nurtured by a single organization, which provides them with career building and training – others train themselves and take responsibility for their own development by switching jobs and gaining insights into leadership by a multiplicity of practical experience. Some leaders believe they can create and develop their own leadership brand, separate and independent from the brand of the organization where they work. Other leaders think their personal brand should reflect where they work now – but this can and will change as they change organizations, based on personal developmental experience.

Leadership options are very often determined by leader experiences in specific management and *leadership functions* – such as the polar opposites of finance and marketing (saving or spending money), or through the human resources (HR) as opposed to production routes. This functional background tends to colour the leader's view of leadership and influence his or her style of operating, and can give the leader a limited view. So an obvious area for leader preference is broad-based or functional, silo-based approaches.

A final dichotomy in ways of leading analysed in this book looks at *leadership practice*, such as questioning if project management represents a unique approach to leadership. If leadership tasks are seen project by project, in what ways is this different from a more continuous and uninterrupted view of a leader in a more long-term situation? And the difference comparing 'interim' or 'temp' leaders on short-term, specialist contracts working in highly specific organizational situations, compared with permanent appointees. How different is the job of leading volunteers, from that of leading paid employees? Increasingly, leaders are under pressure to take into account ethical and corporate social responsibility (CSR) considerations – but they still need to be pragmatic and practical to run a business. The need to promote diversity in leadership is often discussed; the challenging task of managing and leading celebrities, prima donnas and big egos is another issue. Then there is the matter of what happens when the leadership environment is no longer healthy and becomes toxic. And many leaders are impacted by their national culture, especially the difference between East and West.

These debates will continue, and new debates will emerge, whilst some old debates may no longer seem worth arguing about. Questions are likely to be based around leadership styles, attitudes, approaches; leader mindsets; leader responses to conflict; leader personality and behaviour preferences; the way that leaders have been developed; the functional roots of individual leaders; and the realities of leadership practice. New questions will emerge, based on other areas of leader involvement, especially in terms of follower reactions and situational demands. But as long as people and organizations see the need for leadership, the debates will carry on, and are unlikely to ever reach a final conclusion!

As you will see, this book is based on a dialectical approach to key concepts to leadership. Throughout we present many exaggerated examples to illuminate these key concepts. In the end, leadership is still about context and situation – about finding the best means of leading in different times, places and within different organizational structures and populations. Above all, leaders need to operate out of sensitivity to these issues and to act in ways which navigate the dynamics of working with others. As a final key concept for leadership, leaders should remember that their work is ultimately about working with others to create environments where all can develop and achieve.

leadership definition, theory and practice

What is leadership? Who are leaders? What do leaders do? These are some of the most fundamental questions of Leadership Studies. Like all fundamental questions, they defy clear-cut answers. Each opens a universe of challenging, complex, dynamic debate and practice. Far from solving fundamental leadership questions, the study of leadership has compounded the complexity but in a way which provides increasingly sophisticated and sensitive ways of understanding leadership as part of situations of collective activity in group and organizational contexts. Before we turn to the dialectics of specific leadership styles it is useful to briefly review the historical trajectory of leadership studies to lay the foundation for entering the muddy waters of leadership practice.

An early – and persistent – approach to viewing leadership has been to point to the achievements of great leaders, and to explain leadership as the effect of their actions and behaviours. This has become known as the 'great man' theory, because that's how history was taught for many years: a saga of the exploits of (mainly male and often military) leaders: Alexander the Great, Julius Caesar, Admiral Lord Nelson, George Washington. These are some of the classics, now joined by more peaceable figures such as Mahatma Gandhi, Martin Luther King and Nelson Mandela. But what is it about these people that makes them able to be 'great'? Did they have leadership qualities that can be discovered or developed in other people? How about the task of developing leadership in women as well as men? In other words, is leadership an essential quality of the individual person, or are there also cultural and political forces that determine who does or does not get a chance to lead, or whose leadership gets noticed?

So if we want to understand leadership in the real world, should we be looking more deeply at individual personalities, at group dynamics, or at social forces? In fact, leadership studies have progressed on all fronts. From 'great man' theories, we have moved to an exploration of leadership traits or characteristics, studied their behaviours and the situations in which they are more or less successful, and then contingency theories. The more recent development of transactional and transformational leadership theories reiterates a consistent theme: the special relationship that exists between groups and their leaders, and the peculiar impact of the leader.

The earliest leadership theories tend to focus on the characteristics and behaviours of singular, successful leaders. Current leadership studies have come to focus on the role of followers and group processes, the contextual nature of leadership, and the relationships between leadership and management. Other contemporary theories look at leadership as a dynamic process involving many individuals rather than seeing leadership emanating solely from a single person, and include perspectives on 'distributed leadership', 'quiet leadership', 'soft leadership', 'authentic leadership', 'aesthetic leadership', 'narcissistic leadership', 'spiritual leadership' and 'toxic leadership'. Modern leadership studies view leadership as a dynamic, subtle, nuanced process emerging from the actions of groups of people – leaders and followers alike – working together to achieve common goals, in group and inter-group relationships. Some also point to the contrast between 'formal' and 'informal' leadership, with its connotations of authority and participation (House and Baetz, 1979). (See the summary in Table 1).

Table 1   Summary of popular leadership theories over time

Great Man Theories	Based on the belief that leaders are exceptional people, born with innate qualities, destined to lead. The use of the term 'man' was an unquestioned assumption until the late twentieth century, as leadership was primarily male and usually military. Few people bothered to look for examples of leadership outside these categories.
Trait Theories	Trait theories studied successful leaders and moments of leadership to identify traits or qualities which appeared essential to leadership practice. These included adjectives describing mostly positive human behaviours, from A for ambition to Z for zest for life. Maturity, confidence, breadth of interest, intelligence and honesty were qualities common across much of the trait theory research. Traits were seen as characteristics of the person. More recently, interest has shifted towards descriptions of what people can actually do, regardless of personality. Thus traits are often referred to as *competencies*.
Behaviourist Theories	These theories, still regarded as currently useful, concentrate on what leaders actually do rather than on their qualities or characteristics. Different patterns of behaviour are observed and categorized as 'styles of leadership', which are then discussed by practicing managers in the field. Some of these 'styles' include charismatic leadership, servant leadership and quiet leadership.
Situational Leadership	This approach (also still widely popular) sees leadership behaviour as determined by the situation in which leadership is being exercised. Some situations may require an autocratic style; others may need a more participative approach. It also suggests that there may be differences in required leadership styles at different levels in the same organization, depending on follower readiness.
Contingency Theory	This is a refined version of the situational view, focusing on identifying the situational variables (contingencies) which best predict the most appropriate or effective leadership style to fit particular circumstances.
Transactional Theory	This approach emphasizes the importance of the relationship between leaders and followers, focusing on the mutual benefits derived from a form of 'contract' through which the leader delivers rewards or recognition in return for the commitment, loyalty and efforts of the followers.
Transformational Theory	The central concept here is of follower change, and the role of leadership in transforming the performance of his or her followers, through influences which impact on their growth and personal development. Transactional and transformational leaders are frequently contrasted but they are not mutually exclusive.

Source: Remme et al., 2008

Most of these theories (summarized in general terms above from several sources) take a rather individualistic perspective of the leader, although a school of thought gaining increasing recognition is that of 'dispersed' or 'distributed' leadership, sharing the leadership function throughout a team. This approach, with its foundations in sociology, psychology and politics rather than management science, views leadership as a process that is diffuse throughout an organization rather than located solely within a formally designated 'leader'. The emphasis thus shifts from developing 'leaders' to developing 'leaderful' organizations with a collective responsibility for leadership. (See Bolden, 2011, for a comprehensive review.)

Below, we look at how theories of leadership have evolved, suggesting the development of different philosophies of leadership reflecting the thinking of different eras.

THE TRAIT APPROACH TO LEADERSHIP

As we have seen, the trait approach arose along with the 'Great Man' theory as a way of identifying the key characteristics of successful leaders. The aim is to isolate and identify crucial leadership traits, so that people with such traits could be recruited, selected and installed into leadership positions. This approach was common in the military and is still often used as a set of criteria to select candidates for commissions. The problem with the trait approach lies in the fact that there is no agreement about what these traits are – countless research projects have identified almost as many traits as studies undertaken. Although there has been no overall consistency in the results of the various trait studies, certain traits appear more frequently than others including: technical skill, friendliness, task motivation, application to task, group task supportiveness, social skills, emotional control, administrative skills, general charisma and intelligence. Of these, the most widely explored – and hardest to define and measure – has tended to be 'charisma'. Table 2 lists the main leadership traits and skills identified by Stogdill in 1974.

THE BEHAVIOURAL SCHOOL

As can be imagined, the results of trait studies were inconclusive, subjective and ambiguous. Traits are hard to measure. How, for example, do we measure traits such as honesty, integrity, loyalty or diligence? Traits are also hard to define. How, for example, how do we define 'self-confident' or 'socially skilled' in any practical sense? Additionally, each trait has positive and negative potential. In one situation, a leader who is being dominant (in influencing others) may be effective in providing a clear direction and mobilizing a team. However, in another situation such a leader may be seen as arrogant and overbearing, resulting in refusals to follow. Another approach to the study of leadership and the identification of leaders had to be found.

McGregor's Theory X and Theory Y Managers

The behavioural theories concentrate on what leaders actually do rather than on elusive 'inherent' qualities. Different patterns of behaviour have been observed and categorized as 'styles of leadership'. After the publication of Douglas McGregor's

Table 2 Leadership traits and skills

Traits	Skills
Adaptable to situations	Clever (intelligent)
Alert to social environment	Conceptually skilled
Ambitious/achievement oriented	Creative
Assertive	Diplomatic and tactful
Cooperative	Fluent in speaking
Decisive	Knowledgeable about group task
Dependable	Organized (administrative ability)
Dominant (in influencing others)	Persuasive
Energetic (high activity level)	Socially skilled
Persistent	
Self-confident	
Tolerant of stress	
Willing to assume responsibility	

Source: Stogdill, 1974

classic book *The Human Side of Enterprise* in 1960, attention shifted to this behavioural mode of theorizing. McGregor was a teacher, researcher and consultant whose work was considered to be on the cutting edge of management thinking at that time. He influenced many behavioural theories, emphasizing the impact of human relationships on output and performance.

Although strictly speaking not a theory of leadership, the strategy of participative management proposed in *The Human Side of Enterprise* has had a tremendous impact on managers. The most publicized concept is McGregor's thesis that leadership strategies are influenced by a leader's assumptions about human nature and the attitude of workers to their work. As a result of his experience as a consultant, McGregor summarized two contrasting sets of assumptions made by managers in the workplace, shown in Table 3. It can be seen that a leader holding Theory X assumptions would tend towards an autocratic style, whereas one holding Theory Y assumptions would prefer a more participative style.

Blake and Mouton's Managerial Grid

Another behavioural or style approach model from the same period is the Managerial Grid developed by Robert Blake and Jane Mouton in 1964. Their work focuses on the task (production) and employee (people) orientations of managers, as well as combinations between the two extremes. The Managerial Grid locates concern for production on the horizontal axis, and concern for people on the vertical axis, and plots five basic leadership styles (see below). In the centre is 'Middle of the Road', referring to an equal balance between the concern for people and the concern for production. Blake and Mouton's Managerial Grid is a useful way of conceptualizing management styles, classified according to a rating on these two key dimensions of a leader's behaviour. In effect these two dimensions extend and popularize the theoretical concepts of 'initiating structure' and 'consideration', which emerged from a series of studies conducted at Ohio State University from the 1940s. The five main styles of management/leadership identified by Blake and Mouton include:

1 *Team Management*: integrating concern both for production and for the needs of people, this is often a precarious state, much desired, seldom achieved absolutely, and probably not applicable for all situations.
2 *Task Management*: this is more concerned with the production or attainment of goals rather than in empowering people to deliver the required tasks. This case is particularly applicable in crisis situations, or where employees are low skilled and easily replaced.
3 *Impoverished Management*: where no attention is given to the task or to the people, the result is usually a lack of confidence and trust in the group and in its shared task, and the outcomes are chaotic fragmentation. But not every group at every moment needs a manager to care for the task or the people, so there are times when 'less is more'.
4 *Country Club Management*: in this case, importance is given to people and not to task. The extreme form is rare, but characterizes some phases of social clubs and care-oriented organizations. People who come from a task-oriented background often find difficulty in communicating in such an environment.
5 *Middle of the Road*: this is common in many organizations, where attention often fluctuates between task and people, but is broadly balanced. It may depend on the leader's aptitude to read and comprehend the situation; or on the ability of different members of the team to fulfil complementary roles.

Table 3   Theory X and Theory Y manager beliefs

Theory X managers believe that:	Theory Y managers believe that:
• The average human being has an inherent dislike of work and will avoid it if possible	• The expenditure of physical and mental effort in work is as natural as play or rest, and the average human being, under proper conditions, learns not only to accept but to seek responsibility
• Because of this human characteristic, most people must be coerced, controlled, directed or threatened with punishment to get them to put forth adequate effort to achieve organizational objectives	• People will exercise self-direction and self-control to achieve objectives to which they are committed
• The average human being prefers to be directed, wishes to avoid responsibility, has relatively little ambition and wants security above all else	• The capacity to exercise a high level of imagination, ingenuity and creativity in the solution of organizational problems is widely distributed in the population, and the intellectual potentialities of the average human being are only partially utilized under the conditions of modern industrial life

Source: McGregor, 1960

Blake and Mouton propose that 'Team Management', showing a high level of concern for both employees and production, is the most effective type of leadership behaviour. This is confirmed by the Ohio State University Studies of Consideration and Initiating Structure – that a leader trusts, respects and values good relationships (participation) and – by contrast – makes sure that work gets done, including pushing followers to get their tasks accomplished (authority). These studies are amongst many that exemplify a behavioural approach (George and Jones, 2002: 393–4, quoting Fleishman and Harris, 1962).

THE CONTINGENCY OR SITUATIONAL SCHOOL

Whilst behavioural theories may point managers to develop particular leadership behaviours, they give little guidance as to what constitutes effective leadership in different situations. For practitioners it leaves open the question of what leadership practices will best suit specific contexts. Virtually all researchers conclude that no one leadership style is right for every leader under all circumstances. Instead, contingency-situational theories were developed to indicate that the style to be used is contingent upon such factors as the people, the place, the time, the task, the organization and other environmental variables. Some of the major theories contributing towards this school of thought are summarized below.

Fiedler's contingency theory

Fiedler's contingency theory (Fiedler, 1964) suggests that there is no single best way for managers to lead. Different situations require appropriate leadership styles, contingent on the factors that impinge on that situation. For instance, in a highly routine-based (mechanistic) environment where repetitive tasks are the norm and worker autonomy is minimal (such as a factory production line), a relatively directive leadership style may result in the best performance; however, a dynamic environment with skilled, creative staff (such as a software development firm) may require a more flexible, participative leadership.

Fiedler looked at three factors that could define the conditions of a managerial task:

1 *Leader–member relations*: How well do the manager and the employees get along, and how much guidance do the employees need?
2 *Task structure*: Is the job highly structured, fairly unstructured, or somewhere in between?
3 *Position power*: How much authority does the manager possess?

Managers can be rated as to whether they are relationship-oriented or task-oriented. Task-oriented managers tend to do better in situations that have good leader–member relationships, structured tasks, and either weak or strong (but not middling) position power. They also do well when the task is unstructured but their position power is strong. Positional power can also help them to overcome moderate to poor leader–member relations. In other words, task-oriented managers do well when they have clarity in at least one of the factors.

Relationship-oriented managers do better in other situations, where the alignment of beliefs and trust cannot be taken for granted, the positional power of the leader is ambiguous and the task is less than perfectly structured. The environmental variables are combined in a weighted sum that is termed 'favourable' at one end and 'unfavourable' at the other. A task-oriented style is preferable at the clearly defined extremes of 'favourable' and 'unfavourable' environments, but relationship-orientation excels in the middle ground. Managers could attempt to adapt their own orientations, and to reshape the environmental variables to match their style.

Another aspect of contingency theory is that the leader–member relations, task structure, and position power dictate a leader's situational control. Leader-member relations help to measure the amount of loyalty, dependability, and support that the leader receives from employees. It is a measure of how the manager perceives how he or she and the group of employees are getting along together. In a favourable relationship the manager has a high task structure and is able to reward and/or discipline employees without any problems. In an unfavourable relationship the task is usually unstructured and the leader possesses limited authority.

Position power measures the amount of power or authority the manager perceives the organization has given him or her for the purpose of directing, rewarding, and disciplining subordinates. The position power of managers depends on reducing or increasing decision-making by employees.

The task-motivated leader experiences satisfaction in task accomplishment, while the relationship-motivated leader seeks to build interpersonal relations and develop teams. Task-motivated leaders aim at measurable improvements in group performance, such as achieving a new sales record or outperforming a major competitor. Relationship-oriented leaders like to see greater customer satisfaction and a positive company image and atmosphere.

The Hersey and Blanchard model of Situational Leadership

Building a very similar set of assumptions, the Hershey and Blanchard model suggests that the developmental levels of a leader's subordinates play the greatest role in determining which leadership styles (leader behaviours) are most appropriate. Their theory is based on the amount of direction (task behaviour) and socio-emotional support (relationship behaviour) a leader must provide given the situation and follower maturity.

Task behaviour is the extent to which the leader engages in spelling out the duties and responsibilities to an individual or group. This behaviour includes telling people what to do, how to do it, when to do it, where to do it and who's to do it. In task behaviour the leader engages mostly in one-way communication and factual exchanges.

Relationship behaviour is the extent to which the leader engages in two-way or multi-way communications. This includes listening, facilitating, and supporting activities. A key function of leadership is to provide socio-emotional support, to evince a sense of alignment and common purpose.

Maturity is the willingness and ability of a person to take responsibility for directing his or her own behaviour. People tend to have varying degrees of maturity, depending on the specific task, function, or objective that a leader is attempting to accomplish through their efforts.

Within the Hersey Blanchard model leader behaviours fall along two continua, as shown in Table 4.

For Hersey and Blanchard, the key situational variable when trying to determine the appropriate leadership style is the readiness or developmental level of the subordinate(s). As a result, four leadership styles have been described:

1 *Directing*: The leader provides clear instructions and specific direction. This style is best matched with a low follower readiness level.
2 *Coaching*: The leader encourages two-way communication and helps build confidence and motivation on the part of the employee, although the leader still has responsibility and controls decision-making. This style is best matched with a moderate follower readiness level.
3 *Supporting*: With this style, the leader and followers share decision-making and no longer need or expect the relationship to be directive. Participating style is best matched with a moderate follower readiness level.
4 *Delegating*: This style is appropriate for leaders whose followers are ready to accomplish a particular task and are both competent and motivated to take full responsibility. Delegating style is best matched with a high follower readiness level.

To determine the appropriate leadership style to use in a given situation, the leader must first determine the maturity level of the followers in relation to the complexity of the specific task that the leader is attempting to accomplish through the effort of followers. As the level of follower maturity increases (or as the leader moves into a more senior role and is working with more experienced reports), it should be possible to shift from task-oriented leadership towards being more relationship-oriented coaching and supportive. Where the so-called followers are more self-directed and less reliant on the leader for direction, much more can be delegated. Thus in this model, the maturity of workers relative to the work they are asked to do is the deciding factor, rather than the traits or characteristics of the leader. However, in reality these styles are as much a part of the culture and embedded in operating processes and organizational structures. Changing a culture is not easy to do and leadership is a big part of it.

Table 4 Directive and supportive behaviour

Directive behaviour	Supportive behaviour
• One-way communication	• Two-way/multi-way communication
• Followers' roles are clearly communicated	• Listening, providing support and encouragement
	• Facilitating interaction
• There is a close supervision of individual performance	• Involving followers in decision-making

Source: Hersey and Blanchard, 1988

Adair's action-centred leadership model

The Adair model (1973) states that the action-centred leader accomplishes tasks through teams, and through relationships with fellow managers and staff. An action-centred leader must:

- direct the job to be done (*task* structuring);
- support and review the *individual* people doing it;
- coordinate and foster the work *team* as a whole.

Adair presents a simplification of the variability of human interaction, but it can help us in thinking about what constitutes an effective leader in relation to the job to be done. The effective leader/manager carries out the functions and exhibits the behaviours related to these three aspects. Situational and contingent elements call for different responses by the leader. The three elements may be more or less important as the situation varies. The challenge for the leader is to manage all the activities mentioned in Table 5.

LEADERS AND FOLLOWERS

The models discussed so far in this brief introductory review of leadership theories and their philosophical underpinnings have focused on the leader as standing out

Table 5 Leader role in managing tasks, teams and individuals

Task	• define the task
	• make the plan
	• allocate work and resources
	• control quality and rate of work
	• adjust the plan
Team	• maintain discipline
	• build team spirit
	• encourage, motivate, give a sense of purpose
	• appoint sub-leaders
	• ensure communication within group
	• develop the group
Individual	• attend to personal problems
	• praise individuals
	• give status
	• recognize and use individual abilities
	• develop the individual

Source: Adair, 1973

from the crowd, being somehow different and 'leading' others. Even within contingency models such as Fiedler's, attention to followers is from the viewpoint of the leader, and the leader's perception of the nature of his or her relationship with followers. The discussion now moves to recognizing the importance of the leaders' relationships with the followers and the interdependency of roles. This shift takes the obvious, yet remarkable, step of recognizing that leadership requires followership. You can't have one without the other. This shows an evolution in thinking from the hero or solo leader (emanating from the 'great man' concept) to a leader as part of a team, group or wider collection of people. Not the leader always out in front, but the leader who has the capacity to follow as well as lead; not only the master, but also the servant. The leader who symbolizes the way a group would like to see itself – its 'social identity' – and is a representation of the its implicit norms and values. (Haslam et al., 2011). This includes the leader who, through symbolic acts and imagined prowess, can defend followers against anxiety, even if he or she is not actually responsible for much else (Bion, 1963; French and Simpson, 2010).

Does this mean that some leaders are always just a function of the undeclared hopes and anxieties of their followers? Does inspiration boil down to this? Only to an extent: leaders must be seen as 'relevant' to the needs of their followers, and where these needs are for emotional reassurance, much of the energy and hope vested in them is likely to include unconscious dynamics of this sort. The same process underpins more sober groups, in less extreme circumstances. Social Identity Theory suggests that leaders are always those who typify the salient features of collective identity. That is, any collective sense of 'us' has some specific characteristics by which we define who is 'one of us'. We will select leaders on the basis of who most typifies this 'us-ness'. But that is not enough: leaders have to show us something of our future possibilities – in the words of the main proponents of this theory, Alex Haslam, Stephen Reicher and Michael Platow (2011), leaders should be 'entrepreneurs of identity'. Through them we discover what we might become, what new achievements might come to define 'us'. This is inspirational, and a real contribution of leaders to followers.

Servant leadership

The notion of 'Servant Leadership', developed by Greenleaf and Spears (1977), emphasizes the leaders' duty to serve a higher purpose, and thus to lead on behalf of the followers, pointing out that leadership can arise out of a desire to serve rather than a desire to lead. As Greenleaf explains, the leader-first and the servant-first are two extreme types, with a wider range of motivations between these extremes; many people find they become more motivated by a desire to serve as they become more experienced.

Ideally, servant leaders place the emphasis on ensuring the highest priority needs of followers are being met, and see this service as exemplifying service to a higher purpose or goal beyond personal gain or advantage. As such, servant leadership is popular with mission-oriented organizations, such as religious, environmental and human rights groups, where task-related performance is important, but only in the context of a shared and supra-personal purpose.

High on the priority list of servant leaders are the health, well-being and growth of followers, because they are seen as partners in a mission, not merely as instruments to task achievement. Servant leaders tend to consider how their decisions and actions will impact the lives of those they lead; more holistically, they place their leadership practice in the context of an impact on the world at large. Such leaders favour collaboration and empowerment, mutual respect and trust, careful listening, a future vision, and perhaps above all, the ethical exercise of power and authority.

As Greenleaf has described, servant leadership is more a philosophy of leadership than a set of specific traits, behaviours or outcomes. Servant leaders serve first and lead second because leadership is necessary to achieve the goals of service. For this reason servant leaders often do not hold typical 'official' leadership positions, at least not in title.

What is most critical for leadership studies from the work of Greenleaf is the emphasis on purpose, and how this changes the focus from the traits and behaviours of the solo, individual leader to the dynamic relationships between leaders and followers in relation to that purpose. This is all part of a recognition within leadership studies that followership is essential to leadership. Followership is a vital constituent of good leadership – not simply a dependent position on the organization chart.

The following part of leading

Katzenbach and Smith, authors of *The Wisdom of Teams* (1994), talk of the 'following part of leading', and suggest that the critical behaviours of leaders include these characteristics, shown in Table 6.

Table 6   Aspects of the following part of leading

Asking questions instead of giving answers	By asking such questions as 'What do you think we should do?' or 'How do you suggest we proceed?' you take a step behind – rather than in front of – another person. But do you intend to actually follow the suggestion or answer of that other person?
Providing opportunities for others to lead you	This goes beyond the traditional idea of looking for growth opportunities for other people. Unless the opportunity in question bears a real risk for your personal performance outcome, you are not actually positioning yourself as a follower.
Doing real work in support of others instead of only the reverse	Rolling up your sleeves and contributing 'sweat equity' to the efforts and outcomes of other people earns you their appreciation as someone upon whom they can depend, regardless of the relative hierarchical or functional position each of you holds.
Becoming a matchmaker instead of a 'central switch'	In addition to following other people yourself, you must learn to help them follow each other. This requires you to get beyond considering yourself the 'central switch' through which all decisions flow. Instead, you need to look for every possible chance to help people find their best collaborators. 'Have you asked them what they think?' is often the only input required to facilitate the effort at hand, although you then must submit your effort and support to whatever the people in question suggest.

(Continued)

Table 6   (Continued)

Seeking common understanding instead of consensus	The pejorative meaning associated with consensus management has nothing to do with either effective leading or effective following. Leaders are those who know when and how to follow, and to build a deep common understanding, not a superficial consensus, around the purpose, goals and approach at hand. They submit themselves and others to the discipline of ensuring that all sides to any disagreement are fully understood by everyone, recognizing that mutual understanding is far more powerful than any particular decision to choose path A over path B. All people will follow strong, commonly understood purposes and goals more easily than the 'put-up jobs' associated with consensus.

The authors suggest that the indicators of when a leader must follow are:

Individual performance	As a leader, you must follow another individual, regardless of hierarchy, if: • that individual, through experience, skill and judgement, knows a task better than you do • that individual's growth needs demand that you invest more in their skill and self-confidence than you would in your own • only that individual, and not you, has the capacity (the time and opportunity) to 'get it done'
Team performance	• the team's purpose and performance goals demand it • the team, and not you, must develop skills and self-confidence • the team's agreed-upon working approach requires you, like all the others, to do real work and get involved in the task
Organizational performance	As a leader, you must follow others, regardless of hierarchy, if: • the organization's purpose and performance goals demand it • the need for expanding the leadership capacity of others in the organization requires it • 'living' the vision and values requires you to do so

Source: Katzenbach and Smith, 1994

Transformational and transactional leadership

James MacGregor Burns (1978) was the first to put forward the concept of 'transformational leadership', a relationship of mutual help and support that develops followers into leaders. Burns suggested that transformational leadership occurred when one or more people work together in such a way that the leaders and followers help to increase each others' motivation. Bass (1998; Bass and Riggio, 2006), however, deals with the transformational style of executive leadership that incorporates social change. For Bass 'transformational leaders' may:

- expand a follower's portfolio of needs;
- transform a follower's self-interest;
- increase the confidence of followers;
- elevate followers' expectations;
- heighten the value of the leader's intended outcomes for the follower;
- encourage behavioural change;
- motivate others to higher levels of personal achievement.

The styles may be contrasted as shown in Table 7.

Table 7 Elements of transactional and transformational leadership

Transactional leadership	Transformational leadership
• builds on the employee's need to get a job done and make a living	• builds on an employee's need for meaning and personal development
• is preoccupied with power and position, politics and perks	• is preoccupied with purposes and values, morals, and ethics
• is mired in daily affairs	• transcends daily affairs
• is short-term and hard-data orientated	• is orientated towards long-term goals without compromising human values and principles
• focuses on tactical issues	
• relies on human relations to lubricate human interactions	• focuses more on missions and strategies
• follows and fulfils role expectations by striving to work effectively within current systems	• releases human potential – identifying and developing new talent
	• designs and redesigns jobs to make them meaningful and challenging
• supports structures and systems that reinforce the bottom line, maximize efficiency and guarantee short-term profits	• aligns internal structures and systems to reinforce overarching values and goals

Source: Bass, 1985

Clearly, both kinds of leadership are to be found in our organizations, and in the normal run of things one may not want a transformational leader all the time. Transactional leadership has remained the model for many people and organizations, but arguably the pace and complexity of modern society create a greater demand for transformational leadership.

Dispersed or distributed leadership

When considering the contributions made by a whole group, and people throughout an organization, it becomes clear that many are involved in leading and supporting the leadership of others. The question 'how is leadership distributed?' has given rise to a broad theoretical field known as 'dispersed' or 'distributed' leadership. Largely developed within the field of educational leadership (see Gronn, 2002, 2008; Spillane, 2006; Leithwood et al., 2009; Bolden, 2011), the essential idea is that leadership may be taken up by people other than the person at the top of the hierarchy. People who may be 'followers' in some instances are leaders in others, and indeed the proper functioning of most organizations depends on this: a teacher must be a leader in her classroom, a team member amongst colleagues, and a follower in relation to the Principal. So hierarchical leaders must recognize both when they need to be actively leading and when they need to authorize others in their leadership roles. There are personal structural aspects to this: firstly, there is the recognition that certain individuals may be better suited to take the lead in certain situations, and the official leader must be ready for this happen. Second, there are the organizational structures that locate power and influence in some roles – such as those controlling budgets or taking an entrepreneurial initiative – that inherently require leadership to be distributed to those roles.

The distribution of leadership underscores the importance of social relations in the leadership contract and the need for a leader to be accepted by others willing to become their followers. Sometimes likened to 'informal' or 'emergent' leadership, the dispersed/distributed leadership approach suggests a less rigid model of leadership, where the leader's role is dissociated from the organizational hierarchy. Ideally, it implies that individuals at all levels in the organization and in all roles (not simply those with an overt management dimension) can exert leadership influence over their colleagues and thus influence the overall leadership of the organization.

Heifetz (1994) distinguishes between the exercise of 'leadership' and the exercise of 'authority' – thus dissociating leadership from formal organizational power roles – whilst Raelin (2011) talks of developing 'leaderful' organizations through concurrent, collective and compassionate leadership. The key to this is a distinction between the notions of 'leader' and 'leadership'. 'Leadership' is regarded as a process of sense-making and direction-giving within a group and the 'leader' can only be identified on the basis of an individual relationship with followers. Thus, the leader can be seen as emergent rather than predefined, and that role of the leader can only be understood through examining the relationships within the group (rather than by focusing on his/her personal characteristics or traits).

The origins of such approaches have their foundations in sociology and organizational behaviour more than the traditional management literature, and draw on concepts such as structure and agency, organizational culture and climate, to highlight the contextual and situational influences on how leadership is actually enacted, and what people believe about it. It is a more collective concept, and argues for a move from an analysis and development of individual leader qualities to an identification of what constitutes an effective (or more appropriate) leadership process within an organization. This suggests a move in focus from the individuals to the relationships and culture within an organization.

THE 'SEVEN LEADERSHIP ACTION LOGIC ROLES'

Many leadership theories examine an individual's philosophy of leadership, personality, or leadership style, but not necessarily how he or she might act, especially in order to progress his or her career. Rooke and Torbert (2005) have a new approach in an article where they define 'action logic' as the way in which a leader decides what to do when there is an attack on their power base. Very few leaders operate on the basis of the two most effective action logics, and most are confined to the less effective styles. According to these authors, in large part, leadership can be learned. They profile seven leader types, based on extensive qualitative research on attitudes to leadership:

1 The *Opportunist*: these leaders see the world in terms of its potential to give them personal gain. People and resources are to be exploited. These leaders may have a place in emergency or tough sales situations, but that might be all. Opportunists constitute 5 per cent of the leaders studied by the authors.
2 The *Diplomat*: these people are driven by a need to satisfy higher-level managers while avoiding conflict. They follow group norms and rarely 'rock the boat'. They have a role in holding a group together and constitute 12 per cent of the leaders, mostly at junior levels, profiled in Rooke and Torbert's research.
3 The *Expert*: experts believe they influence control through their knowledge. They largely see collaboration as a waste of time as they 'know' the correct answer. They are good as individual contributors and make up the largest proportion of leaders – 38 per cent of those analysed by the authors.
4 The *Achiever* – these leaders focus on creating a positive work environment and also on the deliverables. They tend not to think outside the box, but function well in managerial roles. They make up 30 per cent of all the leaders profiled in this study.
5 The *Individualist*: these people tend to ignore rules with a view to getting things done. They recognize and work on tensions between principles and their actions, or between organizational values and the implementation of those values. They work well in venture capital and consulting roles and constitute 10 per cent of the leaders profiled by Rooke and Torbert.
6 The *Strategist*: strategists are different from individualists in so far that they recognize organizational constraints which they are prepared to discuss and transform. They have the ability and desire to focus on personal relationships, organizational relationships, and national and international developments. They are characterized by their need for inquiry, vigilance and an ability to focus on the short and long term. Effective as transformational leaders, they make up only 4 per cent of the random group of leaders analysed.
7 The *Alchemist*: these people differ from strategists in their ability to renew or re-invent themselves and their organizations in historically significant ways. Typically charismatic, they live by high moral standards. They are good at leading society-wide transformations and make up only 1 per cent of the leaders looked at in this study.

The authors argue that leaders can, and do, transform themselves, and to a certain extent these types can be taught, so you do see transitions from one leader type to another. One of the largest bottlenecks within organizations, however, is from the leadership role of *Expert* to that of *Achiever*. Because people such as engineers, lawyers and other professionals can often demonstrate *Expert* characteristics, the transition to *Achiever* can be difficult, but it is possible and can be positive for an organization.

The authors propose that the most effective teams are those with a *Strategist* culture, though strategist leaders constituted only 4 per cent of the sample, where people see challenges as opportunities for business growth and learning. Few organizations operate this way. Most operate with an *Achiever* culture focused on goal achievement. The rarest but most transformational kinds of leaders are *Strategists* and *Alchemists*. The latter can transcend a narrow role in business to take on more truly a national role, becoming a cult figure.

This brief introduction to a subjectively selected series of leadership theories and perspectives is intended to serve as a background and framework to the 'Key Concepts of Leadership' entries discussed in more detail below. These theories underpin and help to explain the origins of these ongoing leadership debates and perspectives.

1

Accommodating Leadership and Competitive Leadership

> The difference here is between finding a way to please everyone else, or needing to win every battle (and seeing every interaction as a battle to win!).

Leaders face conflicts. This goes with the territory. Successful leaders have to develop skills in conflict resolution to be successful. Few leaders, if any, are able to lead without encountering some level of conflict between (or within) themselves, team members, differing goals and aspirations, and so on. One of the greatest dilemmas is between competitive and accommodating styles of leaders and followers – because the competitive style of leader wants to win, whilst the accommodating leader is prepared to lose in the interests of building harmony, and strengthening relationships and maintaining progress.

One tool for assessing how leaders approach conflict is the Thomas–Kilmann Conflict Mode Instrument (1974) (see related entries on Avoiding Leadership and Involved Leadership, and Knee-jerk Leadership and Reflective Leadership). This can be used to test how a leader typically responds in debate and discussion, particularly in an area of disagreement, where competitive and accommodating behaviour can be seen as opposites. Thomas and Kilmann's five conflict modes contrast the highly competitive (always wanting to win) with the accommodating mode (allowing others to win). Other modes, which can be combined with competitive and accommodating behaviour preferences, include: being compromising and deal-making; avoiding conflict wherever possible; and being collaborative, seeking win/win solutions.

When a leader's strategy and approach – delivered and insisted upon in a very competitive and forceful way – is different from that of the majority, he or she tends to use competitive behaviours. One of the most popular or commonly used preferences of a leader facing a conflict situation, which impacts on the way he or she leads and manages, is competitive behaviour. The opposite – less commonly seen and perhaps less often recognized – is an accommodating style.

How do we define Competitive compared with Accommodating Leadership? A leader who is very competitive is at the top of the assertiveness scale and at the bottom of the cooperativeness scale. A leader who is accommodating is at the bottom of the assertiveness scale but at the top of the cooperativeness scale. Competing is win/lose – someone wins, and someone else must lose. Accommodating, the opposite, is lose/win, because winning this battle is not the most important issue. The leader has deliberately chosen to let the follower or colleague win, which is in contrast with avoiding – this is when he or she has chosen to walk away from the conflict, and is taking a lose/lose approach.

A competitive leader often operates in a power-oriented mode, and uses whatever sources of power available to win ground. This can include legitimate power, his or her ability to argue, to pull rank on another and to exert economic control. The competitive leader may be standing up for his or her beliefs, and may also be anxious to assert his or her primacy. This competitive leader behaviour is often at another's expense. If there are competitive leaders, there must be subordinates who are willing to give way and allow the competitive leader to have what he or she wants.

By contrast, the accommodating leader tends to neglect his or her own concerns to satisfy the concerns of the others first. Sometimes this is purely the result of conflict avoidance. However, accommodation involves self-sacrifice, generosity and yielding to another point of view even if it clashes with one's own. Accommodating-style leaders spend so much time helping others that sometimes they lose sight of what they personally want to achieve. Accommodating leadership can be seen as related to servant leadership (see 'Servant Leadership' section in 'Leadership Definition, Theory and Practice'), but the latter can be more proactive.

The competing mode is common in fields where results are easily measured and compared – sales and investment banking, for example – and in many organizations promotion and rewards are closely linked to competitive behaviour. It can drive decisiveness and clarity, even if insight and understanding are lacking, so can often come to the fore under the pressure of an emergency, even though the desire to win every argument can be very dysfunctional when ideas must be pooled from many sources, and emerging crises require leaders to back down and change direction. Highly competitive leaders can be surrounded by yes-men, people who agree with the leader because they have learned that disagreement may be unwise, or is just not listened to. This can prevent the leader from receiving vital information. Are subordinates afraid to admit uncertainties?

However, a low score for competitiveness could mean that a leader feels powerless in some situations, is unaware of his or her power base or is unable to use it. Does the leader have trouble taking a firm stand? This may be because he or she is overly concerned with others' feelings.

Accommodating as a conflict mode is useful when a leader needs to show they can be reasonable, as well as accepting their own fallibility. Accommodating is appropriate when the issue being discussed is more important to others. It is more than a goodwill gesture, helping to maintain cooperative relationships, building friendships for future benefit and possibly eliciting useful ideas. The accommodating mode is best when continued competition would damage a cause or issue, or when it is most unlikely that the leader in this situation can win. Accommodating helps to preserve a harmonious environment, and also helps subordinates to try things by themselves and learn from their own mistakes. However, the leader with a high score on 'accommodating' may feel that his or her ideas are not getting much attention. Allowing others to keep advancing their concerns can deprive the leader of influence, respect and recognition. Some accommodating leaders may feel that their own contribution will not be obvious. They may not be able to effectively impose discipline at work, but it depends on the extent to which this is needed.

Leaders who are low on accommodating may have trouble building up goodwill with other people, who may see them as unable to admit when they are wrong. It can be challenging for such leaders to recognize legitimate exceptions to rules, and when to give up a line of argument.

Here, we look at an example of a fiercely competitive manager who caused problems even before starting work in a new position, due to her highly competitive nature. In a contrasting case, a junior manager is overwhelmed with conflicting responsibilities due to an accommodating nature.

A consultant working with public-sector organizations tells the story:

A new leader was recently appointed to a senior position in a public-sector organization. Usually, the government is very strict in terms of advertising vacancies and going through proper procedures before appointing anyone. But this particular lady, highly qualified with an MBA and a PhD, who is quite job-hopping and is always going for promotions, put the organization under pressure to hire her quickly, especially as she threatened to try to get another job and then would not be available. The government has a very slender majority in the country and the opposition party is very strong, so this episode became controversial front-page news. If she hadn't been so competitive by insisting that she was appointed – if she had waited for the due processes to take place – maybe this government department would not now be under such fire in the media. So she hasn't started work yet but is already causing difficulties due to her competitive nature. This country where she lives and works has also encouraged this tendency to be competitive among women, as it is very male dominated, so any female who reaches a senior position is bound to be very competitive, because she has to be in order to rival the men.

A trainer working in emerging markets offers this case:

In my work I visit many training institutions and have contact with those who manage them – they give me training assignments and administer the courses I teach. In one particular institution, there is a junior manager (I suppose she has very little hope of ever being promoted) who is so accommodating that she has made her life very difficult and works very long hours, but it's all part of her personality, the corporate culture and the nature of her job. Basically the trainers have certain requirements – such as photocopying training materials – and she always says yes to them to help them out. Then her boss has told her to cut down on photocopying to save money. So she sneaks into the copy room when the boss isn't looking, or asks friends in other departments to help her out. She has two staff members but doesn't trust them much, and gives them only simple tasks to complete, doing nearly all the work herself. The boss gives free places on the courses to friends and contacts, so she lets these 'students' in. But then the trainers ask – 'who is this?' and she has to hope they won't mind. There are rules associated with training and academic standards, and she is constantly in a conflict with these rules, trying to please everyone. She tries to please her bossy boss, her demanding trainees and her difficult trainers – she never says no to anyone. Her behaviour would appear to be out of fear, job-security worries, natural friendliness and warmth, and an anxiety to please everyone. But her workload is huge and she gets home very late every evening, and comes in on weekends when many of the training events take place to make sure everything is running smoothly and to see if she can do anything to help.

Being competitive and accommodating are wide extremes – the one always wanting to win and gain personal advantages, the other prepared to sacrifice personal time to keep everyone happy. Again, neither mode is totally effective as leadership roles as these extremes of behaviour can backfire. It is impossible to win all the time, and probably not advisable to allow others to win all the time. Competitive leaders can appear unapproachable, selfish and too aggressive. Accommodating leaders can be too compliant and insufficiently assertive. Neither necessarily successfully gains the respect of their peers.

FURTHER READING

Bass, B.M. (1985) *Leadership and Performance Beyond Expectations*. New York, NY: Free Press.

Bass, B.M. (1998) *Transformational Leadership: industrial, military and educational impact*. Mahwah, NJ: Lawrence Erlbaum Associates.

Bass, Bernard M. and Riggio, Ronald E. (2006). *Transformational Leadership*, 2nd edition. Mahwah, NJ: Lawrence Erlbaum Associates.

Blake, R.R. and Mouton, J.S. (1964) *The Managerial Grid*. Houston, TX: Gulf Publications.

Bolden, R. (2011) 'Distributed leadership in organizations: a review of theory and research', *International Journal of Management Reviews*, 13 (3): 251–269.

Bolden, R., Hawkins, B., Gosling, J. and Taylor, S. (2011) *Exploring Leadership: individual, organizational and societal perspectives*. Oxford: Oxford University Press.

Dawkins, R. (1976) *The Selfish Gene*. Oxford: Oxford University Press.

Gronn, Peter (2002) 'Distributed leadership as a unit of analysis', *Leadership Quarterly*, 13 (4): 423–451.

Gronn, Peter (2008) 'The future of distributed leadership', *Journal of Educational Administration*, 46 (2): 141–158.

Jones, S. (2010) *Psychological Testing*. Petersfield: Harriman House.

Katzenbach J., and Smith, D. (1994) *The Wisdom of Teams*. New York: Harper Business.

Leithwood, Kenneth A., Muscall, Blair and Strauss, Tiiu (2009) *Distributed Leadership According to the Evidence*. New York: Routledge.

Maxwell, John C. (1993) *Developing the Leader Within You*. Nashville, TN: Thomas Nelson.

Pfeffer, J. (1994) *Managing with Power: politics and influence in organizations*. Boston, MA: Harvard Business School Press.

2

Analytical Leadership and an Intuitive, Instant Leadership Approach

> *Detailed organization charts and an emphasis on planning characterize the approach of several leaders; by contrast, others 'fly by the seat of their pants'.*

Closely related to Involved Leadership and Reflective Leadership (see Avoiding Leadership and Involved Leadership, Knee-jerk Leadership and Reflective

Leadership) is the issue of analysis and structure. What does it mean to be analytical in your leadership practice, particularly as compared to being more intuitive in your leadership practice? Analytical leadership involves:

- Making a systematic decomposition of activities to understand how they add up. Does it make sense? Why are we doing this?
- Interpreting events and working out the relationships between them. Why are they happening? Does this mean that we can predict future events? Or shall we just go with the flow as there is no pattern to events?
- Understanding the organization's disparate component parts. Do we have a clear picture of how they interact? Does our current structure make sense? Should we really be concerned with a structure at all, or just follow the needs of our business?
- Searching for the essential meanings of structures and systems. Why do we adopt certain formats? Is it for a reason, and does it help us? Or is it restrictive, and a lack of confining structure would serve us better?

Analytical leadership is primarily about the role of the leader in analysing structures and systems, making sense of these, and – ideally – using them to help create logical organizational structures (e.g. organizational charts), which best suit the organization, and running the business accordingly. How can we identify and make use of the strengths and assets of the business?

By contrast, a more intuitive leader – one who is generally not analytical by nature – may not spend much time analysing events and what they mean, and may not seek to cognitively understand how things work: it may not matter much in the day-to-day running of the business. This leader is less structured and works from gut instinct; in some situations this is more relevant for employees, if – for various reasons – they don't ask about why their work is structured the way it is. Sometimes this type of less structured leadership can be a by-product of Avoiding Leadership. It can also slip into autocratic and even totalitarian leadership, when the only reason for doing anything is because the boss wants it. Anyone who questions it must be disloyal, as there are no grounds for reasoned debate.

Ann Langley (1995) describes the dangers of either extreme as 'analysis paralysis' and 'extinction by instinct'. One of the criticisms often levelled against MBA programmes is that they teach young, inexperienced people how to analyse businesses, but not how to manage them – because that is far messier and complicated, and depends on social and personal skills that are not easily taught or measured. Although the letters MBA supposedly stand for 'Master of Business Administration', they might more properly be taken as 'Master of Business Analysis'. What would the opposite be like – 'Master of Business Action'?

Here, we consider examples of analytical leaders, and a few examples of leaders who work primarily from intuition. Both can be effective and ineffective. Having an analytical understanding of a business can lead to a more sound structure and a more logical approach to operations, but it may not be the difference between success and failure. Analysis is a good tool, but it's not the only one available.

An emerging markets consultant – on overly analytical leadership:

I'm thinking of a Managing Director I know who is very analytical and loves drawing organization charts. However, he doesn't always think through how this might work in practice. He had an idea of different units acting as partners of the organization reporting to each other in a kind of hub and spoke system. But every time we challenged him about a particular hub and individual reporting line – especially one that obviously would not work due to political or cross-cultural reasons – he backed off and said that wasn't a good example. He became more and more defensive the more we attacked his organization charts for being unrealistic. But he still kept the chart and presented it to the Board. His hubs then came back as 'Strategic Partnerships'. But at that point no-one had any faith in it being implemented. If he had conducted the analysis in a more consultative way, it would have received much more attention.

Analytical leadership can be quite academic and theoretical. In this case, it was shallow analysis – a more in-depth analysis might have worked. For example, in this case the MD had decided that the Vietnam operation should report to China. This shallow analysis did not take into account the obvious politics of the region. For the Vietnamese office this would have been admitting the Chinese were more important, like a reversion to the old colonial system, and flying in the face of centuries of struggle to remain independent from China. He might as well have made Vietnam report to France. Similarly, the Managing Director wanted to make the Kuwait branch report to Egypt. But in Kuwait, the people who are the poorest and do the least-paid jobs are often Egyptians, and the Kuwaitis tend to treat them as inferior. So how would that work? The analysis just didn't make sense, it was not deep, nor sensitive enough. That was what was wrong with it.

In any case, it was obvious, and clear to see on paper, that this Managing Director was centralizing power to himself, and using his new organization chart as a technique to achieve this. He had both support functions and profit-making functions all under the same division – his. He was just accumulating power under his direction, so the abstract models of the organization seemed designed to give a veneer of reason to what was actually something quite different: a political manoeuvre beneath the cloak of a rational pre-organisation. When he was challenged in a staff meeting, he couldn't really justify it – the logic was all against it. No-one in the meeting understood why the organization was structured as it was – the only logical explanation was that it was structured to ensure his continued domination of the operation.

Another project manager I have worked with was also over-keen on taking an analytical approach. He sat in his office poring over flow-diagrams showing his way of planning the scope of his project, and which activity had to come first. If this activity was delayed, what could he do instead? What was his contingency plan? He did so much planning that he wasn't physically on site, and he didn't really know what was going on in reality. It was overkill.

So there are three principal dangers to watch out for. First, successful analytical leadership requires deep reflective thinking about all the issues in play. Analysis must take into account subtleties of politics, cultures and the organization's history. These are often too complex, and too ambiguous, for clear-cut analysis, which is why really advanced analysis blends into its opposite: synthesis, which is rather more an art than a science. Second, the abstract models and charts that are central to analytic techniques are apparently neutral, and can be used by anyone.

But actually they usually depend on privileged information, and are manipulated in the interests of specific people. The analytic leader must also constantly evaluate the analytic process vis-à-vis the benefits to the organization, as opposed to personal benefits or those of specific elites. Third, analytical leadership should not get in the way of practical leadership: it can easily delay or prevent necessary action from being taken. While analysis and planning is important, leaders must still lead in a proactive way to achieve objectives and connect with their people.

Here is an HR/development consultant talking about a lack of analysis in leadership, in contrast with the above cases:

> I used to know two Hong Kong Chinese brothers. They had so many business interests it must have been hard for them to remember them all. They had no structure or organization plan whatsoever in any of their businesses. They did not analyse their portfolio and did not try to exploit any synergies. They had properties, holiday homes, investments in restaurants, a training operation, a recruitment business – and one had a day job working in a multinational. He never told his multinational employer about all his outside business interests – some of which conflicted. But he didn't stop to analyse the issue of a possible conflict of interest. The staff members who worked for the brothers were employed in different parts of the business interchangeably, according to the changing needs of the moment. They couldn't plan and had no career-development structure because the brothers didn't think about that and didn't analyse their future strategy. They hired people they liked and relatives and friends without proper interviews or proper contracts – some were quite good but some were completely unqualified, as the brothers never analysed job requirements. The brothers didn't make an organization chart and barely carried out any budgeting, but they were savvy business people and were quite profitable. Even if one of their businesses was not doing very well, it was subsidized by others. It all worked out somehow without them making a complex analysis of anything. But the erratic nature of their unstructured management style meant they lost more professional employees because it was felt that their lack of analysis suggested poor management and a lack of long-term stability.

A leader managing an unstructured, free-flowing approach to running a business may find that he can be surprisingly successful, such as Yvon Chouinard of Patagonia. This outdoor sportswear company based in the USA thrives on an organic structure, with a flat organization and informal communication lines. Chouinard wants everyone involved in helping to design new products, thinking through the strategy for next year, interacting with customers and living the outdoor lifestyle. The company's reputation for corporate social responsibility and not harming the environment is as well known as its lack of hierarchy. All ideas are welcome. Some old Patagonia products sell on eBay for thousands of dollars. New ones outsell competitors' even if much more expensive. There are 900 applications for every vacancy in the company, so he must be doing something right.

But being ad hoc has its limits. Knowing where in particular your revenues come from is essential. Which are our most profitable customers? When we advertise, which strategy and campaign is most effective? Which of our sales people is the most high-performing? These are on the dashboard dials and navigation instruments which tell us how we are doing, and we can't do without them. If we don't know how much fuel is in the tank or water is under the keel, how can we plan a journey?

This was obviously much of the thinking behind Jack Welch's restructuring and culture change of General Electric (GE). There were too many layers between the bosses and the factory floor. The essential meaning of the organization had got lost in the bureaucracy. He looked at the different businesses within GE – hundreds of them – and discovered in his comprehensive analysis that many were lagging behind or not performing at all. They must be number one or number two in their business sector – said Welch – otherwise we must fix them, close them down or sell them. It doesn't make sense to have non-performing businesses subsidized by performing ones. Welch also analysed the vast human resources within GE considering employee performance and buy-in to the values and culture of GE. Those who were performing well and exemplified the values and culture of the company were rewarded. For those who had a strong commitment to GE but who were performing below their potential Welch sought ways to help them improve. Those uncommitted to GE values and the Welch-style GE mission were let go. The analysis paid off and led to a dramatic culture change and vastly improved performance.

Analytical leadership approaches help us to understand how our organization works – and how we can make it work even better. It helps us to know when we are winning – and when we might be falling dangerously behind. But we don't need to obsess about it. There is such a thing as 'analysis by paralysis' and 'extinction by instinct' (see Mintzberg, 1994; Langley, 1995)! Completely unanalysed and unstructured businesses still thrive, but this might be more due to luck than judgement. The analytical mindset is still a very valuable addition to the manager's toolkit, but culturally it is not universal.

FURTHER READING

Alvesson, M. and Spicer, A. (eds) (2010) *Metaphors We Lead By: understanding leadership in the real world*. Oxford: Routledge.

Casey, Susan (2007) 'Patagonia – the coolest company on the planet', *Fortune*, 12 April, http://money.cnn.com/magazines/fortune/fortune_archive/2007.

Creaton, Siobhan (2007) *Ryanair: the full story of the controversial low-cost airline*. London: Aurum Press.

Gosling, J. and Minzberg, H. (2003) 'The five minds of the manager', *Harvard Business Review*, November, 81(11): 54–63.

Langley, Ann (1995) 'Between "Paralysis by Analysis" and "Extinction by Instinct"', *MIT Sloan Management Review*, Spring, 36(3): 63–76.

Mintzberg, H. (1994) *The Rise and Fall of Strategic Planning: reconceiving roles for planning, plans, planners*. New York: Free Press.

Rooke, D. and Torbert, W. (2005) 'The seven transformations of leadership', *Harvard Business Review*, April, 83(4): 66–76.

Welch, J. (2005) *Winning*. New York: HarperCollins.

Western, Simon (2008) *Leadership: a critical text*. London: Sage.

3
Authoritarian Leadership and Participative Leadership

> *Many leaders make their own decisions in isolation; others seek the support of team members among the management team and wider afield.*

These extremes have long been the subject of debate: should a leader ask others to participate in decision-making, or should he or she simply exert authority and take control? How much should a leader exert power and authority to get things done, and how much should a leader involve others and seek their participation in the running of the organization? Similarly, how much should a leader remain detached from the group that he or she leads, and how much should a leader be directly involved in their activities? Debates around these questions have considered the significance of the personality of the leader, the demands of the organizational context, and the regional, national or transnational locations of the organization, as national culture can play a part here. Is there a time and place for exclusivity one way or the other, or should there be a mix of leadership approaches, to be recommended as a universal theme? Because sometimes there appears to be a need to be authoritarian, and sometimes to be participative.

Participative leadership can be seen as focused on teamwork, and depends on the leader gaining a high degree of loyalty and buy-in from others. A participative leader needs to build trust and confidence amongst his or her team-mates, and they have to be ready to contribute, sharing and supporting each other. Participative leaders work hard to gain commitment and trust and show that they care, and this can then grow and develop: 'If you want to be a participative leader and a team player, you have to create loyalty and trust. Being autocratic is quicker and easier, but risks catastrophic failure' (Jones and Gosling, 2005: 124). Participative leaders see themselves as first among equals. 'We are in this together' is one of their maxims, and they work hard to handle mistakes and failures in a supportive way, avoiding cliques, and avoiding being domineering.

The tension between participative and authoritarian leadership has been considered in many contexts, and can be clearly seen in Hersey and Blanchard's theory of Situational Leadership described in the Introduction. They argued that this simple polarity actually includes four distinct styles, because the amount of authoritarian direction that a group needs depends on both the complexity of the task and the sophistication of the team members or employees. A highly complex kind of work, such as management consultancy, could involve relatively junior people who need a good deal of direction, and very experienced people who bring the most value when they are able to use their own initiative and are free to command the resources of the consultancy firm. In some situations a group will have to figure out its own way forward, because there are no recipes or route-maps. So highly directive leadership would be inappropriate. But in reality it seldom so straightforward, and leaders and their colleagues have to figure out the best balance as they go along.

The discussion also goes back to trait theory (see 'The Trait Approach to Leadership' section of 'Leadership Definition, Theory and Practice', above). This includes the idea of dominance: '...an individual's need to exert influence and control over others, [which] helps a leader channel followers' efforts and abilities toward achieving group and organizational goals' (George and Jones, 2002: 391–392). In the best-case scenario this is like authoritarian behaviour combined with the emotional maturity to accept criticism, an inevitable part of participation and discussion between leader and follower. A leader's tendency to reward and punish feedback is crucial, as well as their personal task-oriented and relationship-oriented styles.

A leader whose power is based on the ability to reward or punish (Lukes, 1974; Handy, 1992; Pfeffer, 1994) may have a tendency to be more authoritarian and directive, but a leader drawing on referent power, legitimized by position, expertise or cultural norms (Watson, 2002), will find others happy to help him or her without obvious coercion; and is therefore more likely to probably operate in a more participative way.

The use of information power – where the leader keeps facts and figures about the organization closely concealed amongst a coterie of close colleagues – reinforces authoritarian rule; participation requires information-sharing as a preliminary requirement. Similarly, an organization in which expert knowledge justifies exclusive access to power also tends to limit participation, because of the tendency to see the sharing of expertise as a dilution of power. (Conversely, in organizations where many people share similar high levels of expertise, such as professional services firms, power is more distributed, and its exercise is often subtle and surreptitious.) So why do some leaders need to use raw authority in their daily work, and view followers in a radically different way than participative leaders do? Is there a dramatic difference in effectiveness either way? It can depend on national and organizational culture. In some cultures 'democracy' is an unquestionable virtue, and cooperatives are just one example of organizations that try to embody participation based on shared ownership (accepting a diversity of expertise as necessary to the work, but not the only legitimate basis for power). Many leaders and leadership commentators would argue that this is a pointer to a more sustainable future, because shared power is equated with shared responsibility, and we have to recognize our collective responsibility for the effects of our lifestyles and business activities on the future sustainability of our planet.

On the other hand, some leaders and observers argue that democracy is just too slow and cumbersome for the decisions that need to be made on behalf of the planet as a whole (and for a fast-moving company), and that we should strengthen the hierarchical systems that enable decisive action. As ever, the problem is that the people who are most likely to make wise and well-considered decisions may not be willing to struggle to get into positions of power and influence, and they may refuse to accept the compromises involved. Can we expect good and wise people to become leaders? Or can we find ways to ensure our leaders act wisely, even against their more selfish instincts? This is the question that Plato asks repeatedly in his dialogues, a question which has understandably obsessed commentators ever since. One of the most important functions of leadership studies, as a field of intellectual engagement, is precisely to keep this question at the forefront of contemporary debate.

Things can change. Authoritarian leaders may behave the way they do because of nervousness and inexperience, and might become more participative as they come to know their colleagues better and grow in confidence. Some stay authoritarian, especially when they perceive it fits with the cultural context in which they are operating. High power-distant cultures (cultures with overtly hierarchical power relations where followers cannot easily access or openly criticize a leader, as discussed in the entry Eastern-style Leadership and Western-style Leadership – Contrasting and Converging National Cultures) tend to make typically authoritarian leaders even more extreme. Participative leaders are fairly unlikely to become authoritarian, unless they have staff members who are reluctant to participate and would rather be told what to do.

Here we profile two authoritarian leaders, and consider the way they operate and the impact on their organizations. Mostly this is interpreted as negative, but in both cases they were effective in their own ways. Then, we consider two participative leaders – one deliberately so, the other more accidentally.

An ex-Chief Executive Officer (CEO)/Management Consultant – on the self-obsessed, authoritarian leader:

> I know a leader who is extremely authoritarian and not at all participative. This individual is the chairman of an organization, yet doesn't even personally know most of the senior executives of the organization, and probably would not even recognize them if he passed them in the street. As an example of the absolutely non-participative approach of this leader, consider the following anecdote. The chairman once invited a VIP to visit the organization and give a talk about doing business in Eastern Europe. I went along, hoping to gain some useful insights. When the chairman rose to speak and introduce the VIP guest he ended up talking only about himself; he hardly gave the VIP time to speak at all, negating the participative point of the VIP's visit to the organization.
>
> This chairman is bossy, arrogant and only interested in himself; he likes to have an audience and for everyone to listen to him, but he's not interested in listening to anyone else, not even VIPs he himself has invited. In this situation, the chairman's extreme narcissism actually undermines the possibility of leadership in practice. In reality, he has no followers. The leader is so obsessed with his status and public persona that he fails to achieve the development of any followership within the organization. For him, his role is not about leading the organization, but about enhancing his status-obsessed figurehead position. He uses the organization to make himself look like a leader, but he really isn't one. Having said that, the organization is profitable and efficient, if not especially innovative and creative, so it must be getting something

from the arrangement – perhaps the Chairman's wealth, profile and contacts are useful, and no-one really expects him to do more.

An emerging market consultant – on the closed-minded, authoritarian leader:

> One authoritarian leader I experienced was my boss at the time. This man could not operate in a participative way, as he didn't listen to anyone else. His mind was always closed to the ideas, issues and concerns of others.
>
> For example, he had an unwavering expectation that staff members travelling on business would invariably bankroll their own expenses and claim them back later. There was no chance of applying for advances. Once, I was asked to go on a business trip at short notice and did not have the cash with me to pay the expenses. He said I should pay by credit card and the accounts department would refund my claim before the credit card bill needed to be paid. But the country I was going to was a very remote developing country, and the hotel where they were putting me up did not accept credit cards. In any case the accounts department usually took around three or four months to refund expenses. Yet he would not tolerate or listen to another point of view even though his arguments did not make sense. He would not listen at all when I tried to explain this, and just ranted on in his own authoritarian way.

In this situation, authority was becoming a problem, as participation in the work of the organization depends on mutual listening and understanding. While authority is important to leadership practice, some participation is almost always necessary, and a leader who feels secure only by ignoring the input of others is damaging leader–follower relations, and this usually leads to a breakdown in the ability to lead.

While both of these examples highlight the need for participation in leadership, a leadership style that is overly participatory can also be unbalanced and ineffective. In the first of the following examples of participatory leadership, the participatory nature is determined by the situation, which often frustrates the leader's ability to exert authority. In the second example, the leader is so participative that she almost neglects her duty to exercise authority.

A researcher on leadership – on being participative by necessity:

> An example of a successful participative leader, though one who also experiences a frustrating lack of authority, is a salaried leader I know within a voluntary church organization (see the related entry Employee Leading and Volunteer Leading). This particular 'free-church' – it is not a government or state-supported organization – is very non-authoritarian and very sharing in its style and approach. It employs very few paid staff and relies heavily on community involvement. Without participation from local people preaching, organizing services, making flower arrangements, serving tea and coffee and running Sunday School classes, the church would not exist.
>
> As a result of the voluntary nature of the organization, this leader must accommodate those willing to give freely of their time and expertise. For example, this leader often finds himself managing many voluntary lay preachers. He describes some of these lay preachers as 'egotistical, demanding and not good at public speaking'. However, he is reliant upon them to maintain the organization's activities. As he said,

'we depend on them, so I have to accommodate them, humour them, give them face and status, and schedule them according to their needs'. He must accept their views and opinions and take them seriously, even if he doesn't want to or doesn't personally agree with them, because an authoritarian style here would soon mean that he would lose their support. They are not obliged to work with him and could go elsewhere, although actually most of them have geographical constraints, and feel identified with this particular denomination of church. But his style ensures their willing involvement.

While this leader appreciates that participatory leadership, something he most often demonstrates, is the only way to get things done in this church, he is often frustrated by the restrictions to his authority. In many instances the participative nature of this leader's focus of activity works and is effective, but the participatory nature of the organization can constrain his leadership authority in delegating tasks to those he feels best suit the job. By contrast, we wonder if he sometimes imagines himself at the head of a charismatic community, in which his word is taken as infallible!

An HR/development consultant – on participation without leadership:

One leader I worked with was participatory to a fault. Her leadership practice was centred around constantly consulting others on organizational decisions. She would ask for opinions all the time. She felt she was engaging followers in a mutually respectful participative environment. However, what was happening was participation without leadership. Many people were consulted because she was afraid of upsetting them if they weren't, and she didn't really have a way of debating differences of opinion or collectively agreeing priorities. This implied that she didn't really value what others said – it was just the ritual practice of asking.

This particular leader suffered from avoidance behaviour, particularly regarding decision-making. Decisions would be delayed, or not taken at all, under the guise of seeking the input of team members. This meant that in the end, after repeated unsuccessful attempts to obtain a decision from her, many junior people made decisions which were above their level, or the decisions just weren't made at all. Though the leader was warm and friendly and thought she was empowering her followers, the lack of authority and guidance did the opposite. Rather than feeling empowered, staff felt that 'power' was just lying around there, for anyone to take and make use of, if they were prepared to take the consequences. There were even some instances of unethical behaviour because of the lack of manager involvement.

Though this leader's participatory intentions were well meaning, they actually negatively impacted on her leadership practice. Engaging followers in participatory dialogue and activity is a very useful practice. It empowers followers with a sense of responsibility, value and respect. However, there must also be a presence of authority, responsibility and willingness to act decisively on the part of the leader. If both sides of the equation are not present, leadership can fail (see the related entries on Avoiding Leadership and Involved Leadership, HR-oriented Leadership and Production-oriented Leadership, Individualistic Leadership and Relationship-oriented Leadership).

Authoritarian leaders tend to be pushy, use legitimate power, and often don't take the trouble to know and trust their subordinates. They thrive on strong position power and make the most of it in highly structured organizations. They dislike attacks on their authority and usually make sure they win. Although many observers and subordinates are highly critical of their behaviour, they can be effective in presenting a powerful image externally. They may give the appearance of confidence, but this could be just a mask, covering deep anxiety about their self-worth (which is why they experience criticism of their decisions as a personal attack, rather than reasoned debate).

Participative leadership has become a commonly accepted ideal, especially amongst educated professionals who are ready, willing and able to participate. But it takes a lot of work on both sides, and authoritarian leadership can be quicker and easier – Churchill allegedly said that 'a dictatorship has six weeks' start on a democracy'. Participative leadership can become an excuse for avoiding decision-making. With volunteers, and where the leader depends heavily on the co-operation of followers, it can be a must. But it should not mean that the leader absolves himself or herself from leadership authority and fails to make decisions at all.

FURTHER READING

Abzug, R. and Phelps, S. (1998) 'Everything old is new again: Barnard's legacy – lessons for participative leaders', *Journal of Management Development*, 17 (3): 207–218.

Ali, M.R., Khaleque, A. and Hossain, M. (1992) *Participative Management in a Developing Country: attitudes and perceived barriers.* Manchester: MCB University Press.

Blake, R.R. and Mouton, J.S. (1964) *The Managerial Grid.* Houston, TX: Gulf Publications.

Bolden, R., Hawkins, B., Gosling, J. and Taylor, S. (2011) *Exploring Leadership: individual, organizational and societal perspectives.* Oxford: Oxford University Press.

Fleishman, E.A. and Harris, E.F (1962) 'Patterns of leadership behavior related to employee grievances and turnover', *Personnel Psychology*, 15: 43–56.

Gronn, Peter (2002) 'Distributed leadership as a unit of analysis', *Leadership Quarterly*, 13 (4): 423–451.

Gronn, Peter (2008) 'The future of distributed leadership', *Journal of Educational Administration*, 46 (2): 141–158.

Handy, C. (1992) *Understanding Organizations.* Harmondsworth: Penguin.

House, R.J. and Baetz, M.L. (1979) 'Leadership: some empirical generalizations and new research directions', in B.M. Straw and L.L. Cummings (eds), *Research in Organizational Behaviour*, vol. 1. Greenwich, CT: JAI Press.

Iszatt-White, M. (2011) 'Methodological crises and contextual solutions: an ethnomethodologically informed approach to understanding leadership', *Leadership*, 7 (2): 119–135.

Jones, S. and Gosling, J. (2005) *Nelson's Way: leadership lessons from the great commander.* London: Nicholas Brealey.

Katzenbach, J. and Smith, D. (1994) *The Wisdom of Teams.* New York: Harper Business.

Leithwood, Kenneth A., Muscall, Blair and Strauss, Tiiu (2009) *Distributed Leadership According to the Evidence.* New York: Routledge.

Raelin, J. (2011) 'From leadership-as-practice to leaderful practice', *Leadership*, 7 (2): 195–211.

Stogdill, R.M. (1974) *Handbook of Leadership: a survey of the literature.* New York: Free Press.

key concepts in leadership

4
Avoiding Leadership
and Involved Leadership

The extent of hands-on leader engagement in all aspects of the organization can vary from non-existent or minimal to 'having a finger in every pie'.

This dichotomy between high and low avoiding styles has been defined by Thomas and Kilmann (1974) within their well-known Conflict Mode Instrument – also discussed in connection with Accommodating Leadership and Competitive Leadership, and with Compromising Leadership and Cooperative Leadership. Of the five possible ways of approaching a situation of disagreement, usually two or three modes of operating are popular with each leader or manager, with one or two being low preferences, and possibly one or two moderate preferences. The preferences reflected in the scores show the following:

- How collaborative a leader may be in working with others to achieve a solution to the problem in hand, rather than trying to score points off the other people in the team.
- How much the leader is prepared to compromise to come to a solution to the conflict.
- The extent to which the leader is able to share ideas and strategies with others in the interests of accomplishing the tasks and overcoming problems.
- Whether or not the leader tends to implement conflict-avoiding tactics, and withdraw from potential conflict, when possible. Would the leader rather get as far as possible from the dispute and remain outside of the issue, even though this means that the opportunity to help make the decision is lost?
- How accommodating the leader is in terms of using the ideas of other people and taking note of their wishes to avoid conflict. Is there a tendency for the leader to try to minimize disputes by calming everyone down? Is the leader happy for everyone to have their say?

Here, we are looking at high and low avoiding styles of leadership. The conflict-avoiding leader feels uncomfortable in any kind of conflict and is therefore likely to be both unassertive and uncooperative. Avoiding disagreements is a great way to lose track of what you are trying to do, and may lead you into making ethical compromises, and pleasing no-one. Characteristic behaviours include postponing action, putting things off until another time, and finding reasons to not deal with conflict in the here and now. A conflict-avoiding leader may also simply withdraw from a threatening situation altogether. This behaviour can be seen to relate to 'management by exception', a characteristic of transactional leadership (see the Introduction; and Burns, 1978, Bass, 1985; Whittington et al., 2009), especially in the passive or laissez-faire mode. It also relates to the impoverished leadership style as identified in the Managerial Grid by Blake and Mouton (1964).

But an avoiding mode may be functional when faced with unimportant issues, especially when more important matters are pressing, and where the leader cannot meaningfully influence the situation. When the potential damage of confronting a conflict is greater than the benefits of resolving it, one may be wiser to let time and events take their course. Much can be achieved by allowing tensions to ease and hot-heads to cool a little. Delaying immediate action is also appropriate when it is necessary to gather more information before coming to a decision. A leader may choose to avoid a conflict when others are better placed to resolve it and when the issue might be outside of the responsibility or knowledge domain of the leader. However, leaders with a tendency to avoid conflict may thereby be unintentionally withholding important contributions to shared problems. Furthermore, they may be using too much energy avoiding issues rather than facing and resolving them, and will soon be overtaken by decisions taken by default.

Leaders who are low on avoiding may find themselves hurting people's feelings or stirring up problems where they did not exist previously. They may need to be more discreet and tactful to avoid causing additional conflict. If they are too busy in their workplace, overwhelmed by too many issues, it may be that they should avoid more, planning to set priorities, and delegate more. Authoritarian Leadership (see the entry above) is often associated with being low on conflict-avoiding and can be the result of corporate culture, personality and circumstances. By contrast, conflict-avoiding leadership is not necessarily leadership in the background (see the related entry Behind-the-scenes Leadership and Leading from the Front) – it might be just as involved, but not so obvious.

Here, we look at an example of both low and high avoiding styles of leadership, which have their advantages and disadvantages. As in the case of many of the other leadership concepts discussed, an optimal approach here might lie in trying to achieve a happy medium.

An author and researcher on leadership studies:

> I have always been interested in the challenge of leading a ship in a wartime/military context, and it would seem that many leaders in the armed services are low on 'avoiding'. Perhaps it is difficult for them to be anything else, because they have an extraordinarily high level of responsibility, including for people's lives, on a 24/7 basis. If you are on a ship at sea, you cannot just go home in the evening. And when you are sailing into a war zone, tensions are running high and the crew members are under a lot of stress. There are also complex relationships between crew members, especially where both men and women are on board, and often more exaggerated than in a land-based environment.
>
> An ex-services leader can't just stop being this kind of leader just because he has stopped being in the armed services – he is likely to go on being very much involved in every aspect of his job (and it usually is a male at the senior levels). So, workaholism,

being a micro-manager and a control freak tends to prevail, even if his crew is no longer counted in the hundreds. Especially at sea, where it is important to be ready for every eventuality and spare parts and equipment can't easily be replaced, the captain will have high anxiety levels and will want to make sure everything is done properly. When a ship is being refitted to prepare for sea, short-cuts and a botched job cannot be accepted, as what if the ship is thousands of miles from home and things start falling apart? A ship at sea is an isolated self-contained operation, which cannot take risks with wind and weather. So, in jobs in remote circumstances, where the community must be self-reliant, a low level of avoidance behaviours on the part of the leader is probably inescapable.

A consultant working in emerging markets:

In many developing countries, consulting operations tend to be quite small-scale, and although each office has a leader, he or she might be only temporarily in that environment, and might be constantly flying around the region (or the world) taking care of a wide span of operations. One such colleague is one day a week working for the parent organization at headquarters, but mostly working in another city a three-hour flight away, and living in a third location – or at least that's where his wife and children are based. It makes sense economically, but the result can be a degree of avoiding behaviour, if only because the colleague cannot simply make all the decisions needed on the ground. He has a BlackBerry and has a plan to answer all emails in two hours – but he focuses on answering the emails of his bosses and his clients, rather than thinking about his subordinates and less influential colleagues. He has a large amount of trust in his office assistant, who would appear to have been promoted above her level of competence and has developed a haughty and arrogant streak as part of an exaggerated feeling of self-importance, being in charge of the office most of the time and making quite big decisions by default as her boss is simply not around most of the time. This scenario is often the result of too much 'avoiding' leadership – but at least this is the result of too much work and too many responsibilities, rather than of not wanting to make any decisions because of fear of doing the wrong thing, which might be more common in cases of high avoiding.

Therefore, we see situations where low avoidance and high avoidance leader behaviours may be to a certain extent inevitable, but there are other scenarios where a leader may be low-avoiding due to lack of trust and a reluctance to delegate, or may be high avoiding out of fear and job security worries. The impact on the subordinates in both cases can be negative, with a similarly negative impact on customers or other third parties. A middle path between these extremes is likely to be more successful, and each leader will have to find their own balance.

FURTHER READING

Alvesson, M. and Spicer, A. (eds) (2010) *Metaphors We Lead By: understanding leadership in the real world*. Oxford: Routledge.

Bass, Bernard M. and Riggio, Ronald E. (2006) *Transformational Leadership*, 2nd edition. Mahwah, NJ: Lawrence Erlbaum Associates.

Bolden, R. (2011) 'Distributed leadership in organizations: a review of theory and research', *International Journal of Management Reviews*, 13 (3): 251–269.

Grint, K. (2010) 'The sacred in leadership: separation, sacrifice and silence', *Organization Studies*, 31 (1): 89–107.

Jones, S. (2010) *Psychological Testing*. Petersfield: Harriman House.

Rooke, D. and Torbert, W. (2005) 'The seven transformations of leadership', *Harvard Business Review*, April, 83(4): 66–76.

Storey, John (2011) *Leadership in Organisations: current issues and key trends*, 2nd edition. Oxford: Routledge.

Western, Simon (2008) *Leadership: a critical text*. London: Sage.

Whittington, J. Lee, Coker, Renee H., Goodwin, Vicki L., Ickies, William and Murry, Brian (2009) 'Transactional leadership revisited: self-other agreement and its consequences', *Journal of Applied Social Psychology*, 39 (8): 1860–1886.

.... 5 ....

Behind-the-scenes Leadership and Leading from the Front

> *'Quiet leadership' and highly visible leadership are the major contrasts in this range of approaches to leadership.*

A key issue in this particular leadership dialectic is the relative visibility of leaders. This presents important questions such as: Why be a visible leader and 'lead from the front'? What are an individual's motivations for being seen publicly to be a leader? Is it important to be seen on a daily basis, or is behind-the-scenes-leadership equally effective? This discussion begins with considering some implications of 'leading from the front' versus 'leading from behind the scenes'. To elucidate these issues, we use cases of front-line versus behind-the-scenes leadership from the UK fashion chain NEXT.

In considering leadership visibility, a central concern of leadership studies now comes into focus: the viewpoint of the followers. How are leaders perceived by those whom they lead, and in the case of overt front-line leadership (such as celebrity executives like Richard Branson or high-profile politicians like Barack Obama), how are they perceived by the public? On the positive side a leader-from-the-front is perceived as inspirational, courageous and confident (see the related entry Inspirational Leadership and Low-key Leadership). These attributes are commonly applied to what in the leadership studies literature is referred to as 'charismatic leadership'. Charismatic leadership practice is generally associated with a highly visible, public presence in which leaders display appealing personalities of charm and dynamism. Charismatic leaders typically express grand visions and great rhetorical abilities. At the same time they are acutely sensitive to, or at least are perceived as being sensitive to, their environments and the needs of those they lead. Charismatic leaders usually score low on uncertainty-avoidance, and are willing to take risks (see Conger and Kanungo, 1998; Ladkin, 2006). This may be contrasted with high and low conflict-avoiding styles of leadership – see the related entry Avoiding Leadership and Involved Leadership.

But are positive attributes such as inspirational, courageous and confident applicable only to highly visible leaders? What about behind-the-scenes leaders, such as are found in most organizations amongst those close to the top, or people such as Rosa Parks (an American civil rights activist who started the Montgomery Bus Boycott), whose example was an inspiration to others even though she had no desire to lead, or publicly acknowledged leaders who prefer to stay out of the limelight, such as King George VI? May they not be perceived as inspirational, courageous and confident too? While these kinds of leaders do not overtly try to develop grand public personas, they are often publicly recognized and praised for their behind-the-scenes leadership of 'doing' rather than 'saying'. Leading quietly is often associated with the values and practices of servant leaders (see related entries on Accommodating Leadership and Competitive Leadership, and Extrovert Leadership and Introvert Leadership). Quiet leadership is typified by pragmatism and a practice focused on values and achieving overall good for an organization, without losing sight of self-interest. Quiet leaders tend to lead by doing, by setting an example (see Badaracco, 2002a, 2002b; Rock, 2009). Servant leadership is similar in that it is often a background practice informed by values and achieving what is considered to be the overall good. However, for servant leaders the needs of followers are placed first and foremost and personal concerns and interests are secondary (see Greenleaf and Spears, 1977, 2002).

While many positive characteristics are attributed to both front and behind-the-scenes leaders, many negative attributes may be associated with both. At extremes, the former can be seen as over-confident, arrogant and egotistical (see the related entry Authoritative Leadership and Participative Leadership) while the latter may be perceived as being weak and timid. In some respects, leadership is always visible – even if no-one sees the leader, he or she still makes a mark. A front-line leader is probably also a purposive leader (see the entry Goal-oriented Leadership and Opportunistic Leadership), but it is still possible to lead quietly from behind the scenes and hold to a purpose.

Leading from the front is more risky and gives the appearance of taking more responsibility. The leader is more exposed when things go wrong, and may lose sight of the big picture if too caught up in constant activity. The old adage 'you can't see the forest for the trees' is applicable.

Below we discuss an example of a remarkable 'behind the scenes' executive, and one who was just quietly effective, but also not frequently visible. We suggest that quiet leadership might be more appropriate for many of today's challenges.

The front-line leader can be very heavily – even emotionally – involved and can be highly effective in motivating followers and leading impressive, innovative development. Such was the case with the exuberant and high-profile George Davis's tenure as

NEXT's CEO (1984–1988). Davis put NEXT on the map in the early 1980s as one of the UK's leading fashion chains, but also took the company to near bankruptcy by 1988. Such leadership can lose sight of practicalities and the bottom line, too focused on a grand vision. Conversely, leading from behind the scenes can allow a leader to see things in perspective and make cooler, more measured judgements. Such was the case with the cautious and quiet leadership of Sir David Jones's tenure as NEXT's CEO (1988–2001). While the former CEO's leadership brought the company onto the national stage with great fervour, the latter's leadership steadied the business in turbulent times and ensured its continued success.

Whereas George Davis created a visionary model for NEXT, but failed to maintain the practicalities which underlay the vision, it was Sir David who put NEXT back on the road to financial stability. Jones – an accountant who worked his way up the ranks from being a 16-year-old messenger in the post room – was a quiet character who let others take the limelight. .

David Jones's story (see *NEXT to Me: luck, leadership and living with Parkinson's*, 2005) describes his rise up the ranks of the mail order and retail sectors in Britain. As a background leader, Jones relied upon the expertise and skills of his teams, and was always the first to praise the contribution of others. He saw himself as relatively pedestrian, plodding and hard-working. His enthusiasm is directed at the people with whom he works and their achievements.

David Jones's attitude to leadership was a function of his personality and the fact that he was suffering from a debilitating, incurable illness: Parkinson's Disease. His natural modesty was enhanced by his decision to avoid the limelight lest his medical problem, which he hid for twenty years, should be discovered and impact negatively on public confidence in the business – an aspect of servant leadership, putting others before oneself. As the CEO and then the Chairman of NEXT, one of the few skills Jones personally acknowledges is his dogged belief that every problem has its solution. This is illustrated by his dedication to work. Waking at 6 a.m. to take enough medication to function by 8 a.m., the only way he could get out of bed in the morning was by rolling over and falling onto the floor. When he finally acknowledged his condition publicly, some observers were relieved to know that his involuntary movements, shaking fits and swaying, were not alcoholism! Typically, he plays down his problems with wry humour.

Jones explained the amazing turnaround of NEXT plc, in which the stock-market valuation increased from £25 million to £3.5 billion sterling, in terms of the contrast between himself and the charismatic founder. He was the 'grey Yorkshire accountant' and 'safe pair of hands' compared with the flamboyant business star found in George Davis. It is here one finds the heart of Jones's background leadership. As a servant leader, he put the interests of his employees and the company ahead of his own problems, often acknowledging and praising the contributions of his team members. As a quiet leader he recognized how others could better handle the more public affairs of NEXT. However, the success in his leadership was not just in recognizing others' skills and accomplishments. He also knew that his careful oversight of financial management was essential. In the background Jones oversaw the 'bean counting', maintaining a pragmatic stance in his leadership decisions, relying upon his considerable skills as an accountant, and operating most actively as a financial leader (see the related entry on Finance-oriented Leadership and Marketing-oriented Leadership). As opposed to the charismatic, front-line leadership of Davis, Jones was far enough away from the front-line action to be able to take in the big picture practicalities of steering NEXT out of financial ruin and into financial prosperity. As a leader he was able to see the problems and issues of the business and to deal with them in measured, practical ways.

Today Jones's success as a behind-the-scenes leader has led him to numerous other business interests, non-executive directorships, investments in fast cars, support of rugby teams and, most significantly, active support of Parkinson's charities. He is keeping as active as possible, and is still inspiring and courageous in the face of the painful process of getting up every morning.

One might well ask at this point, is behind-the-scenes, quiet leadership the answer to all leadership situations? Are we in an age of leading quietly? After all, one can point to a significant number of public, charismatic leaders who have been tragically toxic, doing immeasurable harm, even leading atrocities of immense proportions. Peter Drucker, an outstanding leadership and management thinker, once said, 'the 20th Century produced three great leaders: Hitler, Stalin and Mao'. The quandary is obvious: these leaders oversaw unspeakable horrors, but they also mobilized action on an unprecedented scale.

If the purpose of leadership is to get things done, everyone can think of examples of unassuming but influential people steering the course of major innovations and changes. Recent research into communities facing complex and uncertain challenges shows that the most effective leaders are those with a sense of repose – a tolerance for uncertainty coupled with self-aware creativity (Western, 2008; Ladkin, 2010). It is significant that this recent research focuses on responses to climate change – transformations over which we can have little individual impact, but requiring sustained action with constant learning and adaptation. Perhaps this exposes an important point about leading from behind the scenes – it recognizes that much is beyond our personal control, and that more activity does not necessarily equal more or better effects.

But is behind-the-scenes leadership the best leadership practice? The answer is contextual. Consider this question: would NEXT plc have been so successful in its first years if it had been led by the quiet, background leadership of Sir David Jones? The most likely answer is no, or at least it would not have been as explosively successful as it was. At that early stage, NEXT probably required the vision, charisma and exuberance of George Davis. He was inspiring, visibly passionate and energetic. For that period in the company's history, it was front-line leadership that propelled the company to prominence. However, over time, the requirements changed. Davis was either unable or unwilling to adapt his style to the financial pragmatism required in the late 1980s and the company suffered. Within that context, the behind-the-scenes leadership of Jones was the better leadership style. Leadership must consider the context of leading and certain leadership styles and personalities – whether front line or behind the scenes – will work in some contexts but not in others.

Though the above discussion considers behind-the-scenes leadership as highly positive, there are many contexts when it may not be as successful. Imagine a scenario where a new company's director always works behind the scenes, and avoids speaking in front of others. She prefers short, informal discussions with just a few people. While the leader is very trusting, not overly critical, and generally supportive, she provides little direction for those she leads and is neither inspiring, enthusiastic or outspoken. She is not portraying a vision of the company's future, but is overly preoccupied with the day-to-day processes of the business and its financial management, as essential as those things are. In this type of situation team members, employees, investors, etc. may become frustrated, demoralized and no longer enthusiastic about the venture, and then the business goes nowhere.

Is it too much to ask for a leader who is adaptable to different contexts; a leader who can be charismatic and inspirational, providing a positive public face to an organization when necessary, but one who can also lead quietly, supplying a more cautious and steady hand approach? Often these two styles are represented in different people: a charismatic CEO and a quieter chief financial officer (CFO), for example. But let's hold on to the ideal of a hybrid, someone who is comfortable leading from the front and from the back, as situations require.

Three 'disciplines' derived from stoic values, as set out by Epictetus and employed by Marcus Aurelius, help summarize the qualities we are looking for here, because it seems that we have a new kind of leader in mind – not the romantic heroism of Admiral Lord Nelson, for example, but rather something more in tune with the stoic values expressed by Marcus Aurelius who was facing times at least as turbulent as our own. These three 'disciplines' of the wise leader equate to mostly behind-the-scenes or quiet leadership:

- non-attachment to one's own emotional responses – hunches and gut reactions are evidence of some sort, but not reasons to act;
- the will to act, to change things for the better, but for the benefit of the organization more than self;
- a sense of proportion that comes from the ability to distinguish between background changes, the impulse to act, and the effects that one might actually have.

These three virtues, detachment, action and reason, are surprisingly common in managers' own descriptions of how they would like to work (see Case and Gosling, 2007). They aspire to lead quietly and behind the scenes, in an empowering way, even if sometimes they admire heroic leadership. In fact, if we look closely at Nelson (see Jones and Gosling, 2005), we find that the flamboyant image of the hero is underpinned by a powerful sense of vocation and tremendous diligence to work at the small things that matter so much. As he took on more senior and complex responsibilities, the stoical virtues came to characterize his leadership style.

But is there really such a thing as a behind-the-scenes leader? Let's face it – leaders are almost by definition people who stand out from the norm, who innovate and sooner or later get noticed. On the other hand, it must be open to all of us to lead from the background.

FURTHER READING

Alvesson, M. and Svenningsson S. (2003) The great disappearing act: difficulties in doing leadership, *Leadership Quarterly*, 14, 359–381.

Badaracco, Joseph L. Jr. (2002a) *Leading Quietly: an unorthodox guide to doing the right thing.* Boston, MA: Harvard Business School Publishing.

Badaracco, Joseph L. Jr. (2002b) 'A lesson for the times: learning from quiet leaders', *Ivey Business Journal*, 1–6, January/February.

Case, Peter and Gosling, Jonathan (2007) 'Wisdom of the moment: pre-modern perspectives on organizational action', *Social Epistemology*, special issue on Wisdom and Stupidity in Management, 22(4).

Conger, Jay Alden and Kanungo, Rabindra Nath (1998) *Charismatic Leadership in Organizations*. Thousand Oaks, CA: Sage.

Greenleaf, Robert K. (2002) 'The servant leader within: a transformative path', in Hamilton Beazley, Julie Begg and Larry C. Spears (eds), *Servant Leadership*. Mahwah, NJ: Paulist Press.

Greenleaf, Robert K. and Spears, Larry C. (1977). *Servant Leadership: a journey into the nature of legitimate power and greatness*. Mahwah, NJ: Paulist Press.

Grint, K. (2010) 'The sacred in leadership: separation, sacrifice and silence', *Organization Studies*, 31 (1): 89–107.

Haslam, S.A., Reicher, S. and Platow, M. (2011) *The New Psychology of Leadership: identity, influence and power*. New York: Psychology Press.

Iszatt-White, M. (2011) 'Methodological crises and contextual solutions: an ethnomethodologically informed approach to understanding leadership', *Leadership*, 7 (2): 119–135.

Jones, David (2005) *NEXT to Me: luck, leadership and living with Parkinson's*. London: Nicholas Brealey.

Jones, S. and Gosling, J. (2005) *Nelson's Way: leadership lessons from the great commander*. London: Nicholas Brealey.

Kort, E.D. (2008) 'What after all, is leadership? "Leadership" and plural action', *Leadership Quarterly*, 19 (4): 409–425.

Ladkin, Donna (2006) 'The enchantment of the charismatic leader: charisma reconsidered as aesthetic encounter', *Leadership*, 2 (2): 165–179.

Lencioni, Patrick (2000) *The Four Obsessions of an Extraordinary Executive: a leadership fable*. San Franciso, CA: Jossey-Bass.

Northouse, Peter Guy (2010) *Leadership: theory and practice*. Thousand Oaks, CA: Sage.

Rock, David (2009) *Quiet Leadership*. London: HarperCollins.

.... 6 ....

Broad-based Leadership and Functional Leadership

> *Some leaders stay close to their functional origins (e.g. finance) whilst others, with short experience of many functional areas, can rise above their silos.*

Many leaders rise to leadership roles through one particular functional route. This may reflect the work specialization of their family or another formative influence, such as a school teacher, the subject they studied at university or college, and their first job. It does not always relate to the main area of interest of the particular leader, who may over time even feel burdened by his or her specialism, and wish he or she had never chosen it to start with! A functional specialization can take a hold on the incumbent in terms of impacting his or her outlook after a few years, and is especially powerful if it was the mode in which the person started work. It can influence the way that a leader sees the world, and what he or she prioritizes as important.

A broad-based leader, by contrast, might have joined a company graduate development programme and gained a taste of many specializations early on, or he or she might have started in a generalist role – such as personal assistant to the chairman. This young broad-based leader might have been in a small business, where the functional silos were not well-developed, or an entrepreneur in a start-up.

Here, we look at the issue of a functionally biased or broad-based approach, and then in later entries we turn to look at leaders with either financially-oriented outlooks, compared with those of a marketing bias – and then highly task-oriented production-based leaders compared with HR – both seen here as extreme ways of looking at a business (see the entries Finance-oriented Leadership and Marketing-orientated Leadership, HR-oriented Leadership and Production-oriented Leadership, and Expert Leadership and Generalist Leadership).

Leaders with a strong functional bias often operate from the basis of their expertise, whereas broad-based leaders are generalists. Functional specialists may have a preference for homogeneity, while generalists hunger for diversity. Generalist leaders are those able to operate in many business sectors – in the way that IBM CEO Lou Gerstner could move from financial services to consulting to retail to the computer industry. Broad-based leadership experience gained across many functions of a business – such as accounting, HR, marketing – shapes their outlook as CEOs. Leaders with narrow functional experience arguably bring this sense of discipline and focus to their way of operating in senior leadership roles.

Functionally oriented leaders often have a background in finance (probably the most popular), marketing/public relations (PR), sales/customer service, HR, production, information technology (IT) and strategy. What are some of the issues of having a narrow focus? Here we consider examples of functional leaders who miss the point, waste resources, fail to keep in touch with the overall business and add no value. These are leaders who fail to move beyond their initial specialist functional roles to embrace the more holistic and broad-framework of leadership. By contrast, we begin with the thoughts of a leader who sees the importance of understanding how other functions operate.

An ex-CEO/Management Consultant – on the broad vision of organizational leadership:

> Although leaders are influenced by their early experiences, I believe you can't allow yourself to be one type of leader. You have to combine your natural style with many types of styles. To do the job of a CEO or Managing Director, I have to understand the needs and priorities of finance, HR, sales and strategic planning – and understand what it takes to lead people and make them accountable with measurable tools. This is also an important part of developing leaders – we have to train people to be multi-dimensional, otherwise we will be training lots of departmental heads and section supervisors but not real leaders, I believe. Leaders need to have a basic understanding

of other disciplines. How can I, as a cross-functional, overall and broad-based leader, help them to gain confidence across disciplines? How can I provide them with better information to make the right decisions? I need to help them to see outside their functional areas – to look from the outside in and the inside out.

I can improve the capability of my managers to be successful functional managers if I can help them to gain a more rounded insight of the whole business by understanding the other functions. To optimize your leadership ability, you need to understand how people with different functional backgrounds think; then you need to take the next step and help them to work together. The final stage is to encourage them to help each other, even when the overall leader is not around.

This ex-CEO is clearly not a one-dimensional functional leader, as he understands the broader holistic view that a leader must have. While a leader may come from a particular specialization or functional role, he or she must learn the basics of the other roles within the organization that he or she leads. In this case the leader is clear about the need to develop multi-dimensional employees who can then become multi-dimensional leaders. The following example highlights one leader, the Customer Service Manager of a large company, who was anything but multi-dimensional in his leadership approach.

An HR/development consultant – on the extreme functional leader:

I was researching a company and how it responded to an emergency situation and I was surprised at how little the Customer Service Manager seemed to know about what was going on. Every question I asked received the response 'oh, that's the responsibility of sales'; 'that's nothing to do with me, that's operations'; 'the boss decides on that' and 'that's for head office'. He managed to side-step every question and didn't seem bothered that he was out of touch with many operations of the business. He had defined his functional role so tightly that he practically did nothing. No decisions, therefore no blame. This can be seen as 'laissez-faire' leadership, of extremely passive leadership by exception, of 'high uncertainty avoiding behaviour' – but it exhibits itself as seeking refuge in a closely defined functional silo. His boss was very frustrated with him, but explained his behaviour in terms of his nationality, advanced age and traditional outlook, and said the strict labour regulations and his family background meant that he had a job for life. There was nothing she could do.

In the next example we find a leader who is very successful at operating at a high level on the international stage. Essentially she is a functional strategic leader. However, she is so occupied with this activity that she neglects the more managerial aspects of her role.

An emerging market consultant – on a functional strategic leader neglecting day-to-day management:

There are leaders who focus on strategy and planning to such an extent that they like high-level deals so much that they are not interested in managing people on a day-to-day basis. There is one I can think of who is very successful in negotiating partnerships and lucrative international deals – but she is high on avoiding at the office. This leader is very business-minded and a great entrepreneur, but is much better at travelling and winning deals than leading her employees. She admits she doesn't like managing people at all, and luckily for her the staff members working for her are able to get on with their implementation work by themselves. But if they had what she might think were small problems, and personal issues, she wouldn't be remotely interested.

Within fields of a particular technical specialization, such as the IT industry, leaders can become engulfed in their functions as technical experts within a specific discipline (see the related entry Expert Leadership and Generalist Leadership). For example, the Google leaders – Larry Page and Sergey Brun – had one great idea which they developed very successfully. However, according to many commentators in the business press (Copeland, 2010) they have a tendency to become bogged-down in their technology. A contrast has been made with Apple – a company which is far more strategic, open-minded and exhibits constant innovation. Google has been accused of currently lacking a vision for the future – and that the company may run out of steam if it doesn't keep up the pace of constant change. There are big pressures on IT companies to continue to be innovative – to not just have one big idea. Leaders with IT backgrounds can be very creative, advanced, with lots of exciting ideas, and good at problem-solving; but they can also be too technical, and unable to express themselves or be responsive to the consumer market. Leaders with this background tend to be very task-oriented, seeing other people (their internal customers, in reality) as getting in the way of 'their' computers operating properly.

All the functionally oriented types of leaders described here are based on aspects of 'expert' leadership, where the leader is stuck in a functional silo. Although limiting, this phenomenon is almost subconscious and involuntary – and very common. Multi-tasking, and multi-dimensional understanding, are clearly rare. The downside is that functionally limited mindsets keep many potentially effective leaders in less-than-senior roles. Each of the different perspectives has its own strengths and limitations. But these are the different coloured lens through which many leaders see their world – and it's not necessarily real, and doesn't help them to progress. Breaking out of a functional specialization is one of the most challenging tasks for the young (and middle-aged) potential leader who wants to gain promotion to a general manager/overall leader role. It may be even more difficult than breaking out of one industry sector to go to another. It could be that the functional influence is stronger.

FURTHER READING

Bevan, J. (2007) *The Rise and Fall of Marks & Spencer…and How It Rose Again*. London: Profile Books.

Bolden, R., Hawkins, B., Gosling, J. and Taylor, S. (2011) *Exploring Leadership: individual, organizational and societal perspectives*. Oxford: Oxford University Press.

Copeland, Michael V. (2010) 'Google: the search party is over', *Fortune*, 16 August, 162 (3): 42–49.

Jones, David (2005) *NEXT to Me: luck, leadership and living with Parkinson's*. London: Nicholas Brealey.

Maxwell, John C. (1993) *Developing the Leader Within You*. Nashville, TN: Thomas Nelson.

Mintzberg, H. (1994) *The Rise and Fall of Strategic Planning: reconceiving roles for planning, plans, planners*. New York: Free Press.

Storey, John (2011) *Leadership in Organisations: current issues and key trends*. Second edition. Oxford: Routledge.

Welch, J. (2005) *Winning*. New York: HarperCollins.

7

Change-oriented Leadership and Continuity-based Leadership

> *Some leaders thrive on constant change and a fast-paced environment; others prefer building on what works well and seeking emerging possibilities for the organization.*

Leaders often have to strike a delicate balance between change and the status quo. They may be expected to be action oriented, but are also required to maintain a sense of continuity. Today, leadership is often closely related to the idea that change has to be made to happen, against a background of inertia, and that leaders are particularly endowed with a desire to change, visions of new possibilities, and the skills to manage the processes of change – what used to be called change management. In fact, a change of leadership is often the precursor to more widespread change. Yet, even in change a certain amount of continuity is inevitable, and definitely desirable: it makes people more comfortable with and supportive of change. In this section we consider the differences and similarities between leadership oriented towards change and an approach to leadership that tries to nurture continuity. It is important to remember that in either case, change always happens, and so does continuity; of course some circumstances have much greater stability than others; and in some situations the leadership of an organization or project must be very active in creating and maintaining the momentum for change. But sometimes the best form of action is inaction – to not interfere, to facilitate or to bide one's time. Leadership action is not always visible as activity.

A leader of change *and* continuity leader is someone who is:

- not frenzied in rushing about, but develops a sensitive awareness of the terrain and capabilities of the team(s), helping everyone to set and maintain their direction – with reflection;

- able to realize the importance of achieving a balance, in combination between all the different elements of the organization, and with synergy between the different units working together;
- able to differentiate between those things which should be changed and those which should be preserved.

In contrast the change-obsessed leader is concerned above all with action, sometimes for its own sake, but sometimes because there is no external stability to relate to. The continuity-oriented leader is concerned with maintaining and preserving an organization's positives, but may also be slow to address its negatives. Neither of these extremes is really optimal. But achieving the right balance for the situation is not easy, and much depends on the capacities of the leaders and their team: especially the capacity for dealing with ambiguity and uncertainty. The pressures to 'do something' can be overwhelming – almost as strong as the resistance to anything one does try to do! Handling change effectively is now central to most leadership positions, and can be approached as the task of balancing change and continuity. In helping people to cope with their natural resistance to change, sometimes the leader has to emphasize continuity as well as change. What do we still have to hang onto with all this change happening all around us?

Leaders facing the task of change in an organization need to assess the readiness of the people who will be affected. It is often useful to distinguish people's responses to change according to their initial responses: enthusiasts, consolidators and cynics – who may turn out to be change killers. The cynics might be narrowly focused on their own department or job, and they might have lived through too many company reorganizations in the past. They may take time to come around, and if they can be persuaded of the value of the changes, can be amongst the best long-term champions, staying true to the core values of the organization. But cynicism can be a contagious poison, and should be neutralized. If they can't be won over, the real change killers may be better off leaving an organization they can no longer identify with – and they might have to be encouraged to go! The enthusiasts can be change agents of, whether or not they are full-blown 'action leaders', and our consolidators encourage our 'continuity leaders'. We can consider that they all play their part.

CHANGE AGENT COMPETENCIES – FOCUS ON ACTION

- risk-taking;
- entrepreneurial and innovative;
- tough – in hiring and firing;
- inspirational, possibly charismatic, leadership-oriented;
- thick-skinned – not over-sensitive;
- pragmatic, project based;
- pushy, aggressive, or perhaps just determined and persistent;
- strong impact and influence skills;
- honest and direct to the point of bluntness, but crafty too;
- uncompromising, revolutionary, but prepared to win one battle at a time;

- savvy, street-smart, curious and adventurous;
- maverick, unconventional, risk-taking.

CONSOLIDATOR COMPETENCIES – FOCUS ON CONTINUITY

- prudent, careful, caring;
- committed to the company as a community to belong to – not just a means to an end;
- reasonable, perceptive, team-building;
- focused on managing resources effectively, and alert to complex risks to operations;
- sensitive to other people and to the operational fragilities of the work;
- long-term oriented, focused on steady and secure growth;
- assertive, not passive, but not so aggressive;
- more discreet and subtle impact and influencing skills;
- diplomatic, culturally aware, able to play the politics;
- flexible according to the needs of the business;
- focused on believing in the company, loyal, supporting company policy;
- fitting-in with the company culture;
- respectful of the 'face' of another person.

Here, we are introduced to a colleague attempting to be an action leader, who appreciates that many other colleagues in the organization value continuity and not all are convinced by the need for change. Leaders who have successfully followed the action route have protected continuity when it was deserved, and when it didn't hold the change process in check. Overall, the need to achieve a balance is strong here, which can be especially helpful in overcoming resistance to change.

An HR/development markets consultant – on the value of a change agent:

> I'm thinking of a senior colleague, the leader of a department, who's a very strong change agent. He has completely restructured our processes and the way we operate in the unit for which he is responsible. It has caused some chaos and confusion, but most of the other colleagues are getting used to it. It's definitely leading to improvements, many of which are long overdue. He's taking into account many different stakeholders, which sounds like a good idea.
>
> My colleague has created the image of a cart being pulled along by a few people, who he sees as the change leaders. There are several other people sitting in the cart, who are fairly passive. These are going along with the change. They are not resisting, but they are not doing a great deal to help. But the worst problem – and we all know who he means – are the people hanging off the back of the cart, trying to pull it in the opposite direction, or trying to keep it in place where it is. These are the ones he has identified as the change killers. They insist on doing everything the same old way, and refuse to consider the changes our senior colleague is implementing. They are behaving just like a brick wall.
>
> However, he is also trying to maintain some continuity, by emphasizing our mission, our unique selling points, our experience, our strong track record, and the quality of the staff members. But he's not afraid to tackle many of the problems in the organization. It helps that he's quite new and doesn't have a lot of baggage.

This leader is primarily an action leader, but one who also encourages continuity. He has come into a department and developed a vision for what it might become and has then gone about implementing the changes necessary to make it real. The change has certainly caused a degree of chaos and uncertainty and groups of people have emerged that were supportive of the change, passive or resistive. Recognizing that not everyone was actively supporting the change, and some were actively subverting it, the leader has emphasized key elements of commonality and continuity. In this instance they have been the elements of the shared narrative of the company – the mission, selling points, experience, track record and the quality of employees.

In the following example, an ex-CEO consultant reflects on how he implemented change and how he was able to balance action and continuity leadership. Important in this example is how the leader was mindful of balancing change and continuity throughout the process.

An ex-CEO/Management Consultant – on balancing change and continuity:

> When I faced implementing a major change, I had to be both an action and continuity leader. The former because the new owners were insisting on radical new ways of creating value, which I couldn't achieve doing things the old way. But I wanted to preserve continuity as much as possible, because many of the things we did in the past were OK. We made a point of not making anyone redundant in the change process. A few people took early retirement, and that was all. We changed people's job responsibilities, but also offered them training and re-skilling. We introduced new products – but all on the basis of our core business. We set ourselves action plans and we were much more proactive and focused on change and improvement – that was the biggest change. We monitored our progress much more frequently. But it was based on a sound business to start with, and we didn't want to lose our strengths.

From the outset, this leader was aware of the need to balance action and continuity leadership. As an action leader he realized changes had to be made to respond to new demands for creating value. Things just couldn't be done as they had been before. However, to maintain continuity he evaluated the best parts of the organization's business practice, conserving these, and making minimal changes in staffing. Key to the success of the action leadership here was the empowerment of the employees. Rather than replacing staff, the business invested in training and re-skilling existing employees to fit new roles. It is also clear that the leader engaged followers in the change process by saying 'we set ourselves action plans…' rather than 'I'. Though action was necessary, the leader brought the followers on board with the action, investing in them and continuing the existing best practices of the business.

Building on existing strengths and involving current employees has a proven track record in many great companies. For example, Lou Gerstner was able to create lasting change at IBM by building on its strengths as a one-stop shop, at a time when the market seemed to favour many of the smaller, more focused high-tech operators in niche areas. But Gerstner knew that the clients appreciated the convenience of this ability of an all-round provider – and it had always been one of Big Blue's strengths. They could handle all the clients' needs and problems from one source, and gave guarantees of service continuity to allay clients' concerns about having all their IT eggs in one basket.

Similarly, Jack Welch emphasized the size, power and long history of GE during the change process, leveraging this status to enter other fields. This building on continuity helped GE in entering financial services – it was already big, respectable, and a strong brand name. This and other quite separate, new businesses complemented the GE operation and helped it to transform itself from a synergyless bureaucracy into a much more vibrant, market-driven organization.

Action leaders tend towards fast-moving change, but their efforts don't always lead to a lasting transformation. Continuity leaders like things as they are, and so they are suspicious about too much action and change for its own sake. Yet they can get left behind, when real change pressures leave them unmoved. Ideally, a leader appreciating both change and continuity can strike a balance, particularly based on a long-term judgement of the strengths and weaknesses of an organization. Appreciating continuity can certainly help in overcoming resistance to change, which is one of the greatest challenges facing the action-oriented leader. The fewer things that change, the more people can cope – but there must be a balance as not enough change will leave the organization where it was before.

FURTHER READING

Adair, J. (1973) *Action-Centred Leadership*. New York: McGraw Hill.

Beach, Lee Roy (2006) *Leadership and the Art of Change: a practical guide to organizational transformation*. Thousand Oaks, CA: Sage.

Case, Peter and Gosling, Jonathan (2007) 'Wisdom of the moment: pre-modern perspectives on organizational action', *Social Epistemology*, special issue on Wisdom and Stupidity in Management, 22 (4).

Champey, J.A. (1993) *Re-engineering the Corporation: a manifesto for business revolution*. New York: Harper Business Books.

Gerstner, L. (2002) *Who Says Elephants Can't Dance?* New York: HarperCollins.

Gosling, J. and Minzberg, H. (2003) 'The five minds of the manager', *Harvard Business Review*, November, 81(11): 54–63.

Grint, K. (2005) 'Problems, problems, problems: the social construction of "leadership"', *Human Relations*, 58 (11): 1467–1494.

Haslam, S.A., Reicher, S. and Platow, M. (2011) *The New Psychology of Leadership: identity, influence and power*. New York: Psychology Press.

Joiner, W. and Josephs, S. (2006) *Leadership Agility: five levels of mastery for anticipating and initiating change*. San Francisco, CA: Jossey-Bass.

Pfeffer, J. (1994) *Managing with Power: politics and influence in organizations*. Boston, MA: Harvard Business School Press.

Puccio, Gerard J., Mance, Marie and Murdoch, Mary C. (2011) *Creative Leadership: skills that drive change* (2nd edition). Thousand Oaks, CA: Sage.

Rerup, C. and Feldman, M.S. (2011) 'Routines as a source of change in organizational schemata: the role of trial-and-error learning', *Academy of Management Journal*, 54 (3): 577–610.

8

'Chillaxed Leadership' and 'Leadaholics'

For some, leading is a drug, and they feel themselves truly alive only when in the hot seat. Others value being able to slip in and out of their leadership roles, and value balance with other aspects of life.

Live to lead, or lead to live? The question of balance is central to leadership practice, particularly in high-profile, high-pressure situations. Many leaders have a propensity to be workaholics, focused primarily (if not solely) on their work activities. Other equally successful leaders seem to be less attached to their leadership roles. In this entry we discuss issues surrounding balance and focus in leadership.

One approach is to consider the relationship between a leader's public and private lives. Many consider the personal behaviour of leaders to be fair game for the press, and privacy is a luxury that leaders cannot be allowed. Under constant scrutiny, leaders may find themselves trying to stay in control all the time, seldom really relaxing. It takes a lot of self-confidence to chill out and relax ('chillax') in these circumstances.

In any case, is work–life balance really commensurate with career advancement? Was anyone promoted or otherwise rewarded for going home from work on time? And who achieved greatness by taking it easy?

Being passionate and completely committed to work can be exciting, absorbing all one's ambition, curiosity and idealism. It is easy to get caught up in the belief that success in a career is the same as success as a person, and to throw all one's energy and time into a career or job. Women have to face this issue more directly than men if they want to have children, but the underlying dilemma is the same: What am I to be? How can I fit it all in? Which of my possible selves will I realize, and what will I lose out on in the choices I make?

The forces that drive people towards taking up leadership roles are many and various: it is not wise to generalize. But there are patterns and commonalities: we all grow up as children having to deal with authority figures, usually parents; the solutions we find become habits, some of which are really ways to deal with the emotional pain we suffered at an early stage in life. An addiction to work – equally other forms of addiction, to alcohol, drugs, collecting, socializing – can be an effective defence against feelings of abandonment; that one has not been properly recognized and admired. The busyness blots out the lack of connection and relationship in other parts of life, and makes one feel that it doesn't matter and satisfied with one's own achievements; yet ironically this attempt at independence becomes a pathological dependency. When a leader becomes addicted to being in charge, a 'leadaholic' who can only relate from that position, he or she is cut off from relationships of equality, and doomed to loneliness. Of course, not all workaholism stems from the same cause, and there are plenty of ways to be healthily engaged in work and a career. Nor is it the case that 'chillaxed' detachment is necessarily a sign of perfect emotional health: distancing oneself from work can be a way to avoid commitments, and is just as pathological. So it is appropriate for leaders to seriously examine their working patterns and the emotional investment in the job. This is healthy for them, and has implications for colleagues and subordinates.

Having an overwhelming focus on your job, committing all your emotional energy into one thing, can mean crossing the line from passion to obsession. Of course truly great works in art, philosophy, science, business, war and diplomacy are fruits of passion, and obsession is for many a route to high achievement: 'Passion is incompatible with balance and challenges established priorities' (Jones and Gosling, 2005: 92). Passion can be the mark of great leadership if it is contagious and inspirational, and demonstrates a dedication to high ideals.

Obsession is often productive in the early years of a career, especially in technical roles where the mastery of complex techniques requires dedicated practice; and in relationship-oriented businesses (such as consulting, merchant banking, private equity) in which relentless networking is crucial to building the personal capital that is embedded in contacts and mutual obligations. But it may stem from a longing for absolute control, a defence against acknowledging the complexity, interdependency and emergent uncertainties of the real world. It might also be to do with the objective conditions of job security. Where employment laws are weak, employees may sensibly be more obsessed with the need to hold down a job. And leadership roles are typically more exposed, more subject to political infighting, and will therefore demand constant attention. In many respects, obsession might be a necessary trait for those willing to give the necessary priority to the pursuit of power and influence. Balance can tone down obsession into a more controlled passion, more in touch with reality. 'Harnessing our passions is not giving up our real feelings, but it is directing them for ideal purposes' (Jones and Gosling, 2005: 96).

Below we first look at an example of a leader who achieved a balance between his work and home life. For this individual it was the recognition and acceptance that although he had achieved an important leadership position, he was not likely to achieve a higher level of promotion. In response to this, he came to balance his activities by enhancing his personal interests and hobbies. Second, we look at examples of passionately focused leaders, who find it hard not to be workaholics.

A researcher on leadership – on the task of achieving such balance:

> This example is about an executive who had achieved a senior leadership role in the building society group for which he worked – he had become a District Manager. However, he admitted to himself that he was unlikely to move any higher in the organization because 'he would rock the boat too much'. He was very critical about the organization and found it hard to keep quiet when there were things going on which he really didn't like. He specifically didn't like what he saw as the irresponsible lending of mortgages – an attitude cultivated before the sub-prime mortgage crisis. He would not hesitate to turn down mortgage applications, even from people he knew,

because he thought they weren't reliable enough. But what this meant was that although he was good at his job, and occupied a senior position as a result, he was not obsessed with leading the organization to higher and higher profits, a stance he recognized would limit his opportunities for promotion.

However, while he didn't have the same focus and passion for the organization which some of his colleagues had, it didn't mean he wasn't capable of being passionate. He was able to take a balanced approach to work versus his non-work life. He had always been keen on playing in a brass band, and loved photography, computers and flying light aircraft. As a result, rather than drive himself to an imbalance, he took early retirement from his job and set up and ran a workers' union for his sector. He was very good at this, and enjoyed it much more than the mainstream building society job. Then he retired and really enjoyed himself.

What this individual was able to do was evaluate his situation, accept it, and find a harmonious balance that fitted (although there was certainly more angst in the process than this short description allows). Rather than over-work or compromise his beliefs, he carved out a satisfactory niche for himself. Many ambitious people, and people passionate about the work they want to accomplish, find this difficult. For example, many people (and this is certainly not limited only to individuals in leadership roles) identify so strongly with, and have so heavily invested in, their work lives that it consumes everything they do. This often has negative results vis-à-vis family, friends and eventually their personal well-being. Paradoxically, it takes a real focus and effort to chill out and relax!

A classic example of this is found in the struggle of a founding CEO of a successful company to relinquish power and control, even when it was obviously necessary to do so. An ex-Executive Search consultant – on the difficulties of letting go:

> The problem did not lie in finding a successor. The CEO had already identified a senior executive in the ranks and promoted her, but he had to learn how to stop being obsessed about the company and give her the room to do the job. He recognized the problem and employed an executive coach to help him let go and give her a chance. This was a very sensible attitude, really – as many succession planning attempts fail because the old boss is still hanging in there, and this especially relates to the micro-managing types.
>
> This particular CEO had married fairly late in life – and his new wife helped in the process of him giving up his tight rein on the business. He also found other things in which he was interested, such as being a benefactor of his old university. He achieved both focused and then balanced leadership, but for him it was a deliberate transition, helped by consultants, taken step-by-step. Key to his success was recognizing the problem, recognizing his personal blocks to solving the problem, and then relying upon the advice of experts (in this case an executive coach) and the support of his wife. As in so many leadership dilemmas, the answer is to be found in seeking advice and accepting help.

Emerging from both of the above examples are key lessons in finding a balance in leadership positions. The first is the ability to step back and look at the situation objectively. In the case of the building society manager, he was able to look at his work situation, decide he wasn't likely to progress further, and come to terms with that. In the case of the founder-CEO he was able to see the necessity of gradually relinquishing control of the organization and transitioning from a highly focused, intense leadership role to one that was more balanced between work and personal life. The second was that in both instances the leaders were able to take action to address the situation.

But what are the consequences for a leader who is unable to move from an intense, obsessive leadership role to a more balanced one? Certainly there is the potential for burnout. Leaders are no different from others who are totally consumed by their work, liable to enter a vicious circle in which they will neglect their personal relationships, and then work harder to avoid the pain as these relationships fall apart. There are also a number of knock-on effects for the organization.

Leaders who find it difficult to achieve a balance in their lives can create toxic work environments (see the entry Nurturing Leadership and Toxic Leadership). In many organizations, an imbalanced leader can elevate stress levels in the work environment, leading to a break-down in trust, commitment and productivity. Additionally, under such circumstances, the development of the next generation of leaders is rather limited. In fact, imbalanced leaders may actually fear the progression of competent deputies. Next-generation leaders – who are clearly talented and potentially highly motivated – receive little opportunity to take decisions; such is the level of control of the overall leader. The leader may be so passionate and controlling that his/her staff members become disempowered, and do not feel they can be passionate themselves, unless absorbed in the boss's enthusiasm. This is a typical effect of narcissistic leadership: the conviction that everything will be all right if the world can be made to fit the image the leader holds in his or her mind.

A leader who takes on too much responsibility takes jobs away from followers, forcing the leader to take on even more responsibility, resulting in a vicious cycle that can typically end in disaster. At the very least, subordinates will quit and move on to other employment opportunities.

Like many aspects of leadership practice, balance and focus have a lot to do with cultural conventions. In the Netherlands, for example, 'specific behaviours' (as described by Trompenaars and Hampden-Turner, 1997) are far more common than 'diffuse behaviours'. In terms of the 'specific' preference, people put their work life and home life in separate boxes. At 5 p.m., it's time to stop work and go home, even if half-way through an email. Trompenaars quotes the example of an employee being asked if he would be prepared to help the boss paint his house over the weekend (1997: 88, Chapter 7, 'How Far We Get Involved'). In China and much of Africa, only a minority of employees (30–40 per cent) would not 'volunteer' to help the boss, and 60–70 per cent would spend their weekend doing this task, even if they didn't really want to. But in the Netherlands – and in Switzerland and Sweden – 91 per cent of employees would unequivocally refuse. Only 10 per cent would feel a sense of obligation: 'It's not my job. It's not in my job description. Why should I?' The concept of work–life balance is very strong in much of Northern Europe, but in many countries it may be seen as a luxury that is not available, and work takes precedence over home life all the time. A job and income are too precious, and a boss may not be refused.

Leadership requires focus if it is to produce powerful results, but an obsessive attitude to work can go too far, becoming controlling and leaving others with no room to develop and grow. A leader who is reluctant to consider handing over to another generation should be prepared to question his or her motives. Leadership – the power and excitement – can become like a drug, and it can be hard to let go.

Chillaxed leadership can be highly effective, but may be more suited to established businesses, where there are systems in place, or to people with a portfolio of interests who are a slave to none. All leaders benefit from not being obsessive and narrow. But there is a time and place for everything: balance could be an excuse for loss of focus and drive. Chillaxed leadership is a great thing if it is seen as a conscious decision, carefully crafted, and its pursuit regarded as a matter for prudent judgement.

FURTHER READING

Bolden, R., Hawkins, B., Gosling, J. and Taylor, S. (2011) *Exploring Leadership: individual, organizational and societal perspectives.* Oxford: Oxford University Press.

Dyer, F. (2005) *Why Do I Do This Everyday? Finding meaning in your work.* Oxford: Lion Hudson.

Fischman, David (2006) *The Secret of the Seven Seeds: a parable of leadership and life.* San Francisco, CA: Jossey-Bass.

Fletcher, Winston (2002) *Beating the 24/7: how business leaders achieve a successful work/life balance.* Chichester: John Wiley.

Jones, S. and Gosling, J. (2005) *Nelson's Way: leadership lessons from the great commander.* London: Nicholas Brealey.

Lencioni, Patrick (2000) *The Four Obsessions of an Extraordinary Executive: a leadership fable.* San Franciso, CA: Jossey-Bass.

Storey, John (2011) *Leadership in Organisations: current issues and key trends* (2nd edition). Oxford: Routledge.

Trompenaars, F. and Hamden-Turner, C. (1997) *Riding the Waves of Culture: understanding cultural diversity in business.* London: Nicholas Brealey.

Western, Simon (2008) *Leadership: a critical text.* London: Sage.

.... 9 ....

Coaching and Mentoring-oriented Leadership and Directive, Telling-what-to-do Leadership

> *Some leaders adopt a supportive, transformational style, whilst others are simply looking to get others to do the job in the most efficient way.*

Mentoring can be seen as the process of coaching and supporting others, and can be especially valuable in developing leaders in an organization prepared to invest the necessary time and effort to make it work. A hands-off style of leadership with a strong developmental base, mentoring requires a mutual buy-in to achieve shared goals: processes that encourage distributed leadership in an organization. Distributed leadership (see the Introduction) avoids the singular leader concept in favour of recognizing the complex, dynamic relationship between bosses and subordinates, and recognizes the distribution of leadership activities amongst several individuals working within a team or across an organization (see the related entry Authoritarian Leadership and Participative Leadership). Rather than expecting a single person to show leadership for all the activities in an organization, distributed leadership recognizes and encourages the spread of leadership activity across a larger number of individuals, empowering a wide range of employees to take ownership and responsibility for running various projects and aspects of organizational governance. This approach was certainly favoured by one of our authors, in a team-based operation managed by himself and his fellow-directors and managers discussed below.

As a method for developing distributed leadership, coaching and mentoring can be highly effective – but it takes time to lay the foundations. Coaching is generally provided by a trained professional drawing on particular skills, but with no line management responsibility for the 'client', helping them to be effective in a leadership role. Mentoring is usually more focused on careers in a specific organization, but in reality there is much overlap between the two: coaches may provide mentoring functions over time, and mentors will use coaching skills. Both are processes in which one person (the coach or mentor) takes some responsibility for overseeing the career and development of another (the protégé or mentoree), usually outside of the normal manager/subordinate relationship – and both can gain important benefits. A mentor is usually an older and wiser person, who has a wide knowledge and experience of the world in general and (usually) of the particular company in question. Mentoring and coaching can be seen as a key strategy for fostering talent and spreading knowledge in an organization, at all levels. Mentoring by senior leaders can help junior leaders to get promoted, as the top executives know the mentoree's or junior's strengths and abilities and can recommend him or her for ideal opportunities. The younger leader, thanks to the mentor, can learn about changes in the organization before they happen; can avoid political landmines, so that fewer mistakes and faux pas are made; and can be plugged into the corporate strategy more actively and effectively.

But there are significant barriers to mentoring in most organizations, as many potential mentors among the leaders of an organization will argue: 'It's not in the organizational culture; there's not enough trust here; it's a gimmick, the management will forget about it after a while; it's time-consuming; people don't want the responsibility of trying to develop others, it's not part of my job; as managers, we may lose authority among our staff if we are not very good at it; I will get stuck at this mentoring stuff – what would I say to this younger person?; it's not focused enough on results; my mentorees might think it's a sign of weakness to confide in anyone, especially me; and '"if it ain't broke, don't fix it", things are OK around here.' In many organizations, mentoring would be just too far from the culture. This is one reason why many experienced leaders who are keen to offer the fruits of their experience to younger managers do so through specialist mentoring and coaching companies; their own employers just don't appreciate the value of this resource (see the discussion of transactional and transformational leadership in the definitions and theories of leadership).

It is, of course, a two-way relationship: potential mentorees may be thinking: 'It won't do any good, the organization does not support us; the managers may think it's a new management fad or fashion and won't take it seriously; no-one wants to take responsibility for me as a young executive, they are too busy doing their own work; won't I be too embarrassed to speak with the mentor openly?; it is just a new way of keeping tabs on us.'

Mentors must be skilled to be successful, and should have the following attributes:

- credibility: has a positive reputation in the organization;
- communication: asks insightful questions; frequently checks for understanding; empathetic;
- organizational know-how: understands the cultural norms and values, and structure, of the organization; can handle cross-departmental tasks and relationships;
- management perspective: experienced in management with different organizations in different functions;
- accessibility: makes time available when the mentoree is in need;
- developmental orientation: provides opportunities for others to perform; gives constructive feedback; contributes to company's training and development events;
- inventiveness: lateral thinker; active supporter of good ideas in the workplace; has creative problem solving skills.

Mentors can play the role of Interpreter/Advocate, helping the mentoree to understand the organization; of Counsellor, in handling interpersonal and private issues; of Coach/Learning Consultant, in helping the mentoree to improve specific skills; and of Process Consultant, to direct the mentoree in achieving a successful conclusion to executing specific processes in the organizational context, such as launching quality initiatives and change management processes.

Mentoring can help build careers for mentorees. It can reframe issues in a broader perspective; consider business realities beyond the mentoree's management perspective; and ask questions beyond the bottom line, even questions that may seem illegitimate when taken out of the privacy of the mentoring dialogue or exercise – such as personal issues. These issues may be holding the person back from further development.

But mentoring can also go wrong: is the organization ready for a mentoring process? It needs to have a developmental attitude (see the related entry Developmental-oriented Leadership and Job-hopping Leadership). Have the aims/goals of the coaching and mentoring programme been defined? Is there commitment from the top? Does the coaching and mentoring programme have a champion? Are there criteria for selecting mentors and mentorees? How are the mentors to be trained? How are the mentors and mentorees to be matched? Are there guidelines for both sides? Are there contingency plans to deal with typical mentoring problems? Most organizations are put off making full-scale coaching and mentoring programmes because of the time commitment, and the need to overcome a directive style, which might be favoured by many managers.

Here, we look at examples of being mentored and being a mentor, and the role of mentoring in creating an organizational culture, and how this might need to be adapted and changed in different circumstances and to achieve different targets.

An HR/development consultant – on an example of a redundant coach:

> One of my colleagues in a previous job had a private coach, outside the company. The coach didn't know anything about the organization; he was not there to help my colleague navigate round the place and get promotion. In fact, it seems the coach was there to motivate my colleague to actually do his job. The employee was a senior member of the organization whose primary role was as adviser to the CEO. In practice this individual's role was actually to motivate the CEO, to help him to write his memoirs, to help the CEO with succession planning, and to help the CEO achieve his personal goals of learning a foreign language and completing his MBA. The situation was rather bizarre. My colleague was in reality working as a coach to the CEO while also having a coach himself to motivate him as a coach. Why did he need a personal coach to push him to do his job? Why didn't he just get on with it by himself?

In this example the coaching seems to be over-the-top. The CEO had an adviser who operated primarily as a coach and motivator. At the same time the CEO's adviser had a personal coach: was this merely a fashion accessory, or a proper level of professional supervision, such as would be required in any normal psychotherapy or counselling work? This vignette illustrates how difficult it is to make a judgement about the value of coaching and mentoring, especially as the effects may not be obvious immediately, and where the human cost of doing something wrong could be extremely high. There is always a tension between the invisible effects of coaching and more measureable outcomes such as problems solved, projects completed, targets achieved. Increased confidence and commitment may be relatively intangible, and sometimes a client will come to realize they are in the wrong job, and quit. Is this a plus for coaching? Perhaps so, if one accepts that there are hidden costs to having an unhappy executive. 'It's better to have a good vacancy than a bad appointment' is how Stephen Cooper, HR Director at Exeter University, puts it.

In some situations, if both parties are fortunate, mentoring can blend into a rewarding colleagueship.

An emerging markets consultant – on the productive mentoring aspects of colleagueship:

> I remember a very productive mentoring relationship I had in Australia. My mentoree (who was actually quite a lot older than me) was a very good 'quality management' consultant but was less familiar with selling consulting services, especially in terms

of working with clients and the people who would implement quality in a client organization. He was very good with things, but his way of dealing with people was to have a few beers together and hope that things would work out. I suppose I taught him something about proposal-writing and doing deals on recruitment projects, and about interviewing and writing candidate profiles for headhunting. But mostly we worked as a team, and he taught me about business in Australia and a different way of operating. We have continued to stay in touch for many years, long after we both left the company.

This particular dynamic worked so effectively because of the mutual respect and learning needs in the process, and the way the roles were reversed from time to time. The older mentoree had a specific role – to teach the younger mentor about quality management and about business relations in Australia. So, the mutual nature of the relationship also saw the mentoree learn from the mentor, taking lessons on selling consultative processes, proposal writing, etc. As such both individuals grew through the process and developed a lasting professional relationship. The concept of 'mentor' hardly seemed relevant any more.

However, the mentoring and coaching approach to leadership development can take time to develop, and sometimes is not seen as sufficiently hands-on and results-oriented. Perhaps it may be the case that mentoring and directing are not extremes, but need to be used as situational leadership tools, according to the needs of the moment. This is why we often speak of a coaching style, or a mentoring approach to leadership. It is a reminder to the leader to draw out the inner capabilities of staff, help them to gain their own insights, and to make their own commitments.

An ex-CEO/management consultant on the task of balancing mentoring and directing leadership to achieve organizational change:

The case of a small, focused and innovative packaging company based in the Netherlands is particularly useful in considering mentoring and directing activity within leadership practice. It was an unlikely candidate for achieving the quadrupling of the return on investment of its American owners (First Atlantic Capital, New York), yet its earnings before interest, tax, depreciation and amortization (EBITDA) rose dramatically in just four years. Now, the firm's prestigious clients – based in Europe, the USA and Asia – include some of the top automotive and electronics companies worldwide.

As the Managing Director, together with my colleagues in the management team, we were able to make this big transition by changing our style from being mentoring and coaching-based to being directive. We would always say that we preferred our old coaching and mentoring styles of leading, but we realized that sometimes it's necessary to adapt to being directive, to achieve certain short-term objectives, by focusing on telling people what to do rather than expecting them just to do it.

With the end of family ownership and the move to the new owners, the company faced new objectives and profit targets. So, in 2002, I announced the changes that were about to happen to the employee team. I called the entire labour force into the staff canteen, and shared with them the news and its implications. I realized I must start with myself: as a European (with what I saw as a coaching and mentoring style) I had to get used to an American style of management (which I must admit I regarded as much more directive and controlling). Although I had studied for my MBA in the USA and had lived there for several years, this involved a big personal transition. My style was always one of encouraging and supporting my teams, giving them a lot of autonomy, and delegating functional responsibility – with an emphasis on coaching and mentoring – but the Americans required a concentrated level of detailed hands-on focus, personal control, clear direction and daily monitoring to provide precise evidence of what was going on in every aspect of the business. If people weren't doing things the way they should do, they were told what to do. The Americans saw this as imperative in order to achieve the big transition they were looking for. This was all quite new to me at the time. But this change from mentoring to directing-style leadership, I must admit, was successful in achieving the results required.

Mentoring people creates a whole new environment in an organization. It gives the impression that the management team members are there to help employees get better and grow in their jobs, not just to extract the labour of each employee. But not all organizations buy-in to this concept, and sometimes the time just isn't right – and it is very time-consuming. Mentoring suits organizations with long-term thinking who like to grow their own talent, and who have access to experienced managers willing to mentor the next generation of leaders (see the related entry on Developmental-oriented Leadership and Job-hopping Leadership). In more short-termist, highly dynamic organizations, it just may not seem appropriate, especially if the organization has a strong focus on rapid change.

FURTHER READING

Blake, R.R. and Mouton, J.S. (1964) *The Managerial Grid*. Houston, TX: Gulf Publications.

Blanchard, K. (2007) *The Secret*. San Francisco, CA: Berrett-Koehler.

de Bono, S., Jones, S. and van der Heijden, B. (2008) *Managing Cultural Diversity*. Oxford: Meyer & Meyer.

Jackson, Brad and Parry, Ken (2008) *A Very Short, Fairly Interesting and Reasonably Cheap Book About Studying Leadership*. London: Sage.

Ladkin, D. and Taylor, S. (2010) 'Enacting the true self: towards a theory of embodied authentic leadership', *Leadership Quarterly*, 21 (1): 64–74.

Leithwood, Kenneth A., Muscall, Blair and Strauss, Tiiu (2009) *Distributed Leadership According to the Evidence*. New York: Routledge.

Maxwell, John C. (1993) *Developing the Leader Within You*. Nashville, TN: Thomas Nelson.

Pfeffer, J. (1994) *Managing with Power: politics and influence in organizations*. Boston, MA: Harvard Business School Press.

Snook, Scott A., Nohria, Nitin N. and Khurana, Rakesh (2012) *The Handbook for Teaching Leadership: knowing, doing and being*. Thousand Oaks, CA: Sage.

Stidl, D. and Bradach, J. (2009) 'How visionary nonprofits leaders are learning to enhance management capabilities', *Strategy and Leadership*, 37 (1): 35–40.

10
Colleague-leading and Leading Prima Donnas

> *Some are experienced at leading people with big egos; others prefer to offer leadership amongst equals.*

How do you lead people who see themselves as extremely important, have big egos, are paid massive amounts of money, and don't like to be told what to do? For example, how do you lead film stars, opera divas and football players? Managing football teams as a coach or manager, especially in a World Cup tournament, can be a case in point. Football analysts, managers and other stakeholders, now forced to analyse what went wrong and why sometimes it went right, consider the performance of participating teams in this event. Even if they performed badly, these teams are full of convinced celebrities, who will continue to see themselves as superstars. Some leaders thrive on managing this challenging kind of person, whilst others would not go near such a responsibility. There is definitely another dimension to the leadership task here, and not everyone will warm to it in practice.

Football management is dominated by the task of celebrity management. The main question posed by many commentators on the football matches of the World Cup, challenging the leaders of the football teams, is often related to why some players appear to be highly motivated and others do not. Ironically, and posing many problems for the leaders concerned, is the fact that some of the most motivated (and high-performing) players are not in the World Cup's best-known teams. Especially in the 2010 competition, countries from the less-developed regions of the world were attacking the premium position of some of the traditionally most famous football nations, usually in the developed countries. The 'unknowns' were attacking the position of the 'knowns'. The obscure were being more successful than the celebrities. What was the role of leadership here? Do some of the developing countries know something that is still unknown in countries where football is very big business? Are they better at managing celebrities – or perhaps their players don't behave in this way?

Managers, leaders, coaches and other stakeholders of the football teams across the world who failed to qualify for the final rounds will ask themselves a very important question: how can we motivate our players to be more high-performing, despite them being hugely well-paid and receiving star treatment? What are the leaders doing which is simply not working?

Industry sources in football discuss 'the annual salaries of the fifty most highly-paid footballers' which 'vary from €4.8 up to €13 million, even up to €40 million per year'. Football players are described as 'celebrity personalities around the globe' and as 'pampered Gods with mansions and massive incomes'. Yet none of the top ten most highly paid footballers made it through to the semi-finals of the World Cup in 2010.

So why has there been a lamentable failure to lead celebrity players by the football coaches and managers? As the authors of 'The Sven-Göran Eriksson way of leadership' study (Birkenshaw and Crainer, 2004) reflected, this task is extremely problematic. Eriksson's initial success as a football manager was based on his attitude of being 'immune to personality, celebrity and the hype that goes with it and therefore he focuses on the task in hand (score goals and win). To do this he needs to treat the players in his team as human beings as opposed to celebrities' (2004: 85). 'He is already very tough. He can speak with the big stars to make them understand his way of thinking. He is very good at that', said Sven-Ake Olsson, Eriksson's first club coach (2004: 79).

For example, 'all of Eriksson's experience has been brought to bear in managing England's star player, David Beckham. Think of what it is like to be David Beckham. He is in his twenties. He plays for the most famous football club in the world. He is married to a pop star. Everywhere he goes in the football playing world he is recognized. The media cover his every appearance, his every gnomic utterance. His tattoos and hair cuts have been photographed from every conceivable angle. Think of how you would manage David Beckham. What motivates him? It isn't money. How could you get the best possible performance from him? What would you do?'

The authors and the gurus they consulted suggested ten strategies, including not treating him as a celebrity, but more as an ordinary person; developing mutual respect and trust and then allowing more autonomy and responsibility; encouraging him to focus on the short-term, immediate task in hand; showing belief in him and his further potential; and tolerating occasional 'off' days (2004: 88–9).

Here, we look in more detail at the challenge of motivating football heroes, and managing them successfully, followed by a perspective of managing a colleague with a celebrity mindset.

An MBA student – on the challenge of managing celebrities:

> I recently completed a study of the World Cup competition in terms of the factors influencing player motivation. I asked seven questions in seeking to pin-point the sources of motivation of these celebrity football players: is the desire to show off expertise and to inspire others a motivating factor (self-actualization, based on Maslow's (1954) Hierarchy of Needs)? Is the desire for esteem/status/fame a motivating factor? Is the desire for achievement a motivating factor? Is the desire for affiliation, including teamwork and mutual support and concern, a motivating factor? Is the desire for promotion/opportunity/recognition/increased responsibility a motivating factor? To what extent is the pay/cash bonus paid to players a motivator? Finally, is the desire for serving your own country/patriotism a motivating factor? Most of the questions will also be familiar to anyone leading highly paid people in a 'star' culture, such as investment banks, and private equity and fund management companies.

> Although it was found that these issues were important, they impacted on different teams in different ways. Players motivated by external factors such as status, recognition and attention showed better performances at this level (especially the team players of Ghana and Brazil), than those who were motivated by internal factors such as autonomy and gaining a sense of achievement (such as the team players of England and France). Players influenced by the need for affiliation, who showed

strong teamwork skills, were also generally better performers at the World Cup level (again, the teams of Ghana and Brazil, rather than England and France). But many of the football leaders don't seem to be encouraging teamwork – which seems like an obvious thing to do – or if they are trying it's not working.

Specific recommendations for the underperforming but celebrity-packed England team from this study (based on a survey of nearly 300 football fans from around the world) included the point that England should focus on developing players with a team spirit and need for affiliation, in order to strengthen this motivation within the team; they should combine the needs for affiliation and achievement; they should encourage players to be more selfless and play for the good of the team; they should help to make football stars more aware that they need other players to make them better in the game.

For France, also failing to come over well in this event and filled with players with big egos, this study suggested that the team managers should make their footballers more aware of their important role as their country's representatives when they play for the national team; they should encourage the need for affiliation; they should encourage the attitude of being more selfless; and they should promote the need for achievement, using their success that had been achieved in the recent years as a bench-mark. Many of these things should be quite obvious to the leaders involved.

A business school academic – on the challenge of leading prima donnas:

> We had a colleague at the university where I worked who regarded himself as a celeb-rity. He has written many well-received works and commands high consulting fees. He is very difficult for the Dean to manage. He turns up fairly rarely and is a law unto himself. He especially doesn't like having to change his teaching style or content. He is particularly vocal if his travelling expenses are not paid rapidly. He is quite a hero to the other professors, as his complaints and threats to quit are taken more seriously, and he can shake-up the support functions more effectively than anyone else. But I would not say he was well-managed. He is allowed to get away with being a prima donna and intimidates the senior management. In universities many of the professors have big egos, and so this is an ongoing leadership problem.

Leading celebrities is actually very varied. Motives differ more than might be expected, as the football study showed. Even the biggest personalities need others around them, and while some reward sycophants, others respond well to those who can 'speak truth to power'. In service firms, celebrity status often comes with leverage, because the brand of the individual may seem to be more valuable than that of the company. Immature celebrities can intimidate their managers, and refuse to respect authority. Often, celebrity is the fulfilment of attention-seeking behaviour patterns. No wonder, most managers prefer not to manage superstars – and this is why those who can handle it are so sought after. This challenge is outside the scope of most leadership and management training courses, which usually assume that the followers are fairly collegial. Leaders in industries where celebrity is rife have to develop a very sophisticated range of approaches, both authoritative and participative (see the related entry Authoritarian Leadership and Participative Leadership), a recognition of diversity rather than homogeneity (see the related entry Diversity Leadership and Leading Homogeneity) and just the right balance of avoiding and non-avoiding styles of leadership (see the related entry Avoiding Leadership and Involved Leadership).

FURTHER READING

Birkinshaw, Julian and Crainer, Stuart (2004) *Leadership the Sven-Göran Eriksson Way.* London: Capstone.

Bolden, R., Hawkins, B., Gosling, J. and Taylor, S. (2011) *Exploring Leadership: individual, organizational and societal perspectives.* Oxford: Oxford University Press.

Bryman, Alan, Collinson, David L., Grint, Keith and Jackson, Brad (2011) *The Sage Handbook of Leadership.* London: Sage.

Grint, K. (2005) 'Problems, problems, problems: the social construction of "leadership"', *Human Relations*, 58 (11): 1467–1494.

Halilaj, Altin (2010) 'Sources of motivation of footballers in the 2010 World Cup'. Maastricht School of Management, unpublished MBA thesis.

Salacuse, Jeswald W. (2006) *Leading Leaders: how to manage smart, talented, rich and powerful people.* New York: AMACOM.

Storey, John (2011) *Leadership in Organisations: current issues and key trends* (2nd edition). Oxford: Routledge.

Valcea, S., Hamdani, M.R., Buckley, M.R. and Novicevic, M.M. (2011) 'Exploring the developmental potential of leader–follower interactions: a constructive-developmental approach', *The Leadership Quarterly*, 22: 604–615.

11

'Company-branded' Leadership and 'Individual-branded' Leadership

> The concept of developing an 'individual leadership brand' which can enable a leader to move from company to company is attractive to some leaders; others foster a sense of service to something greater than themselves.

Building a personal leadership brand – where an individual leader fosters a reputation for leadership which is uniquely his or hers for the long-term – has become increasingly popular. CV-writing advisers encourage job-hunters to promote themselves as the special ingredient of organizational success, associating stories of remarkable achievements with an individual name. The idea is that each leader has a distinctive style that an employer might select: How do you answer the question if an employer asks you to describe your particular brand of leadership? This sounds useful and interesting – but the million-dollar question could be – how to develop a unique personal brand, and how to do this in such a way as to not go on a collision course with current or future employers and their own carefully developed corporate brands? Some 'branded' leaders can be inspirational individuals, but this might not mix with the corporation's style and culture (see the related entry Inspirational Leadership and Low-key Leadership). An own leadership brand can also be associated with a purpose, rather than a style – following a specific mission or goal – which might chime with what the organization wants to achieve. On the other hand, an executive willing to fit in with a company's branding might be seen as a good company servant – or merely opportunistic (see the related entry Goal-oriented Leadership and Opportunistic Leadership).

This career-oriented brand-building concept was described in a *Fortune* magazine article (Hyatt, 2010), which points out that it is a double-edged sword: Who benefits the most? What if there's a conflict? Sometimes the personal branding can benefit the employer, but if it looks like the individual is really only looking for personal advancement, and is using the employer as a temporary pawn in the game, it can be a liability for the employer concerned and may ultimately backfire for the employee. But it is easy to see why people start to build their personal leadership brand: someone trying to break out of a reputation as a functional specialist might have to re-brand themselves by emphasizing generic leadership abilities (see the related entry Expert Leadership and Generalist Leadership). Organizations can benefit from this ambition and desire for transformation, but it is not good for morale if staff feel they are being used just to 'big up' the boss.

Here we look at different styles of leadership brands created by two individuals – one not so successful, one more so. Much depends on the alignment of the personal leadership brand with the organization concerned, and how effectively these two brands can work together.

An HR/development consultant – on the problem of the lack of an accurately aligned leadership brand:

A previous boss I worked with used to be very keen on building relationships with aristocratic people, and he networked extensively with people with whom he had been at school, and with whom he had served in the armed services. He had lots of connections with the British royal family. He was probably more interested in keeping in touch with all these contacts and attending a lot of upper-class outings and functions than in his job. He was supposed to be working in Corporate Communications, but our company used to get a very bad press from the journalists in London, so obviously his contacts were not very useful, or he was reluctant to keep calling on them for help. His personal brand didn't really fit with the needs of the organization; the two brands were misaligned. Luckily he was about to retire when the company underwent a huge transformation of culture. He was definitely associated with the old culture, of being gentlemanly, colonial, social class-oriented. The new culture of the organization was more workaday, practical, results-oriented, and was built around people who wanted to achieve success in this way, so were not yet 'brands' in themselves. My previous boss no longer fitted in at all.

As this case illustrates, there needs to be a good fit between organizational and personal brands, so they enhance each other, but this does now mean they should always be in harmony. There can be tensions between them – for example, companies wanting to show they are serious about sustainability sometimes hire well-known environmental campaigners, individuals with a reputation for criticizing that particular industry. For the environmentalists, this is a way to enhance their own brand by showing they are willing to do more than shout on the sidelines, and to engage with corporations they have previously lambasted. Here the apparent contrast between brands works in favour of both – at least so long as they each remain distinct, even while cooperating.

Personal brands are about much more than the personal qualities and achievements of an individual. They are powerful because they refer to distinctive social identities. One might be seen as a leader amongst a particular group or movement because you represent its most characteristic qualities. For example, Mick Jagger might be seen as a leader within rock music, not because he has any formal leadership role, but because he encapsulates so much of what the rock era means. Jack Welch is seen as a business leader not just because he leads a particular business (though he did lead GE for many years), but because he stands for what many regard as the best of business leadership. The same can be said of many well-known business leaders – Anita Roddick for ethical business, for example, who was strongly associated with The Body Shop, the cosmetics business she started with a strident opposition to animal testing.

Personal brands are about a symbolic representation of values, not so much about a political representation of constituencies. Mick Jagger is a potent brand to have associated with any rock-related activity because of the values he symbolizes, not because he can organize a protest movement (though he might be able to do that too!). Some recent social networking protests have shown how leadership can be effected without the use of personal brands. For example, a group calling itself 38 Degrees organized massive online petitions and mail campaigns in opposition to the British government's plan to sell off ancient woodlands in 2010. There were no famous people running the organization, though they did sometimes allude to well-known people who were supporting them. They made use of these personal brands to support their cause, but not as leaders of the cause.

So the ability to organize a network is not integral to personal brands, but personal brands always depend on a network or group for whom the brand represents something valuable.

Anita Roddick stood for animal welfare and fair trade in business, which was important for a specific group of consumers, a group that widened to include more and more people concerned about the moral basis of business. This group expanded to such an extent that many other businesses were established on similar values, and eventually The Body Shop itself was bought by L'Oreal to gain a foothold in what was now a substantial market segment. That was possible only because Anita Roddick herself was no longer working in the business (she sold it shortly before her death from hepatitis C); while her reputation is still strongly associated with the birth of ethical consumerism, The Body Shop brand carries only a nostalgic hint of the values it once represented.

Personal branding is integral to some professions, so much so that employers will attune their strategies to make the most of the personal brands of their star employees. This is clearly the case in the movie business, for example, where it is the leading actors more than the movie as a whole that sells tickets (but not always – a bad movie can seriously dent the reputation of a great actor). The same dynamic also exists in many other walks of life – some of which are quite surprising.

An MBA teacher – on an aligned leadership brand:

In the world of the academic, for example, personal brand-building is encouraged. High-profile academics bring prestige, research investment money and students to the institutions for which they work. Some business schools use this in their advertising. A prime example is Michael Porter at Harvard Business School. However, the profile of the academic must be aligned with the thrust of the organization. My specialization as an academic is leadership and culture in emerging markets. This is the research area I work in at my institution, and helps to define the academic brand I have built and continue to build. I spend considerable time researching in this area, giving lectures/ seminars and publishing articles and books.

However, in my free time I have a passion for sailing, and I'm also interested in preserving heritage sites. While these hobbies are important to my life, and I write and publish on these topics as well, I keep these pursuits for outside of working hours and when I'm not so busy, writing on Sunday afternoons and publishing articles as limited circulation pieces, just for fun.

My own individual brand has these many aspects to it, and although people I relate to through my sailing are probably not at all interested in my work on emerging markets, it is all part of what makes me who I am. My employer is of course primarily interested in my academic reputation, and that is what they advertise on the university website. But my other interests don't do any damage and probably enhance the university brand if anyone cares to look. I suppose that if my hobbies were more contentious, and I had a reputation for something contrary to the values of the university, it would be a challenge to the vaunted ideals of academic freedom. And even now, I am not too sure what the response would be if my reputation for heritage conservation outstripped my academic reputation.

Good work can be its own advertisement – but, having said this, we should not hide our skills and accomplishments. There is a need to achieve a fine balance between making the most of our achievements by making sure others know about these, but also avoiding arrogance and too much pride.

Branding plays an important part in leadership development. Many organizations like to indentify a cohort of people tipped for the top, to subject them to intense measurement and to give them special opportunities. Being identified as one of these 'high potentials' is to 'be branded', and often becomes a self-fulfilling prophecy. Research shows that people who know that they are part of a group of 'high performers' make special efforts to succeed precisely because this is the shared identity of that group. The shared identity can be enhanced by branding – so we have seen such groups identified by names such as 'deep gold', 'aspiring leaders', 'G10', and so forth. Once branded as a 'deep gold' leader, one is likely to make special efforts to embody the values of hard work, corporate loyalty and success that are associated with the term. It works in just the same way as identifying some children as 'monitors' in schools: being branded has an effect on behaviour, self-image and status. It can work well for both parties, but it can also be constraining. The individual becomes obliged to self-regulate his or her behaviour and emotions in order to stay within the brand values, and this can sometimes lead to an unbearable compromise. And all these brands exist in specific arrangements of power. It is all very well to be identified as 'deep gold' leader so long as the CEO who sponsored the programme is in power. If he or she is unseated for some reason, the 'deep gold' branding might become a liability. The only way around this is to refer to objective measures of performance and use these to convince the new CEO that 'deep gold' really does indicate substantial capabilities.

So personal branding, like corporate branding, requires constant attention. Developing a personal brand is something all leaders do to some extent, because leadership always has a symbolic aspect – it always stands for something in the eyes of others. Even if a potential leader is being developed by a specific organization down a particular career track, his or her personality and individual ambitions will ensure the creation of an individual brand. But if it is at odds with the organization, for example if it is extremely individual, the growing tension between the two may lead to a parting of the ways.

FURTHER READING

Alvesson, M. and Spicer, A. (eds) (2010) *Metaphors We Lead By: understanding leadership in the real world*. Oxford: Routledge.

Bryman, Alan, Collinson, David L., Grint, Keith and Jackson, Brad (2011) *The Sage Handbook of Leadership*. London: Sage.

Colvin, Geoff (2009) 'How to Build Great Leaders', *Fortune*, 4 December, 160 (10), http://money.cnn.com/magazines/fortune/fortune_archive/2007

Groysberg, Boris, Nanda, Ashish and Nohria, Nitin (2004) 'The risky business of hiring stars', *Harvard Business Review*, May, 82(5): 92–100.

Hyatt, Josh (2010) 'Building your brand (and keeping your job)', *Fortune*, 16 August, 162 (3): 50-55.

Jones, S. (1989) *The Headhunting Business*. London: Macmillan.

Snook, Scott A., Nohria, Nitin N., and Khurana, Rakesh (2012) *The Handbook for Teaching Leadership: knowing, doing and being*. Thousand Oaks, CA: Sage.

Storey, John (2011) *Leadership in Organisations: current issues and key trends* (2nd edition). Oxford: Routledge.

12
Compromising Leadership and Co-operative Leadership

Leaders willing to give a bit and take a bit to get things done will approach things differently to those who look towards new opportunities and concentrate on actively building the alliances to make them possible.

This might not be the most obvious distinction; compromise and co-operation appear to be quite close in meaning, and are not mutually exclusive: compromise could be one of the ways in which collaborative ventures proceed – both sides giving a bit in order to carry on. But we believe it is an important distinction because compromise occurs when people agree to shift their existing positions, while collaboration is when parties create new positions and possibilities by working together.

It is true that in order to collaborate, they might have to compromise a bit; and in order to reach a compromise they have to collaborate in negotiations. But there are important differences that become clear when we consider how people approach conflict situations. An easy way to approach this is through the Thomas Kilmann exercise (1974) (see the related entries Avoiding Leadership and Involved Leadership, Accommodating Leadership and Competitive Leadership). By identifying different modes for resolving conflict, the exercise shows how politically sensitive a leader is; do they treat people with diplomacy, or do they lack tact (see the related entry Individualistic Leadership and Relationship-oriented Leadership)? Do they use bargaining and trading to get things done? Do they keep sight of the larger issues in spite of the outbreak of conflict? How much are they prepared to give in? Do they sometimes appear unreasonable? Are some approaches to leadership, such as coaching and mentoring, more associated with compromise, or with cooperation? Leaders strongly focused on achieving a task might be more prepared to compromise along the way, but what if they have a strong competitive drive and don't want to give in to anything? (See the related entry Coaching and Mentoring-oriented Leadership and Directive, Telling-what-to-do Leadership.)

The Thomas Kilmann model suggests that when people's concerns and desires come into conflict, their behaviours can be described along two dimensions: (1) assertiveness, which is the drive to get what one wants, and (2) cooperativeness, which attempts to satisfy the other person's concerns. These are not opposites – it is possible to be highly assertive and highly cooperative. The Thomas Kilmann assessment instrument uses these two dimensions to identity five possible ways of approaching a conflict:

1   competing, highly assertive and uncooperative;
2   accommodating, unassertive but highly cooperative;
3   avoiding, unassertive and uncooperative;
4   collaborating, assertive and cooperative;
5   compromising, moderately assertive and moderately cooperative.

Leadership involves many situations of conflict and disagreements, real and imagined. Changes to the status quo inevitably unsettle some vested interests, and disputes between people very properly come to leaders when they represent alternative perspectives and strategies. How a leader approaches these conflicts can be a significant factor in their success. It is seldom possible to say with any certainty what is the best way to approach these conflicts (though many pundits will offer opinions); but leaders are often characterized by their preferred styles. Most people find that they prefer one or two of the approaches identified in the Thomas

Kilmann model, with a moderate preference for one or two others. This means there are some approaches that seem out of the question for them: potentially a serious limitation. The preferences reflected in the scores allow us to ask questions such as:

- How collaborative may the leader be in working with others to achieve a solution to the problem in hand, rather than trying to score points off them?
- How much is the leader prepared to compromise to arrive at a solution to the conflict?
- To what extent is the leader able to share ideas and strategies with others in the interests of accomplishing the tasks and overcoming problems?

A compromising leader is exactly in the middle of all the scales. It is unlikely that a leader can be both competing and collaborative, or avoiding and accommodating, i.e. they will be either assertive or unassertive. Leaders who are either assertive or unassertive could also be compromising. It is likely that a high score in assertive qualities will be matched by low scores in avoiding and accommodating, and vice versa. Being highly competitive and highly accommodating at the same time is fairly unusual. Co-operative and collaborative styles are unlikely to be matched with a high preference for compromising – these are opposites. However, sometimes when a leader is unsuccessful in encouraging collaborative or co-operative behaviours in others, he or she might default to being compromising, especially when facing time-pressures.

It is also possible to see the five conflict preferences in win/lose dimensions. Competing is win/lose – someone wins, and someone else must lose. Accommodating, the opposite, is lose/win. The leader has deliberately chosen to let the follower or colleague win, which is in contrast with avoiding – this is when he or she has chosen to walk away from the conflict, and is taking a lose/lose approach. Compromising can be seen as a combination – win/lose, lose/win and lose/win, win/lose. Both parties are winning and losing, depending on the particular points they are succeeding in gaining or giving away. But collaborative leadership is win/win.

How do we define collaborative and compromising leadership? According to specific examples of leaders, confirmed by the explanatory literature provided with the instrument and adapted for our purposes (see www.kilmann.com/conflict.html), we can see that the different types of conflict styles of leaders can have a big impact on the way they operate and their impact on an organization. Our 'voices' quoted in many of the entries confirm these reflections.

The collaborating leader is keen to work with others to find a solution which satisfies all, and takes a lot of time probing an issue to identify the underlying interests of the people in conflict. He or she puts a lot of effort into exploring disagreements from a variety of viewpoints, concluding issues clearly. Collaborative leaders typically have a lot of patience. Many of them work in the voluntary sector (see the related entry Employee Leading and Volunteer Leading), and increasingly in cross-sector roles building alliances between companies, non-governmental organizations (NGOs) and regulatory or government agencies. This kind of work is crucial for the economic changes facing us as we try to deal with the effects of climate change worldwide. However, consultation processes can go on too long and decisions do not get made fast enough: this usually indicates some conflict avoidance.

Compromising leaders try to find an expedient and mutually acceptable solution which at least partially satisfies both parties. As such, compromising leadership is closely related to collaborative leadership. Compromising can mean giving up more than in the competing mode, but giving up less than when accommodating. Compromising leaders address an issue more directly than leaders in an avoiding mode, but they do not explore it in the same depth as leaders in the collaborating mode. Compromising may mean dividing differences, exchanging concessions or seeking a middle-ground position. It can be seen as highly pragmatic (see the related entry Pragmatic Leadership and Principles-driven Leadership). Compromising leaders can be seen as flexible and easy to work with by subordinates; but the latter might be concerned about how far the compromising is going to go. What are the ultimate standards and values of the organization, which cannot be compromised? They might not be sure, which can be a point of worry or concern.

The use of the collaborating mode is an important way to find a solution when a compromise between leader and subordinate concerns is difficult. Collaborating helps the leader to test assumptions and to understand the inputs of others, helping to merge insights from people with different perspectives. Collaborating can help gain a commitment through consensus, and can also help to get over problems in interpersonal relationships. However, leaders focused on collaborating should ask themselves if they spend too much time discussing issues in depth, especially those which perhaps do not deserve such time expenditure. Collaborating takes a good deal of time and energy, and consensus decision-making can sometimes represent a desire to minimize risk by diffusing responsibility and delaying action. Is the leader's collaborative behaviour encouraging collaborative responses from others? In a conflict situation others may disregard co-operative overtures, and the trust and openness which a collaborative leader may use, especially if insufficiently assertive, may be abused, being seen as too friendly and even weak, verging towards compromise.

The leader with a low preference for co-operating and collaborating (i.e. highly competitive or avoiding) may not be able to see differences as opportunities to help solve problems. If the leader doesn't like conflict at all, this mindset can prevent him or her from seeing collaborative possibilities, and can prevent a successful collaboration. Leaders low on co-operation may find that subordinates are not committed to their decisions, as perhaps their concerns are not being included in the leader's plans.

The compromising mode is useful when goals are moderately important but not worth risking the potential breakdown of a relationship which can be a result of using the more assertive modes, such as competitiveness. Compromising is also useful when two opponents with equal power are very keen on goals that are in conflict with each other. Compromising can achieve temporary settlements to complex issues, and can help the parties to arrive at expedient solutions under time pressures. Compromising can be a useful back-up mode when attempts at collaborating or competing are not working. But compromising leaders should ask themselves if their focus on the practicalities of compromise means that they might lose sight of the larger issues, such as core values and long-term objectives. An emphasis on bargaining and the trading of concessions can create a cynical climate. This might then undermine interpersonal trust and deflect attention away from the key issues at stake.

A leader who is low on compromising may be too sensitive or embarrassed to be effective at bargaining, finding it hard to make concessions and having trouble avoiding mutually destructive arguments and power struggles.

Collaborative or co-operative leaders try to gain 100 per cent successful outcomes and work hard to achieve these. Compromising leaders are often protecting their own situation and can be willing to make some concessions, but these can work against them if there are not clearly defined limits to the trading and bargaining. Here, we consider practical examples of co-operative and compromising leaders, and some of the positive and negative issues they are facing.

A consultant in emerging markets:

I met a doctor working in a specialist hospital in Tanzania. He was the chief executive of a large clinic, funded by donations from Europe. He is an extremely co-operative and collaborative person, especially because his job is problem-solving. Although his hospital faces cash and resource constraints, he is completely focused on providing for patient needs. To meet these needs he is constantly finding new partners to work with, creating openings in government ministries that help them achieve their goals, working with community leaders and funding agencies. He seems to know just what they want to achieve and how to present his 'needs' as an opportunity for them. The medical profession is not always co-operative and collaborative in the way it operates, but it has to be if it is to maintain the focus on patient care despite difficult circumstances. This doctor attended a training course on leadership and took part in the Thomas Kilmann exercise, and his preference for collaborative behaviours was very dominant. What made this powerful was his constant attention to the purpose of his work. He was well-informed about the possible extent of healthcare options, even if they could not be obtained in Tanzania at this point, and kept these ideas alive in his mind, as motivating ideals. These kinds of leaders are much admired, especially because they face daily temptations to compromise on the level of service offered – which would be only too easy to do.

An example from politics:

By July 2010 the US debt crisis was critical. The massive level of national debt – $14.3 trillion – was at its legal limit, and the government had only $72bn in reserve (less than the cash pile amassed by Apple Corp). If the debt ceiling could not be raised by 1 August, the US would default on its loans and lose its AAA credit rating. It would very soon have to prioritize payments, and troops stationed in Afghanistan asked if they would get paid for their services to the nation. The budget deficit was symptomatic of a long term malaise, but the scale of debt or the shortage of reserves was not in itself critical: what brought it to the brink was the inability of the Republican and Democrat parties to reach a workable compromise. The Republicans (their position hardened by newly elected Tea Party members) wanted no more taxes, while the Democrats wanted to protect health and social payments. By the morning of Sunday 31 July, just a few hours before the absolute deadline, both sides had agreed to raise the debt ceiling, but were intransigent about the timing – was this agreement for just six months, or for long enough to see the country past the next election?

Eventually, literally at the last moment, an agreement was reached by negotiators on both sides: to raise the debt ceiling by $2.4 trillion, and to commit to cutting the deficit by the same amount over ten years. This was a classic compromise: both Republican and Democrats had to give up much of what they had hoped for; and no progress was made on reforms to the underlying structure of the tax system or the way that spending was determined. The deal was simply a compromise made necessary by the inability of the political parties to collaborate. But it should not be played down: as president Obama said announcing the deal on Sunday night 31 July, 'This compromise does make a serious downpayment on the deficit reduction we need and gives each party a strong incentive to get a balanced plan done before the end of the year. Most importantly it will allow us to avoid a default, and end the crisis that Washington imposed on America ... Ultimately the leaders of both parties have found their way towards compromise, and I want to thank them for that' (CNN, 1 August 2011).

This overall analysis of behaviours in a conflict situation can be useful in finding the patterns in the way leaders react to disputes, and can aid our understanding of political and organizational processes. Generally, avoiding and compromising styles are not associated with the most forward-looking leadership and management, although compromise is necessary in some contexts. Collaborative approaches require a leader to be highly participative, whereas a leader driven by the need to competitively assert his or her will over others is likely to be more directive in style. The idea that people approach conflict in characteristic modes, developed by Thomas and Kilmann, is widely used to study how leaders and managers behave in negotiations, but in theory it has a much wider application, and can help us understand how different leaders operate. There are also cross-cultural issues here, as behaviours that might be categorized as 'avoiding' in a culture that values self-assertiveness are seen as tactful in cultures that value collective agreement more highly; and compromise is integral to cultures based on trading favours and obligations (see the related entries Eastern-style Leadership and Western-style Leadership – Contrasting and Converging National Cultures, and Global Leadership and Worldly Leadership).

FURTHER READING

Bolden, R. (2011) 'Distributed leadership in organizations: a review of theory and research', *International Journal of Management Reviews*, 13(3): 251–269.

Grint, K. (2005) 'Problems, problems, problems': the social construction of "leadership"', *Human Relations*, 58 (11): 1467–1494.

Jones, S. (2010) *Psychological Testing*. Petersfield: Harriman House.

Katzenbach J. and Smith, D. (1994) *The Wisdom of Teams*. New York: Harper Business.

Leithwood, Kenneth A., Muscall, Blair and Strauss, Tiiu (2009) *Distributed Leadership According to the Evidence*. New York: Routledge.

Northouse, Peter Guy (2010) *Leadership: theory and practice*. Thousand Oaks, CA: Sage.

Western, Simon (2008) *Leadership: a critical text*. London: Sage.

13
Developmental-oriented Leadership and Job-hopping Leadership

> *Some leaders thrive in an environment favouring employee growth and constant training; others like staff members who can 'hit the ground running' as soon as they are brought on board.*

Organizations handle the need to develop and establish leadership talent in different ways, and the leaders they employ as part of the process are also different, or should be, if the organization is to successfully maintain their focus either way. There are essentially two approaches here. In the first, companies look to their existing employees for future leaders. They then invest in their development, using existing leaders to nurture future leaders. The second approach is to hire mid-career talent from outside the company to take over leadership positions, according to the needs of the moment.

Companies who grow their own talent from within – who hire entry-level staff and train them to be future leaders – can be seen as predominantly developmental in emphasis, and attract developmental-oriented leaders. After recruiting and training this talent, they then try to retain them with individual career plans, personally tailored benefits, a strong corporate culture and building a family environment in the unit or department. They also give them ownership of specific processes and applications, award them with stock options, pay for their MBAs and use several other techniques to lock them into the organization, all with the carrot of continual career growth and more and more opportunities. These opportunities are designed to specifically create leadership talent that will flourish in that company's particular corporate culture and fulfil its future needs. This requires existing leaders with the right attitude, who are likely to be more participative in style, employing coaching and mentoring approaches. They might also be inspirational and extrovert in style, but not necessarily (see the related entries, Authoritarian Leadership and Participative Leadership, Coaching and Mentoring-oriented Leadership and Directive, Telling-what-to-do Leadership, Extrovert Leadership and Introvert Leadership, and Inspirational Leadership and Low-key Leadership).

By contrast, the companies who hire mid-career executives (and sometimes very senior leaders) from outside the company essentially rely on other organizations to do their training and development work for them, and they don't mind paying the price. But they can't wait. They want executives who can hit the ground running, and the existing leaders in the organization appreciate this and fit in with them – they may be fairly opportunistic in style, or very focused on achieving a narrow set of targets (see the entry Goal-oriented Leadership and Opportunistic Leadership). These new leaders and those above them know that this process could create fragmented cultures within the organization, but this is part of the deal. Many of these companies will develop a patchwork-quilt of sub-cultures, each with its own leadership and membership characteristics, which might be integrated over time, but may create separate enclaves within these companies. Some of these new leaders may have their own individual leadership brands, but in companies attracting mid-career talent, they are more easily accommodated than in grow-your-own companies. Diversity rather than homogeneity can also be a feature of the mid-career oriented company (see the related entry Diversity Leadership and Leading Homogeneity).

Leadership development has become a significant focus in organizational life in recent years. Efforts by organizations to develop leadership in their ranks have become more specific, nuanced and dynamic, but the results are still widely contested. When an organization actually decides it wants to try to take on this difficult but important job in a scientific way, what does it do? And how does it measure success? *Fortune* magazine tried to answer this question in an extended article (Kowitt and Thai, 2009). One of the cases discussed was that of IBM, which sent ten senior employees to Ghana for four weeks to explore possible CSR activities. An observer not convinced of the value of CSR, observing this initiative, might question the value of sending senior people on a non-essential and non-business-related mission. Those who took part seemed to think it was worthwhile. It built trust and confidence in each other, and deepened their bond with the company. Separately, the Board of Directors of IBM spent an entire day assessing how the company was developing leaders for the future. The company (number one in the *Fortune* magazine top 25 for developing leaders, 19 November 2009 issue) spends almost $700 million a year on leadership development. But perhaps the question should be asked – is this a lot or a little out of $103.6 billion in revenues and nearly 400,000 employees?

The *Fortune* article suggests that leadership-building involves extra risks and costs because of the approach used of

i pulling a leader out of a job where he or she is performing;
ii putting a leader into a job he or she doesn't know.

However, the leader in i) is not learning anymore because he or she knows what to do and finds it quite easy, so it's not very challenging. But perhaps it makes sense for the company to keep him or her in this job in the interests of efficiency and fewer mistakes – or is that not the point? And how about the risks associated with ii), of the trainee leader struggling with a difficult job which another leader could manage much more effectively? So, when a difficult task comes up for a company – what is the first reaction of the senior management? 'Great, here's a super leadership development opportunity, we can send in someone who doesn't know anything about it, and he/she will learn so much!' Or, are they more likely to say, 'The *&%$ is about to hit the fan, let's send in our best leader in this area and get this sorted out ASAP!'

Another important area for leadership development is sending potential leaders to set up new businesses in new countries. Again, should the company send their most experienced, knowledgeable, culturally attuned leaders? Many organizations only allow leaders aged 45+ to take up such projects – they have shown their loyalty, they can be trusted, they know the priorities, requirements and culture of the organization, they can do the job far away from head office without careful monitoring. But are they really open to learning? And do they want to go? What about their partners and children, are they also mobile? Other companies are more ready to send eager young and single employees who are keen to travel. This poses different risks for the company, but can produce fast results, develop leadership talent, build skills and networks for the future, and get the job done. Increasingly, really worldly companies develop talented people with a cosmopolitan outlook, for whom working across cultures is the norm. These companies are also more likely to find the talent they want in situ, from local sources, and thus avoid the expenses and risks of using expatriate leaders.

And how long do companies expect to keep their leaders? When might they break even on their investments – or are their (particularly senior) employees simply milking the system? And what if their expensively trained would-be leaders don't make it to the top? What if unsuccessful candidates for CEO succession (such as the also-rans in Jeff Immelt's drive to head up GE after Jack Welch) then go to other companies? Is the leadership investment wasted, or is it all part of the company's commitment to leadership development? Some organizations have a fantastic reputation as training-grounds for great leaders and business-people – Mars, Unilever, GE, ICI, and McKinsey's are just some of the well-known corporations in this category. Other organizations include the armed services and the diplomatic services, and there are a few names in almost every sector that, over many years, consistently develop leaders who come to prominence later in their careers in other places. In UK universities, for example, Southampton and Warwick have produced brilliant administrative and academic leaders for the whole sector. This reputation has great benefits – such institutions attract the best applicants for junior and mid-level positions – but is the investment financially worthwhile?

These are very difficult questions to answer for many companies. Perhaps not surprisingly, the top 25 companies worldwide for leadership development (according to *Fortune* magazine and the Sixth AON Hewitt HR Barometer (Sforza and Perret, 2011)) are large organizations, highly profitable and well established. Perhaps they can afford the costs of training, which may not be confined to the $700 million spent by IBM on training courses. Do they factor in failed assignments and the costs of mistakes? How about smaller organizations and start-ups – to what extent can they afford leadership development? Or to what extent is normal, everyday life in these organizations a development opportunity for their leaders in any case?

It's also a question of how leaders learn – through mentoring and coaching, or being closely directed? And what are the results for the organization? Does mentoring take too long and use up too much management time, and suit a consolidating period of a company more than an active change or growth period? Does a directing style – 'sink or swim', or 'my way or the highway' – have more instant results? And does it depend on the organizational and national cultures involved?

Another important question here is the extent to which companies take a developmental attitude, recruiting first-level entry staff members and nurturing them into leadership positions. Many of the (mostly) big-name multinationals profiled in the *Fortune*/Hewitt survey (Kowitt and Thai, 2009) are doing this extensively. By contrast, companies hiring mid-career heroes are buying the results of the time and effort of their competitors – and their investment dollars. The latter companies, who hire from outside, can be less clannish, have more new blood, and may be more agile – but the new talent doesn't always make the transition (see Groysberg et al., 2004) or just keeps moving after a short interval, and may not represent a return on investment in hiring, even if the new employer saved on the training.

Here, we look at experiences of working in developmentally oriented organizations, compared with those that recruit people who are already up-and-running and can be slotted into a key responsibility straight away. There are advantages and disadvantages to both approaches, and most executives are in one groove or another. Some people are in a fast track of their own, switching from one company to another, constantly in the market for the next opportunity, and talking to head-hunters all the time. By contrast, many developmentally geared companies grow their talent from the bottom to the top, and being able to promote leaders from within is regarded as the ultimate success of their approach to leadership development.

An ex-CEO based in emerging markets – on developmental thinking, old-style:

> I have worked for only two organizations in my life, after completing military service – Cadbury's and Reckitt & Colman. They were both very traditional. There were fantastic overseas opportunities with both of these companies, and in both companies overseas staff had a huge amount of autonomy. Even when I was in my 20s and 30s, as I was when I was with Cadbury's, I was given vast territories to manage. It was a hangover from the colonial period. Most companies hired young people and trained them up. We rarely changed jobs, and if we did it was often because we had a boss we didn't like – something personal. The companies I worked for were both similar in style – paternalistic and trusting. I never had a job contract. You were expected to just do your job, and if you looked after the businesses OK, you were given more to look after, and generally left to get on with it. It was also a function of communications – we were a long way from headquarters, we didn't have the advanced technology we have now, and the pace of life was much slower.

An emerging markets consultant – on developmental thinking in a changing world order in a major multinational:

> When I was living in the Middle East I knew a senior oil-company executive who had a very long-term career with Shell – he had been there for most of his career – and there are so many developmental opportunities and internal training programmes, sometimes he wondered when he had time to do his job! Especially here in the Middle East, we are trying to localize. So we are training the local people all the time. The senior expatriate managers such as myself are usually involved in attending the courses with the local trainees, to try to reinforce the training – which makes sense.

When it comes to the more practical, technical training courses, these are taken more seriously. We're always doing simulations of oil rig shut-downs, for example, we know exactly what to do! I'm very much a Developmental Leader – it's my main job. Although sometimes I think we're not very successful, because some of the locals are very privileged and not always interested in learning what we want to convey. Our training efforts are very Western in style and don't always match their culture or their priorities, and sometimes they don't get much out of it. But we must keep working on it. It's an important goal for Shell as an organization.

Part of the developmental process is to keep building our corporate culture. It's very easy to get sucked-into the culture – it takes over your life. There are so many corporate functions such as parties and outings where families are also invited that no-one can leave Shell because the families would pressure them to stay, because socially work and home life is very interrelated. But I've never wanted to leave, because there is always a new job to do and new training courses to attend. I'm always getting new opportunities and assignments. We are well looked-after, and the company is prestigious here. I suppose one drawback is that we could do with new blood, and not just young people, but senior guys who might shake things up – but that doesn't happen much. We use a lot of consultants but we don't take them as seriously as we do our own people. My role focusing on development work definitely impacts on the way I operate as a leader and manager. I'm looking for lessons learned and areas for improvement all the time.

In both of these examples it is clear that the developmental company which invests in its employees' development tends to keep its employees – at least in the relatively predictable, Western-dominated corporate landscape to which both these managers refer, where growth is fairly continuous and stable.

The client of an executive search consultant on the challenges of recruiting from outside the company:

I work for Reckitt Benckiser, a household products company formed from the merger of the British company Reckitt & Colman, and the Dutch company Benckiser. The latter, in particular, are mostly interested in hiring mid-career talent. Most of us come from P&G, Unilever, Kimberly Clark or other companies where they do a lot of training. As a result of our company hiring people who can hit the ground running, we don't offer many developmental opportunities – we don't need to, but we pay a lot for these people. Our culture is much tougher, it's quite a rat-race, we work much harder but we get paid more. People come and go more often. We headhunt others and we get headhunted ourselves. Our corporate culture is just a mix of other companies' cultures. We are very market-driven, so if people don't make the grade, they are kicked out. Some people are not as successful with us as they were with their previous company, especially if the culture there was more structured and traditional. But if they are hard-working and ambitious and like a challenge, responsibility and variety, they will like our organization. For me, this culture definitely affects my leadership and management style. I have much less job security than I might have elsewhere. I'm not quite sure how long I can carry on changing jobs every few years. At the moment it's fun and interesting, but I'm still quite young and have the energy and aptitude for it. I don't know how I will feel when I'm much older, when I might want more stability.

Certain types of leaders will thrive in a company that is constantly headhunting from the outside. These typically high pressure organizations are fertile ground for those who are exceptionally ambitious, competitive and challenge driven. The benefit to the companies is that they hire leaders who need little preparation and development. Companies that depend on headhunting to attract talent also find that this process maintains the pressure and competitive culture that they seek. However, there is a negative aspect here too. High turnover rates, either because leaders couldn't survive or they were head-hunted away, mean such organizations can lack continuity at leadership levels. The corporate climate can become toxic through an unhealthy level of overt competition. There is also a negative effect on cost. Companies that rely on leadership development invest very heavily in their future leaders tend to keep them; they need to if they want a return on the investment. However, for companies that rely on headhunting, the often much higher salaries and benefits they have to pay are risky investments, as there is no guarantee a leader will succeed or stay. At the very least, though, a transient leader might bring diversity to the 'ideas gene pool', even with a brief tenure (see Dawkins, 1976).

The way people are developed can thus impact on leadership style considerably. Mentored leaders often like mentoring others; directed leaders may boss others around. Companies with a strong developmental focus are good at producing leaders who see their job as helping others to grow; mid-career hirers and the headhunters who work for them can encourage opportunism and a level of job-hopping.

FURTHER READING

Bryman, Alan, Collinson, David L., Grint, Keith and Jackson, Brad (2011) *The Sage Handbook of Leadership*. London: Sage.

Colvin, Geoff (2009) 'How to build great leaders', *Fortune*, 4 December; 160 (10): 48–54, http://money.cnn.com/magazines/fortune/fortune_archive/2009

Cotter, David A., Hermsen, Joan M., Ovadia, Seth and Vanneman, Reece (2001) 'The glass ceiling effect', *Social Forces*, 80 (2): 655–681.

Groysberg, Boris, Nanda, Ashish and Nohria, Nitin (2004) 'The risky business of hiring stars', *Harvard Business Review*, May, 82(5): 92–100.

Jackson, Brad and Parry, Ken (2008) *A Very Short, Fairly Interesting and Reasonably Cheap Book About Studying Leadership*. London: Sage.

Jones, S. (1989) *The Headhunting Business*. London: Macmillan.

Maxwell, John C. (1993) *Developing the Leader Within You*. Nashville, TN: Thomas Nelson.

Snook, Scott A., Nohria, Nitin N. and Khurana, Rakesh (2012) *The Handbook for Teaching Leadership: knowing, doing and being*. Thousand Oaks, CA: Sage.

Stidl, D. and Bradach, J. (2009) 'How visionary nonprofits leaders are learning to enhance management capabilities', *Strategy and Leadership*, 37 (1): 35–40.

Valcea, S., Hamdani, M.R., Buckley, M.R. and Novicevic, M.M. (2011) 'Exploring the developmental potential of leader–follower interactions: a constructive-developmental approach', *The Leadership Quarterly*, 22: 604–615.

14

Diversity Leadership and Leading Homogeneity

> *There are leaders who enjoy managing a diverse team and the challenges and benefits that go with it; others prefer to lead a group of like-minded people.*

Diversity management as a job in leadership involves leading culturally diverse teams and encouraging cultural diversity within the leadership of organizations. One of the key issues here is a need to understand the benefits of diversity, and to buy into this philosophy. This is not a matter of homogenizing organizational diversity – encouraging apparent diversity with the goal of showing how everyone is really much the same – instead it is the process of embracing diversity for the richness of the differing perspectives, ideas and traditions that are brought to the table and committing to making good use of the debate and even conflict that might ensue. For example, a leader coming from a different ethnic background to that of other senior colleagues can bring a different viewpoint and, as business globalizes, organizations are coming to appreciate this – if they listen to them, use their ideas and address majority reactions such as stereotyping and in-group clannishness. In some organizations the presence of women in leadership roles is felt to be quite radical, and unsettling enough to challenge old assumptions and suggest new possibilities. The literature on diversity studies has grown exponentially in recent years, with 'cross-cultural management' and 'gender management' becoming popular MBA modules, as well as discussion of this topic in ethics and CSR, and in HR.

One might imagine that leaders who themselves appear to be different from the norm – to personify 'diversity' – would be effective at managing a diverse workforce, but this is not necessarily so; nor is it the case that managers from homogeneous backgrounds cannot manage diversity. Sometimes it helps if the leader of a diverse workforce has a developmental or coaching and mentoring background, because of the inherent interest in each person as an individual, and beneath the surface appearances (see the related entry Developmental-oriented Leadership and and Job-hopping Leadership) – but not always. Collaborative and co-operative styles of leadership, and a participative leadership approach, might also be beneficial – but there is more to managing diversity than this (see the related entries Individualistic Leadership and Relationship-oriented Leadership, and Authoritarian Leadership and Participative Leadership).

But to what extent has the concept of diversity really taken hold in the senior echelons of management and leadership? Not much, really – otherwise the statistics would tell the story. Especially in the field of women in leadership, some emerging markets – especially in Africa – are making more progress than in the West (see the related entry Eastern-style Leadership and Western-style Leadership – Contrasting and Converging National Cultures). The key question, though, is whether minorities make a difference through being genuinely different, or are these minorities being sucked into the system and behaving like the majority? So, are successful Chinese heading up US companies succeeding because they have become 'American'? Are successful women heading up any organization succeeding because they have become 'masculine'? In such cases diversity is defeated by homogenizing systems, even though a team or a leader may appear to represent diversity and may also appear to be encouraging the process.

What are the dynamics of sameness and difference in organizations? A valuable perspective is offered by Social Identity Theory (Haslam et al., 2011), which emphasizes the crucial importance of being part of a 'we', a collective sense of 'us'. Any group will select and accept leaders who seem to represent the features that most characterize their shared identity, and leadership is the opportunity to extend the range of what it is to be 'one of us'. Strong corporate branding (see the related entry Company-branded Leadership and Individual-branded Leadership) may enhance the social identity of an organization, but it is rooted in something much deeper – in the personal 'sense of self' of the organization's members. An homogeneous organization is one in which members feel a commonality only with others who look and behave in similar ways; it may be a sign of intrinsic insecurity and uncertain external circumstances, where there is felt to be a real and present threat from competitors or other factors. An organization that is more obviously diverse is one in which surface-level differences can be tolerated because the sense of 'usness' is based on deeper commonalities; a clear strategy often helps, but the main condition is security in relation to the external environment. This is one reason why large, long-lived and successful companies can be surprisingly diverse in their membership, and also NGOs with a clear mission that overrides other identities. So back to leaders: Haslam et al. (2011) describe them as 'entrepreneurs of identity' because they see leadership as primarily representing the current and possible social identity of an organization. From this perspective, a leader should be both 'one of us' and also hold out the possibility that 'we' might become something more. The question here is, 'What is the difference that counts?' It might not be ethnicity or gender (though it could be, if having a woman leader, for example, represents new opportunities for many people in the organization and among its stakeholders). If diversity is about more than how people look, and has real meaning in terms of diverse skills, attitudes, cultural resources, and so forth, leaders must pay attention to the underlying strategy, values and purposes that are the foundations of tolerance.

But there is an even darker side to diversity in leadership. We have all heard of the so-called 'glass-ceiling effect' (Morrison et al., 1987; Cotter et al., 2001), referring to the myriad subtle and not-so-subtle ways in which institutions will create barriers preventing people who don't fit the 'top management' norm from rising to the top. The 'glass cliff' refers to the predicament of those few people from minorities who do make it. The original research by Michelle Ryan and colleagues (2005) questioned the relatively high failure rate of companies headed by women CEOs. They found that boards would often appoint a woman as a last resort, when failure was imminent. And this pattern is repeated further down organizations: women are more likely to be given (and to accept) projects with a high risk of failure. Of course none of this is necessarily conscious or systematic: but it is systemic behaviour that is deeply embedded in the group psychology of organizations, and another factor that militates against diversity in leadership.

Here we look at the perspective of a typical business leader on the value of diversity – but there are warnings here, and a refusal to generalize. We also look at some practical reflections on the impact of diversity. But, despite paying lip-service to the concept, there is still a long way to go before diversity is sincerely valued, such that leaders can readily and easily be people who don't conform to taken-for granted assumptions about what is normal.

An ex-CEO/Management Consultant – on the benefits of a diversifying approach to leadership:

> People with a different ethnic background who are leading an organization can add an extra dimension to the typical leadership style of that environment. It can be beneficial – but if his or her different background turns out to be the basis for just another dogma, it is not about diversity at all. Diversity should bring a range of views – not just one new one replacing one old one. Some leaders are open to a high degree of diversity, whilst others are not.
>
> A new way of looking at things can be a blessing or a curse. The organization can have a new perspective, can have multiple views instead of one view, can be more creative, and can have more competitive advantages. There's an organization for which I consult which is predominantly Dutch – our consulting firm is in the Netherlands – but it has a handful of Anglo-Saxons and others – British, American, Canadian and Indian employees. These staff members provide a new interpretation – but the trouble is that the organization doesn't listen to them, so they are frustrated. And the Dutch people there, who listen to these foreigners, can be a bit unsettled by them. They're not sure if they have any power in the organization, and if their influence competes with theirs.
>
> Women sometimes bring a different perspective to leadership where everyone has got used to men in the top jobs. Maybe they have less need to be seen as the leader, standing in front of the group, looking as if they're telling people 'you're looking at the leader – me'. Men often want this dominant position, but I think a lot of women don't (though there are clear exceptions). Some women seem to be happier facilitating on the side of the group, encouraging everyone with a shared sense of purpose – 'we all need to make progress' – and often are more consistent in what they say they will do compared with what they actually do. Actually some men prefer this approach, but if they behave like this they aren't recognized as leaders – it's not seen as manly. Some people think that there are inherent qualities to being a woman, that they have a stronger sense of empathy, a closer sense of the feelings of others, and are more interested in people generally. This certainly fits the stereotype, so some women feel that the only way they can get to the top and be a leader is behaving more like men, which has its own problems. Overall, it seems to me as a diversity-sympathizing male leader that

a gender balance in organizations is preferable. Men have more camaraderie and women more rivalry, so a balance between the two might cut out too much chummy behaviour, and too much cut-throat in-fighting. But it depends a lot on circumstances.

The stereotypes fly thick and fast in the foregoing quote, and are typical of much discussion about diversity: a desire to pin down the essential qualities of being a man or a woman, an Easterner, or a Westerner. If only we could do this, we would be able to say that 'men are like this, women are like that, and we are all better off with a bit of this and a bit of that'. But reality is not so neatly partitioned; people don't conform to stereotypes. In fact stereotypes are notably important for the people who do the stereotyping, and tell us more about their need to categorize and normalize. They are also effective ways of securing a group identity: a clear 'them and us' distinction. This is why stereotyping is so common in debates about diversity – and why it is so poisonous of true tolerance and giving people a chance.

An emerging market consultant offers differing perspectives on diversity. The first example shows how recognizing the diverse characteristics of customers and markets can open up new opportunities; the second and third examples show how the desire for homogeneity can be deeply rooted into the fibre of a company. Example 1:

> We once had the privilege of attending a lecture by C.K. Prahalad, who has now sadly passed away. As an Indian by origin, but with huge experience in the UK and the USA, he was able to offer a very fresh perspective. He challenged the previously widely accepted, and biblically referenced, belief that 'the poor will always be with us' – by suggesting ways in which this is a market segment that may be tapped and brought into the global economy. If poor people cannot save, and have money available only on a day-by-day basis, then they want to buy consumer products in small sachets – shampoo, margarine, jam, cheese, etc. They can't afford to buy big quantities and they may not have facilities for safe or temperature-controlled storage. But they can purchase and use smaller units in a practical way. And Prahalad also suggests ways in which the poor – especially by sharing resources, such as access to one mobile phone per village – can leverage their collective bargaining power and work their way out of poverty.

Example 2:

> A friend of mine working in the shipping industry is a Norwegian, but he's based in the Mediterranean. He takes an entirely different view – much more long-term, more strategic, and shipping is in his blood. The contrast between Northern and Southern Europeans can be quite remarkable, in his view. Mediterranean people work to live – he lives to work. His problem, as he sees it, is how to infect his south European staff with his north European commitment for the business, hard work, a sense of responsibility and enthusiasm for ships and the sea. But he finds that most of his staff members are just going through the motions. He likes to manage in an homogeneous way as he finds it hard to cope with the mentality of different ethnicities, and thinks his is the best.

Example 3:

Another homogeneity-preferring leader I know was in the British Royal Navy. Although he regarded his officers and crew as a mixed group socially and in terms of class and educational background, he felt that the Navy's culture was a unifying force that united diversity and made it more homogeneous. Then, half-way through his career, the Navy decided to admit women to jobs at sea. He found it very challenging, and felt that the ensuing problems on board ship added around 30 per cent to his workload. He still sees women and men in specific roles – women as nurses, men as soldiers – and strongly believes in many gender stereotypes. Although he is not misogynistic by any stretch of the imagination, he is not likely to change this perspective. He really believes that the armed services, especially in wartime, are a man's world.

Diversity can be valuable, but is often unappreciated in reality, possibly because of the tendency to promote and trust others of a similar background, so homogeneity in organizations is a powerful norm. Leaders from minorities (however defined) are perceived to involve a high level of risk, so few boards of directors will appoint them, except in advisory capacities. This may be one reason why so many people who don't fit the most obvious ethnic and gender norms of big companies turn instead to their own businesses, and become entrepreneurs.

FURTHER READING

Bolden, R., Hawkins, B., Gosling, J. and Taylor, S. (2011) *Exploring Leadership: individual, organizational and societal perspectives.* Oxford: Oxford University Press.

Bryman, Alan, Collinson, David L., Grint, Keith and Jackson, Brad (2011) *The Sage Handbook of Leadership.* London: Sage.

Cotter, David A., Hermsen, Joan M., Ovadia, Seth and Vanneman, Reece (2001) 'The glass ceiling effect', *Social Forces*, 80 (2): 655–81.

Dowd, Maureen (2005) *Are Men Necessary? When sexes collide.* London: Headline Book Publishing.

Due Billing, Y. and Alvesson, M. (2000) 'Questioning the notion of feminine leadership: a critical perspective on the gender labeling of leadership', *Gender Work and Organization*, 7(3): 144–157.

Morrison, A., White, R. and Van Velsor, E. (1987) *Breaking the Glass Ceiling: can women reach the top of America's largest corporations?* Cambridge, MA: Perseus Books.

Northouse, Peter Guy (2010) *Leadership: theory and practice.* Thousand Oaks, CA: Sage.

O'Connor, Karen (2010) *Gender and Women's Leadership: a reference handbook.* Thousand Oaks, CA: Sage.

Parker, Patricia Sue (2005) *Race, Gender and Leadership: re-envisioning organizational leadership from the perspectives of African American women executives.* Mahwah, NJ: Lawrence Erlbaum Associates.

Ryan, M. K. and Haslam, S. A. (2005) 'The glass cliff: evidence that women are over-represented in precarious leadership positions', *British Journal of Management*, 16: 81–90.

Storey, John (2011) *Leadership in Organisations: current issues and key trends* (2nd edition). Oxford: Routledge.

Western, Simon (2008) *Leadership: a critical text.* London: Sage.

15
Eastern-style Leadership and Western-style Leadership – Contrasting and Converging National Cultures

> *There are leaders who typify their origins and culture and are successful in their own environment; others are cosmopolitans who can operate anywhere, bridging East and West.*

In today's globalized world, leaders work increasingly in cross-cultural contexts, with teams comprising members from widely differing national backgrounds. They have differing viewpoints and behaviours, and often diverse ideas about work, careers, hierarchy and authority. Similarly, leaders are now more globally active, working in many different countries in which they have to respond to widely differing expectations. This raises significant issues regarding what counts as proper leadership activity and requires leaders to develop sensitivities towards disparate cultural backgrounds so as to inform and better orient their own leadership practice. It is now difficult for a leader to operate from one cultural perspective.

Cultures are dynamic, changing, adapting all the time; and they are each full of their own complexities, diversity and contestation. Whatever generalization one might make about a culture – such as 'that we value democracy' – there will be numerous exceptions and disagreements. The same can be said for all manner of so-called cultural norms: attitudes towards authority figures, the roles of men and women, relationships between generations, attitudes towards family and community. But nevertheless, cultural stereotypes persist, and some generalizations are helpful. In particular, we frequently hear of a distinction between 'East and West' referring in very general terms to Asia on the one hand, and the Americas and Europe on the other. These are assumed to embody two distinctive cultures, with implications for leadership practice. Developing Eastern and Western cultural competencies is often seen as an ideal, even though some may be contradictory or mutually exclusive – this is all part of the challenge. For example, authoritarian leadership may be more accepted in some 'Eastern' countries whilst organizational norms in Western countries increasingly value participatory leadership. Some cultures are seen as more competitive and directive, with a more individualistic approach to leadership (see the related entries Authoritarian and Participative Leadership, and Individualistic and Relationship-oriented Leadership). These are just two of the many attempts to define the dimensions along which cultures differ. In the remainder of this section we balance a common-sense East–West distinction as related to leadership practice, with a more analytical consideration of underlying values, based on one of the most well-established systems for categorizing cultural differences: Geert Hofstede's (2001) 'Culture's Consequences'.

Here, we look first at the East–West leadership divide in the form of a set of direct contrasts, compiled by one of the authors of this volume and a student. Then, we look at the example of Vietnam, shared by our emerging markets consultant, considering a characteristically 'Eastern' country which is facing up to the challenge of 'Western' (as well as 'Eastern') business, and discussing specific cultural manifestations which can be challenging to leaders struck by an East–West divide. Then, we consider Hofstede's (2001) constructs of Power Distance and Uncertainty-Avoiding behaviour as helping us to understand the differences, with practical examples.

A compilation of stereotypical characteristics as if West and East are direct mirrors of each other can be useful here (see Table 8). This format of comparison, typical of many descriptions of Eastern versus Western leadership, looks plausible at first sight, and may reinforce assumptions and make sense of impressions. Thus, Western leaders may be seen as more task-oriented, focused on the here-and-now, collaborative and co-operative and opportunistic – with Eastern leaders more in contrast with these attributes. However, a closer examination shows how problematic this can be. Because each row of the table is supposedly addressing a 'common' concept (such as delegation, trust, centralization, and so forth), it forces an apparent opposition between the two: East must be the opposite of West. This might be true on a compass or a map, but it is a strange way to describe cultures, which are different in their own ways, with interconnecting histories and influences. The great bureaucracies of India are derived from an amalgam of Moghul and British colonial forms, imbued with specifically Indian values of dharma (poorly translated as 'duty'), for example. Are these 'Western' or 'Eastern'? Meanwhile, the value of meritocracy underpins bureaucratic norms in China and Europe, but no-one would claim that all leaders are promoted on merit alone in either region. Thus, broad generalized bifurcations between East and West are of little use, more likely to hinder understanding than to help it. But an awareness that particular circumstances differ is a precursor to working with, rather than against, the flow of different cultures. The following is an example.

An emerging market consultant on trying to find practical examples of leadership and culture, in this case in the context of Vietnam:

Leaders coming from Western cultures often experience confusing challenges when working within Asian contexts. One particular example of this is highlighted in Borton and Ryder's 'Working in a Vietnamese Voice' (2000), who show how Vietnamese cultural conventions differ, and may clash with Western cultural conventions. For example, Vietnamese culture is highly community focused, as opposed to the generally individualistic focus within most Western cultures. In the work environment this is enacted through an indirectness of conversation and decision-making that may be frustrating to a Westerner. One particular instance of this is the *'xinphep'* consultative process common in Vietnamese society and organizations. *Xinphep* is a

Table 8 Western vs Eastern leading styles

Western leaders	Eastern leaders
Someone has to do the job, it can be me	A duty, a calling, no argument, no choice
For excitement, challenge, adventure	It is what I have been brought up for
Task-oriented, on the spot, urgent, now	Relationship-oriented, building harmony
Short-term thinking, opportunist	Longer-term, visionary, committed
Making own choices and decisions	Consciously following a role model
Reluctant leader, happy delegating, hands-off	Strong ambition, controlling, responsible
Large span of command – need to trust and empower	Manage through a group of acolytes
Seeing self as expert in motivating people	Concern with own leadership progress
Climbing the ladder of seniority as manager	Coming in at a high managerial level
Know the business to gain credibility	Know business to avoid being fooled
Supervising experts to get on with the job	Supervising for control/gaining respect
Finding a new team in a new job	Team follows him from job to job
Has to be visible, duty to be seen, build trust	Wants to be visible, to monitor/control
Must proactively help out in a tough job	Must show concern/support in tough job
The team must solve their own problems	Problems must not go any higher up
Vacations mean a long break from work	Vacations are short, work contact is kept
Delegation during vacation is a plus	Reluctance to delegate during vacations
Delegation helps to develop young leaders	Delegation is limited to a trusted few
Work is for work time only	Work is all the time
Time management is an important skill	Time management is impossible
Away from home so work is priority	Family obligations are a priority too
Wants strong teams of able people	Wants teams to be loyal and supportive
The leader is the first among equals	The leader has followers
Culturally low power-distant	Culturally high power-distant
Decentralized leadership/management	Centralized leadership/management
Build trust and then delegate	Lack of trust is a barrier to delegation
Delegation is based on ability and merit	Delegation is based on close relationships
Bosses do leadership and management	Boss is the leader, others manage
Appreciate followers' needs and goals	Followers exist to support the leader
Followers have to be won and convinced	There will always be followers
Managers must achieve the financial goals	Managers must keep control
Leaders do the job and move on	Leaders build a reputation in the community
Leaders are one-off individuals	Leaders are members of their families

community-focused process designed to show mutual respect, enforce team relationships and ensure those people involved understand and feel comfortable with the decisions being made. Essentially it is an exercise in maintaining community cohesion. Because Vietnamese typically link directness (a common feature of Western leadership styles) with arrogance, they tend to be indirect using proverbs, parables and anecdotes during discussions. Additionally leaders tend to avoid saying things like 'We must do this…' or 'I believe this must be done…' in favour of phrases such as 'Be kind enough to listen to me…' or 'If you agree, we thought we might…' (Borton and Ryder, 2000: 23.)

A leader with a Western cultural outlook who has a low level of cross-cultural competence may view this type of interaction as inefficient, aggravating and evidence of a lack of leadership. However, the *xinphep* consultative process is not a relinquishing of power or delegation, or a waste of time – it is culturally relevant and necessary. Because the communal outlook (as opposed to an individualistic one) is highly salient in this cultural context there is a requirement to continuously show mutual respect and rein-force community cohesion. From a Western perspective, this process may be experienced as cumbersome, as everyone discusses details exhaustively, leading to 'almost too much democracy' (Borton and Ryder, 2000: 23). However, if a Western-oriented leader showed frustration with this process and attempted to assert an individual dominance over the situation, his/her leadership may be perceived as disrespectful, arrogant and offensive, negatively impacting the work environment and the leader's ability to lead. By developing awareness and understanding of the cultural background of working in Vietnam, a leader can adapt his/her leadership practice to respect this type of organizational interaction, engage in this process, and more effectively lead.

This is an example of different ways of doing things; cultural theorists try to understand the deep-seated beliefs and assumptions that underpin behaviour. One such framework, already mentioned, is the Cultural Dimensions index constructed and developed by Geert Hofstede (2001). The five dimensions are power-distance, individualism, masculinity, uncertainty avoidance and long-term orientation. Cultures may be characterized by how the population responds to questions on each of these dimensions, with the whole set adding up to a profile of the culture (as represented by the respondents, usually educated employees of large organizations). The issue of power-distance (the perception of tolerance of a wide or narrow gulf between a leader and followers) raises particularly important questions for cross-cultural leadership: for example, are interactions between leaders and followers in Asian or Arab countries more structured, rigid and formal than in Western cultures?

Hofstede's findings contrast 'high power-distance' cultures, such as many Asian countries (the Philippines, India, Singapore, Hong Kong), South American countries (Mexico, Venezuela, Brazil) and many Arab and African countries, with 'low power-distance' cultures such as North America, Australasia, Scandinavia and Great Britain. The former countries emphasize the importance of rank in organizations and the deference shown to authority figures; the latter indicate less rank-consciousness and much more familiarity (Hofstede, 2001). Generally, insights regarding Asian countries suggest that they exhibit 'high power distance' and 'ascribed status', as defined by another guru of cross-cultural management, Fons Trompenaars: 'acting as it suits you even if nothing is achieved' (Trompenaars and Hampden-Turner, 1997: 105).

The emerging market consultant again, looking to apply this concept from experience in a practical way:

For example, a low power-distant leader in a high power-distant environment – such as an Irishman working in the Middle East – will shock local managers as he greets low-level (in terms of the organizational hierarchy) immigrant workers as 'buddies'. They will not understand why he is consulting cleaning staff about building materials – but there is method in his madness. From the perspective of the low power-distant leader such as the Irishman, he is cultivating an organizational culture of inclusion, regardless of hierarchical position – a strategy not dissimilar to *xinphep* – but with completely different underlying causes, because in Vietnam the consultative behaviour is motivated by wanting to avoid upset and exclusion, while the Irishman is simply talking to whoever might have the answers and insights into his problems.

However, cultural differences are far too myriad and dynamic to be reduced only to these generalizations. The above example of *xinphep* is a prime example of how 'high power-distance' is not necessarily present in all Asian contexts. Even the sources for respect and authority afforded to leaders can be widely different. Whereas in Western cultures leaders are given respect mainly for their accomplishments (education, career success, wealth, etc.) and personality traits (being confident, decisive, dependable, adaptable, etc.), Trompenaars and Hampden-Turner point to how leadership in Arab countries is highly dependent on family background and connections (1997: 106).

Another related issue is the amount of risk or uncertainty individuals from different cultures are comfortable coping with, what Hofstede (2001) refers to as relative levels of uncertainty avoidance. This might be shown in higher or lower levels of avoiding behaviours – following the stereotypical view that Eastern cultures are high avoiding, and Western is low avoiding – but the concept is more complex than this. The construct of uncertainty avoidance assesses levels of comfort or discomfort in unstructured or unfamiliar situations. Hofstede's research has indicated significant national trends in the overall acceptance or avoidance of uncertainty within organizational cultures. For example, the research points to Germans as having relatively high levels of uncertainty avoidance as compared to people from Singapore. In practice this means that German organizations tend to avoid unstructured or unfamiliar situations, employing highly structured processes, rules and regulations to decrease uncertainty. On the other end of the spectrum, members of an organization in Singapore will typically be more comfortable with emergent processes with far less structure than their German counterparts.

An MBA teacher, considering progress in cross-cultural research and looking at opportunities for practical learning:

> Developing cultural competencies, including national cultural awareness, is essential for the twenty-first-century leader. For leaders this has to be a continuous process, as not only are cultural behaviours multiple in nature, but they are ever-changing. In terms of teaching national culture to leaders, it is obvious that much of the research into the characteristics of various national cultures is now 25–30 years old, and the norms and conventions of economies and social groups have changed.
>
> Exemplary of this is a recent study of Peru compared with the Netherlands (More Torres and Jones, 2010). A sample of the inhabitants of Lima revealed diametrically opposed cultural characteristics and preferences compared to a similar sample conducted by Hofstede in the 1980s.
>
> What this research shows is that countries with high economic growth rates (e.g. 8–10 per cent), such as Peru, change significantly over relatively short periods of time as compared to countries with relatively stable economic conditions, such as the Netherlands. Many of the writers on cross-cultural management assumed that the descriptors they developed were of permanent value in describing these countries. But they were not!

In terms of leadership this has significant implications for how leaders lead – both in how they act themselves and in what they can expect from those they lead. Imagine for a moment the problems and potential chaos that could arise if a low uncertainty-avoiding leader, reliant on emergent rather than prescriptive processes, was leading a team of primarily high uncertainty-avoiding individuals. Team members would likely feel lost, confused and ultimately frustrated with the lack of process and structure. At the same time the leader may not understand why the team cannot just get on with the work by orienting towards the overall goal rather than prescribed step-by-step processes.

Here again the onus is on the leader to develop cultural competencies to be able to identify such issues and adapt leadership styles accordingly. This is a very complex process and one which cannot rely upon the stereotypes of any particular country or region. As shown above, while research suggests many Asian cultures feature high power-distance organizational structures there are exceptions, such as the *xinphep* consultative process in Vietnam. Similarly, overall generalizations regarding uncertainty avoidance cannot always be relied upon. Germany's neighbour Denmark has, according to Hofstede's work, a much lower uncertainty-avoiding culture while a scan of the highest uncertainty-avoiding cultures will find countries from across Europe, Asia and South America present. While there are national, regional and local trends to culturally informed behaviour, there is no definitive map for leaders to rely upon.

Although an awareness of differing national, regional and local cultural norms and conventions (such as low versus high uncertainty-avoiding behaviours) is useful, the issues are more complex than merely seeing leadership–followership relations in terms of national culture. Abstract concepts such as national culture, nationalism and national type are highly problematic when put into active situations and practice; they do not account for the subtle complexity of individual personalities and particular market conditions of a specific company. After all, while citizens of a particular country tend to share many aspects of cultural background, each individual has a unique life history which informs how they interpret and enact cultural norms and conventions. They may also be a mix of cultures.

Leaders must develop an awareness of their own cultural biases and develop toolkits to build an awareness of other cultures. They must be able to see the presence of specific cultural perspectives and behaviours and also be able to accept this diversity and work with it for the betterment of all involved and the successful completion of tasks and projects. While developing such competencies, leaders must be sensitive as well to the unique individual perspectives of differing cultures and open to how cultures change over time. National cultural differences cannot necessarily be easily predicted and understood and, with the presence of so many other variables, it might make more sense for a leader to keep an open mind in an unfamiliar environment, rather than searching for patterns and boxes in which to put people and their attitudes.

FURTHER READING

Andrews, T. (ed.) (2009) *Cross-cultural Management: critical perspectives on business and management*. London: Routledge.

Borton, Lady and Ryder P.R. (2000) 'Working in a Vietnamese voice', *Academy of Management Executive*, 14 (4): 20–31

de Bono, S., Jones, S. and van der Heijden, B. (2008) *Managing Cultural Diversity*. Oxford: Meyer & Meyer.

reward in being good at something, to have independently chosen to do it and, above all, to have a sense of purpose, which must be constantly present.

Not-for-profit organizations come in various forms, many of which are not strictly speaking 'voluntary'. They include NGOs staffed by professional scientists, policy think-tanks, universities, arts and culture groups, cooperatives and numerous other organizations for whom making a profit is not a requirement. Most have salaried staff with expectations of fair pay for their work, and hopes of promotion and a career. These are not strictly speaking volunteers, but many such organizations couldn't function without the contributions of unpaid volunteers. They can operate and have structures very like private companies but have humanitarian rather than financial goals. They have objectives but rarely profit targets, except to stay within a budget or achieve specific funding goals. Many still have donors to answer to, and need to be seen to be spending money wisely rather than making a monetary return on the investment.

Here, we meet two volunteers who are reflecting on their experiences, and two people running NGOs who have to cope with specific management and leadership challenges. These are mostly very different from private-sector businesses, but have to be run in a businesslike way, while seriously engaging the participants (we can't really call them staff).

A willing volunteer – on the volunteer–follower perspective:
Example 1:

> I'm volunteering to help with the maintenance of a heritage site. Generally, the long-term volunteers have been given an area of the site to look after, and they can clean paths and restore walls and look after the trees and flowers in this area according to what they think needs doing. Most of them quite enjoy this and come regularly once or even twice a week. Some of them are good at specific tasks needing experience of equipment, such as lawn-mowing and hedge-trimming. But several of the volunteers stopped coming when the former leader was critical, bossy and demanding.

Example 2:

> I used to volunteer to help out in church, showing visitors to the pews. We are in a popular tourism area and have a lot of visitors. The church is very old and picturesque, and many people want to have christenings and weddings here. So I volunteered to help direct people to free spaces in the pews. But the Vicar shouted at me and said I was showing them to the wrong place. I was very upset. So I would not do anything at the church anymore, and soon I stopped going altogether and attended another church.

In both these examples, criticism from the leader elicited a very negative reaction from the volunteer. Leaders within volunteer organizations have to be very careful in balancing encouragement with constructive criticism. It is not that leaders in volunteer organizations cannot be critical; they have to do this from time to time, but they have to be more acutely aware of how that criticism will be received by volunteers, and what the consequences might be.

An emerging market consultant – on the not-for-profit leader perspective:
Example 1:

I'm running a major NGO to encourage business and investment in Africa. We have a small staff, not paid much, and working in rather difficult conditions here in Tanzania. For example, the internet connection comes and goes, and the telephone lines aren't very reliable. I've really put everything I've got into this project, and brought my family out with me, and I've been here for two years already. I've been successful in attracting a lot of funding, but we have to manage it carefully as the European donors are strapped for cash themselves. I'll be talking to the Chinese next, as they are very ambitious in Africa. With my staff, I have deliberately recruited young people who have a personal mission to be in Africa and help African people to run businesses and be independent. We have built a family atmosphere here where we all help each other. My staff members go on leave (locally and home) quite often as it's tiring and frustrating being here, and I want them to love Africa and care about these people and our mission. Luckily, we've been able to retain our staff but I make a much bigger effort with them than when we are back in Europe, where they have their own lives and see the job as more nine-to-five, which they don't have here, and can't have.

Example 2:

I work for a faith-based organization, created and funded by a church, where the participants receive subsistence allowances but not substantial wages. They are motivated by the cause, and not by earning money. We run clinics and schools, and build wells and roads. Those who work with us are either here for the short term or for the long term. The latter have to be ordained as priests, and the short-term participants must at least be keen church-goers and believe in our mission and attend all the religious services as well as helping with the projects. We have to find a balance between the spiritual life of our participants, and their practical life of digging and farming and nursing and teaching. Some people are more interested in one than the other. We want people here to be genuinely having missionary zeal, but they have to be practical too. We have to manage the church funds, report back to the donors, manage our support staff, achieve the project objectives and communicate the results back to all the people who contribute. We also need to find projects worth supporting and see them through to completion, which sometimes includes coping with bureaucracy and corruption.

It can be a big mistake to treat workers in voluntary organizations and not-for-profits like private-sector staff – their agendas are quite different. They need a completely different leadership and management approach. Although effective systems have to be in place so that people are accountable for the disbursement of funds and other resources, these people should be given more opportunities to do what they like doing best, and get better at it. They should also usually be allowed to do things in their own way, with more freedom and autonomy, as this also contributes to job satisfaction. They particularly need to be thanked regularly for the worthwhile and important work they are doing, both as a group and individually.

FURTHER READING

Agard, Katherine A. (2010) *Non-profit Organizations: a reference handbook*, Sage Reference Series on Leadership. Thousand Oaks, CA: Sage.

Bolden, R., Hawkins, B., Gosling, J. and Taylor, S. (2011) *Exploring Leadership: individual, organizational and societal perspectives*. Oxford: Oxford University Press.

Colvin, Geoff (2009) 'How to build great leaders', *Fortune*, 4 December, 160 (10). http://money.cnn.com/magazines/fortune/fortune_archive/2009

Maxwell, John C. (1993) *Developing the Leader Within You*. Nashville, TN: Thomas Nelson.

Stidl, D. and Bradach, J. (2009) 'How visionary nonprofits leaders are learning to enhance management capabilities', *Strategy and Leadership*, 37 (1): 35–40.

Thach, E. and Thompson, K.J. (2007) 'Trading places: examining leadership competencies between for-profits vs. public and no-profit leaders', *Leadership and Organizational Development Journal*, 28 (4): 356–375.

17

EQ-oriented Leadership and IQ-oriented Leadership

> There is a school of thought in leadership prioritizing self-awareness and relationship management through empathy and social skills; others prioritize cognitive intelligence.

Typically, management has been analysed and interpreted in terms of its normative functions (such as organizing, planning and controlling). Scholars also look at the unintended or phenomenological effects of leadership (such as linking, defending, buffering); the political relations of leaders as agents of capital or the state; or the skills and competences embodied in leaders and managers themselves. But a distinct line of theory has explored the possibility that managers – and others – operate within a range of distinct intelligences. In 1990 Salovey and Mayer published a model of 'emotional intelligence' (later popularized by Goleman, 1998). The origins of the theory go back to the 1930s.

Since then, when considering leadership and how it is related to personality and behaviour, it has become popular to look at the concept of emotional intelligence. It used to be that leaders and others could be measured with a simple focus on IQ. Many still measure people this way – especially those who favour expert leadership (see the related entry Expert Leadership and Generalist Leadership). Over the last decade, many scholars and leadership developers have decided that this simple, one-dimensional view should be discarded in favour of a more complex, and to them more useful perspective – that of EQ. Leaders can be seen (especially in the Goleman study of 1998) as being high or low on five elements of emotional intelligence: self-awareness, self-regulation, self-motivation, empathy and social skills. For many, a high score in these factors is seen as crucial for a move from management to leadership, where raw IQ or technical expertise is not enough on its own. Clearly, leaders who are high on EQ factors are likely to adopt a coaching and mentoring style, to be comfortable with more emphasis on collaboration and co-operation, and to promote a relationship-building and people-oriented approach – as discussed in related entries (Coaching and Mentoring-oriented Leadership and Directive, Compromising Leadership and Co-operative Leadership and Individualistic Leadership and Relationship-oriented Leadership). One might also expect people with a high EQ to be alert to the value of life beyond work, and thus to be less at home in very results-driven cultures – but it is seldom as simple as this observation might suggest.

EQ is defined as 'the ability to know and manage oneself along with the awareness and ability to manage one's relationships with others'; the concept may be new, but its definition is time-honoured. Aristotle said: 'anyone can become angry – that is easy. But to be angry with the right person, to the right degree, at the right time, for the right purpose, in the right way – this is not easy.' Not everyone is convinced of the usefulness of the concept of EQ in leadership, as it says nothing about practical business skills, product knowledge and handling customers – or does it?

EQ can be divided into five aspects:

- *Self-awareness* can be seen as the start of emotional intelligence. Self-aware people know their weaknesses. If you know you cannot work under tight deadlines, you plan your time carefully. This self-awareness mode is the ability to recognize and understand your moods, emotions, and drives as well as their effects on others.
- *Self-regulation* means being able to control impulses or channel them for good purposes, the ability to control or redirect disruptive impulses and moods and the propensity to suspend judgement – to think before acting.
- *Motivation* is the passion for achievement for itself, and not simply the ability to respond to whatever incentives are on offer, the enthusiasm to work for reasons that go beyond money or status, and a tendency to pursue goals with energy and persistence. Leaders in interim positions, and those handling projects, need to be self-motivated (see the related entry Interim Leadership and Tenured Leadership).
- *Empathy* is the ability to relate to others, taking into account the feelings of others when making decisions, as opposed to taking on everyone's troubles. This is the ability to understand the emotional make-up of other people, which requires skill in treating people according to their emotional reactions.
- Finally, *social skill* is the ability to build a rapport with others, and gain co-operation – particularly valuable for leaders of volunteers (see the related entry Employee Leading and Volunteer Leading). Managers who try to be sociable, while lacking the rest of EQ characteristics, can fail. Social skill is friendliness with a purpose, a proficiency in managing relationships and building networks, and an ability to find common ground with others.

Here, we look at three examples where an understanding of EQ can help in appreciating different leadership styles, their strengths and drawbacks. We look at a leader lacking self-awareness; another lacking empathy; and one with an apparently high level of EQ. A leader with high EQ scores across all of the five areas can be highly effective, but developing personal EQ takes experience and judgement. In particular, few leaders really understand how others see them – self-awareness is one of the most challenging of the EQ elements.

An emerging markets consultant – on the unaware leader:

I met a senior colleague who holds a very senior position but who has no idea about self-awareness. He comes over as pompous and arrogant, but he doesn't see himself this way at all. Once he pressed me to tell him what I thought of him and give him feedback – he probably thought it was going to be very positive, I think he actually thought I really liked him, and so he poured himself a glass of wine and sat back comfortably to listen. He was really surprised by my comments – I didn't really mean to be so candid but I couldn't help it, he had asked me directly. He was quite shocked. If you had asked him about EQ he might have said he agreed with the concept, but that doesn't mean he embraced all aspects of it, or had thought about himself this way.

However, all he ever talked about was himself, how brilliant he was, and what he liked to do. He originally came from quite a poor developing country but had gained American citizenship and kept talking about himself as American. We were in a tourist city in Europe one afternoon having lunch. He was a Moslem, and made a point of criticizing this poor waitress in the restaurant for bringing a salad with bacon bits in it and not explaining that it was with pork and therefore not suitable for Moslems. But he was drinking wine at the same time! So he could go on about being a Moslem when it suited him, but not otherwise; he saw no discrepancy or inconsistency. This must have been unsettling for his staff – it certainly made me think this way. He would talk about how senior and important he was and how he was going to be promoted to this even more senior job, but his actual authority seemed to be rather limited in spite of his position on the organization chart.

He thought he was very creative and original, but he borrowed other people's materials all the time and never created his own. This must have been obvious to his staff, but clearly wasn't to him. He thought he was very culturally sensitive but constantly criticized colleagues from other countries in a negative way. Again, the contradiction between his view of himself and the reality must have created a lack of confidence and even some hilarity amongst his subordinates. He was disorganized and left everything to the last minute, but expected others to understand this was the way he worked and there was nothing wrong with it, it was their fault when things were late. His intolerance and inability to handle others – despite his assertions of his strong leadership ability – made him look unconvincing. This lack of an important dimension of EQ undermined his effectiveness as a leader, big time.

A researcher on psychology – on a leader without empathy, and – by contrast – one with high EQ:

A colleague, a senior leader for many years, has very little empathy. He doesn't react to how others feel. He was talking about a project in which he was involved as a 'great experience' and didn't seem to appreciate that another person who had helped him a great deal at that time saw it as 'a nightmare'. The staff members who help him cannot express any personal feelings or concerns – he ridicules them and encourages the others to do the same. This works, up to a point, in an urgent situation, but not for the long term. His subordinates don't have a life at all when he's around – nor does he, for that matter – but he doesn't care either way. He doesn't read emails carefully or listen well, so he often responds inappropriately – 'how super' he might say when someone is trying to tell him about their problems. He simplifies relationships, makes massive assumptions, and takes the help and support of others completely for granted. Even people who have helped him a lot he would criticize negatively. If someone is sick or ill – well, that just happens, so what? They must get better quickly and get on with their work, or they are no use. Probably they are just being lazy. He has no time for staff members like this. He is completely unmoved by stories which others feel are highly emotional, and cannot respond in a way which reflects their feelings. He has very little respect for the possessions of others – even when he knows how much they might value them – and would lose them, break them, or just leave them lying around. Occasionally he would be sorry when confronted about this behaviour, but most of the time he just carries on as always. Staff members who are also lacking in empathy and are only interested in practical expertise seem to admire him, but others feel that they are not treated as human beings, and that there is no concern for their life outside work. He would make fun of a worker whose wife asked him to come home!

However, there is another respected business contact I have who exhibits very high EQ. This leader understands his strengths and they way he behaves – he takes a clear overview and reflects before taking action. He tends to see the best in people and prefers coaching and delegation to authoritative direction. Micro-management is just not his thing – he exhibits a high degree of trust with his team-members. He knows the way he operates and has a strong sense of work-ethic and self-discipline when he needs it, but can also relax and have fun and enjoy himself. He is comfortable with himself, and has a style all of his own – authentic, reflective, appreciative, and generous. He's reflective, and mostly a generalist leader, but appreciates the expert contribution of others. When he's being critical, he tones this down with humour, and always combines it with praise. When one of the organizations he managed achieved a significant objective, he happily gave out big bonuses to everyone, because he really appreciated the contribution of everyone, in a very sincere way. When he achieves something through others, he is more than happy for them to accept recognition, being highly people-oriented. He doesn't need a big ego, and is embarrassed by this in others. He seems totally in charge of his career and where he's going, and gives the impression that he always has been this way, but without arrogance or assumptions. He's caring, sensitive, insightful and relates to and understands the problems of others when this is appropriate. He is at home in any group of people and is constantly in demand for speaking at very high-level gatherings, and joining corporate boards.

So EQ can be a useful measure of effectiveness in leadership – a high EQ doesn't of itself guarantee success, but it might be argued that a low EQ will almost certainly cause problems. A highly technical environment will value IQ and expertise more, but can suffer like any other from leaders with a low EQ leadership. This may be especially the case in terms of employee engagement and empowerment. Can low EQ leaders be as effective? Are there some occasions when it simply doesn't matter? Even when highly directive leadership is required, leaders need to know themselves and handle themselves and be self-motivated, even if they lack empathy or social skills. Often, subordinates have to develop high EQ to cope with their leaders, and some leaders compensate by working closely with a colleague who can 'do the soft stuff' for them.

Can a leader boost his or her emotional intelligence? Some observers think that leaders who are set in their ways will never change. But Goleman argues that EQ can be learned – but not with traditional training programmes that target the rational part of the brain. Extended practice, feedback from colleagues and personal enthusiasm are essential to becoming an effective and emotionally intelligent leader, suggests Goleman. Overall, it would seem that a leader would need a very strong wake-up call to make a big change, but it has happened. It all starts with looking in the mirror and proceeds with seeing oneself through the eyes of others.

FURTHER READING

Abelson, R.P., Gregg, A. and Frey, K.P. (2004) *Experiments With People: revelations from social psychology.* Mahwah, NJ: Lawrence Erlbaum and Associates.

Goleman, D. (1998) 'What makes a leader?', *Harvard Business Review*, November–December, 76(6): 93–102.

Goleman, D., Boyatzis, R. E. and McKee, A. (2002) *Primal Leadership: learning to lead with emotional intelligence.* Boston, MA: Harvard Business School Press.

Jones, S. (2010) *Psychological Testing.* Petersfield: Harriman House.

Maxwell, John C. (1993) *Developing the Leader Within You.* Nashville, TN: Thomas Nelson.

Salovey, P. and Weaver, J.D. (1990) 'Emotional intelligence', *Imagination, Cognition and Personality*, 9: 185–211.

18

Expert Leadership and Generalist Leadership

The source of comfort for some leaders is their expertise, knowledge, skill and focus on a particular area of business or management; other leaders could more or less manage anything they turn their hand to.

What are the issues along the continuum of generalist to expert or focused leadership? Generalist leaders are concerned with the act and process of leadership, and apply their leadership talents to a wide variety of organizational and business contexts. They are leaders first. The situation in which they are leading comes second.

Expert leaders, on the other hand, rise to the top of their specialist profession (e.g. academics, engineers, artists) and gain leadership status through their unique, specific focus, knowledge and expertise, developed over many years, perhaps helped by patrons or mentors in the same sector. Their credibility comes – at least initially – through their commitment to their vocation and accumulation of knowledge and skills in this area, which they then leverage to move on to higher things. A generalist leader, for example, may be a CEO of a specialist organization such as a pharmaceutical corporation, but have no technical expertise in pharmaceuticals. In contrast, a specialist leader may be the dean of a university faculty who has reached that position largely based on his or her academic accomplishments in the discipline.

We might expect generalist leaders to succeed through their generic skills and contacts amongst the elites of the business and public sphere in which they operate. Expert leaders have a stronger sense of commitment to their discipline and sector, and see their chosen specialism as particularly meaningful and worthwhile ('expertise with feeling' as discussed in *Nelson's Way* (Jones and Gosling, 2005: 45–6)). Leadership here is the pursuit of their profession, a continuation of a lifelong commitment, and something for which they are prepared to make sacrifices. In a sense, both expert and general leaders have a vocation – one to be a leader, one to be at the top of a specific discipline or industry – but both are leadership roles.

Expert leaders are likely to have a commitment to their profession, to their employer, and to their colleagues, customers, patients or students. But sometimes these commitments can be in conflict with each other, so the expert leader can have a difficult juggling act: many experts find this too stressful, and prefer to stay out of line management roles. Additionally they must keep up to date in the chosen field, continuously managing and adding to the body of knowledge in which they garner their expertise legitimacy. For expert leaders, with their deep technical knowledge, it can be a challenge to remember (and respect) that a complex organization requires other areas of competence, including generic functions such as finance, marketing and human resource management (HRM). Leadership, whether by experts or generalists, requires an overview of the system as a whole, with all the parts in proportion.

Expert leaders flourish in an organization that can help them develop and expand their expert skills and knowledge. They are more likely to build a career in the same organization, or at least in the same sector, because this is their vocation. As such, expert leaders are often, though not always, purposive leaders (see the related entry Goal-oriented Leadership and Opportunistic Leadership). It may be more of a challenge for an expert leader to make the leap to senior management from an operational job, because he or she will no longer be in the comfort zone of their expertise.

By contrast, generalist leaders can and must keep moving. The more diverse their organizational experience, the more effective they can be as generalists, and the more rapidly they can rise to more senior positions. As such, generalist leaders are often, though again not always, opportunistic leaders (see the related entry Goal-oriented Leadership and Opportunistic Leadership). An example of this kind of leader gaining a wide range of experience to broaden his skills is Lou Gerstner.

With positions at McKinsey, Nabisco, Amex and then IBM, each new experience built upon his ability as a change agent and master of strategic reform. Organizations needing a new brand of leadership, away from technical and narrowly focused views of the way the business should be run, welcome generalist leaders from varied backgrounds. Hence Gerstner's wealth of generalist leadership expertise enabled him to see IBM's problems in a more objective light than a technical expert – of which IBM had many.

Overall, senior posts are more usually filled by generalist leaders, as advancing up the managerial hierarchy inevitably means managing others in mysterious and unfamiliar departments. Effective generalist leaders let go and give their experts space to operate, not trying to micro-manage them and look over their shoulders all the time. Generalist leaders like being leaders and like managing people, but they need technical help and advice from experts, or risk simplifying decisions and missing some of the consequences that only the experts could foresee.

Expert leaders have the advantage of a strong capability in their particular calling, which can gain them credibility and respect. Having crossed the first few major barriers to career advancement, some are able to take a more generalist view, as it will be necessary for them to lead people whose jobs they don't entirely understand. This is the greatest hurdle for the expert leader to cross: expert leaders tend not to trust people who are not also experts, and dismiss the views of others unless they have a comparable level of expertise.

We now reflect on different generalist and expert leaders, how their thinking evolved and their attitudes to their role as a leader, including their prospects for further development. Considering the reflections of one executive coach/consultant on an expert leader, and the reflections of a self-described generalist leader, we explore the benefits and challenges of generalist and expert leadership.

A researcher on leadership – on the transition from expert to generalist:

I remember meeting a very senior leader in the oil industry. This individual rose through the ranks as an expert, having gained a PhD in Geology. As his successes accumulated and he rose in the ranks he was promoted to a managerial role. For him this was a big transition, from being a successful 'lone' scientist to leading a major corporation with many people.

As a manager, he quickly found a drastic change in his work priorities. No longer responsible for overseeing geological surveys, planning exploratory drilling, etc., he found he had to manage people. Rather than exploring and managing natural resources, he was managing and leading human resources. While he knew a lot about the jobs and roles of the corporation related directly to the discovery, extraction and refinement of petroleum he knew little to nothing about jobs in IT, finance and marketing, among others. In fact, he soon discovered his leadership job was mostly battling for talent with other parts of the organization, and attracting new recruits. He had to change from being a scientist to being a people-person whose priorities lay in human resources.

During his tenure at a large branch of the business in a Middle Eastern country, the country experienced a significant political crisis. Everyone in the head office realized that the operation he oversaw would be on hold for a few weeks. They began raiding his best people for short secondments in other offices. He would not have been concerned with such issues as a geologist, but as an overall leader he had to be.

In this case, key issues regarding expert to generalist leadership emerge. While this individual succeeded first as an expert scientific leader, he was eventually placed in a generalist leadership position. What he encountered there is typical for people who follow this type of trajectory. First, he realized that the work of a generalist leader is very different from that of his previous expert leader work – the priorities change. Rather than working with natural resources, this leader found that the priorities lay in leading human resources. He also found the context had changed. No longer was his leadership focused on specific geological problems, but distributed across the human resource problems of operations for which he was responsible. The oil company leader had to take on diplomatic and political responsibilities to manage the people resources of his operations within the wider context of the corporation. As a leader he had to communicate and argue his personnel needs with head office and be a voice for his projects and people in the corporation in general. Additionally, the expert leader realized he actually lacked the expertise necessary for leading other areas of the business, areas like finance and IT.

Ultimately this individual was successful in moving from expert leadership to generalist leadership. He succeeded in the transition because he was able to identify the changing dynamics of his work and to adapt to them. He recognized the different priorities, embraced the political role he had to take on and developed trust in those who offered the expertise he lacked.

An ex-CEO, now a Management Consultant – on generalist leadership:

I see myself as a generalist leader, having worked in leadership roles in private-and public-sector businesses, in all kinds of sectors. However, in my experience, many generalist leaders also have an area of expertise, often a finance background (see the related entry Finance-oriented Leadership and Marketing-oriented Leadership). This was particularly true 15–20 years ago. At that time individuals with a finance background moved to CFO positions and then transitioned to CEO. You can understand why this would happen: owners and investors were not able to keep in touch with the day-to-day running of the business, the key relationships and product developments, but they wanted reassurance that the finances were sound, and generally trusted an expert to tell them. But the problem with this approach was that managers who had grown up with a close eye on the accounts were not always best suited to sizing up the risks and opportunities when it came to new product and service innovation, creating new sources of revenue, and thinking through a strategy for the future.

Today, generalist leaders often have a consulting background. However, there are problems here as well. Consultants are familiar with being in an advisory role, telling people in organizations what to do. Even consultants who have specialized in strategy, and might be best suited to having a overview of the business and its markets, often have little experience of implementing strategies, and motivating people on the ground to cope with change and move to a new perspective. There is a world of difference between advising senior managers and developing followership across the organization. Consultants are usually very bright but because they have built their careers on looking for confirmation from senior managers, they may not have a feel for the ordinary operations and the people who make them work.

The consultant-turned-leader must, therefore, develop followers throughout the organization. Leader as 'colleague' might work well in professional services firms, but not in most businesses – where the leader has to be seen to be the boss!

In these reflections, central concerns for generalist leadership emerge. As with the oil executive in the previous example, our ex-CEO notes that many generalist leaders begin as expert leaders in the sense that they come from a specific profession or discipline – for example, finance. One of the dangers for this in generalist leadership is the challenge to an individual to step beyond the lens of their expertise. As he points out, an expert finance leader may stifle innovation through obsessive bean-counting. However, generalist leaders, such as those coming from consulting backgrounds, can also encounter serious issues. Consultants are typically good at generalization; they often work in widely differing business environments, industries, fields, etc. Such generalists are typically successful at adapting to new conditions of work, new priorities, and recognizing where they lack expertise and need to rely upon that of others. However, as leaders, being a generalist is not all that's needed: being responsible for action is quite different from analysing the situation and advising others on what to do. Not all generalists turn out to be good leaders.

Generalist leaders have often evolved from expert roles but can cope with more and wider responsibility, developing the ability to manage uncertainty and take risks, and see situations 'in the round'. Some start off as generalists but then recognize the need for experts and have to learn to trust and empower them. Generalist leaders who try to do everything and become micro-managers will struggle to motivate those working for them.

By contrast, expert leaders continue to build up their expertise, because this is how they feel able to keep a grip on things, and they believe – perhaps rightly – that their authority depends on this expertise. But they should beware creating an increasingly comfortable zone around themselves, made up of experts similar to themselves, and remain open to the insights brought by generalists. Expert leaders must learn to adapt to more generalist roles. They must be able to identify changes in priorities, develop new competencies (such as diplomacy and negotiation) and recognize when they themselves lack specific expertise in other areas.

FURTHER READING

Alvesson, M., and Sveningsson, S. (2003) *Managers Doing Leadership: the extra-ordinarization of the mundane*. University of Lund Institute of Economic Research Working Paper.

Bolden, R., Hawkins, B., Gosling, J. and Taylor, S. (2011) *Exploring Leadership: individual, organizational and societal perspectives*. Oxford: Oxford University Press.

Bryman, Alan, Collinson, David L., Grint, Keith and Jackson, Brad (2011) *The Sage Handbook of Leadership*. London: Sage.

Cotter, David A., Hermsen, Joan M., Ovadia, Seth and Vanneman, Reece (2001) 'The glass ceiling effect', *Social Forces*, 80 (2): 655–81.

Fryer, B. (2004) 'The Micromanager', *Harvard Business Review*, September, 82(9): 31–40.

Gerstner, L. (2002) *Who Says Elephants Can't Dance?* New York: HarperCollins.

Grint, K. (2005) 'Problems, problems, problems: the social construction of "leadership"', *Human Relations*, 58 (11): 1467–1494.

Handy, C. (1992) *Understanding Organizations*. Harmondsworth: Penguin.

Haslam, S.A., Reicher, S. and Platow, M. (2011) *The New Psychology of Leadership: identity, influence and power*. New York: Psychology Press.

Jones, S. and Gosling, J. (2005) *Nelson's Way: leadership lessons from the great commander.* London: Nicholas Brealey.

Ladkin, D. and Taylor, S. (2010) 'Enacting the true self: towards a theory of embodied authentic leadership', *Leadership Quarterly*, 21(1): 64–74.

Leithwood, Kenneth A., Muscall, Blair and Strauss, Tiiu (2009) *Distributed Leadership According to the Evidence.* New York: Routledge.

Pfeffer, J. (1994) *Managing with Power: politics and influence in organizations.* Boston, MA: Harvard Business School Press.

Rooke, D. and Torbert, W. (2005) 'The seven transformations of leadership', *Harvard Business Review*, April, 83(4): 66–76.

Snook, Scott A., Nohria, Nitin N. and Khurana, Rakesh (2012) *The Handbook for Teaching Leadership: knowing, doing and being.* Thousand Oaks, CA: Sage.

19
Extrovert Leadership and Introvert Leadership

> *Some leaders derive energy from people around them; some feel drained by the constant demands of others and thrive if they have time and space to themselves.*

Extroversion and introversion are commonly supposed to be important characteristics when it comes to social behaviour generally, and leadership in particular. The distinction has been very influential in leadership development and assessment because it is one of four fundamental characteristics measured by the hugely popular Myers Briggs Type Inventory (MBTI). What are the different characteristics and how can they impact on the way a leader operates?

Being described as an extrovert means that a leader probably relates more easily to the outer world of people and things than to the inner world of ideas. Extroverts are thus often people-oriented, and can be inspirational because they are excited by interaction with others, so put a lot of effort into it. They may prefer a participative approach, and like co-operation and collaboration. But they can also be authoritarian and competitive, liking to lead from the front. They quickly make friends and contacts, so they often don't mind interim and project-based work. An introvert, on the other hand, is more aware of what is going on inside his or her own mind.

The MBTI is based on Jung's division of people into groups who like action and activity, and those who like their own space. This is a question of where the leader gets his or her energy and drive from, and what takes away his or her energy and leaves a feeling of being drained. In extreme cases, it is sometimes hard for an extrovert to understand an introvert's form of activity and attitudes, and vice versa. Extrovert leaders can find it difficult to understand their introverted team members, and may be negatively critical of them. Introverted leaders struggle with the extrovert-oriented activities required of them, such as making presentations and talking to journalists and investors, but for this reason they can be good at delegation, if they are willing to let go of the reins. Introvert leaders can be reflective, analytical, behind-the-scenes leaders who are thoughtful and sensitive about other management styles, and can be purposive implementers – but not always. (See the related entries Inspirational Leadership and Low-key Leadership, Authoritarian Leadership and Participative Leadership, Accommodating Leadership and Competitive Leadership, Behind-the-scenes Leadership and Leading from the Front, Interim and Tenured Leadership, Long-term Leadership and Project Management Leadership.)

This discussion of extroversion and introversion (E–I) needs to be understood in the context of the Myers Briggs Inventory as a whole. Besides the E–I scale, the MBTI also identifies a second dimension, described as that of sensing compared with intuition. Leaders who are sensing prefer to work with known facts rather than look for possibilities and relationships. Those with a high preference for intuition would rather look for possibilities and relationships than work with known facts. Sensing leaders are practical and handle routine well but, by contrast, intuitive leaders don't like routine, and prefer the world of ideas. Sensing leaders are more common than intuitive leaders, but the latter can be more effective in handling people. These can be combined with E or I.

The third scale of the MBTI is concerned with preferences for thinking compared to feeling. What does the leader do when he or she has gathered the necessary facts and impressions? A thinking leader is likely to base his or her judgements more on impersonal analysis and logic than on personal values, whereas a feeling leader will base judgements more on personal values and sentiment. Feeling leaders can be more empathetic and can be seen as considerate and warm with their team members. Again, E or I leaders can also be thinking or feeling leaders as well.

Finally, the fourth dimension looks at judging as opposed to perceiving. The leader with a judging attitude probably means that he or she likes a planned, decided, orderly way of life, more than a flexible and spontaneous way of operating. The opposite of this is a perceptive attitude which probably means, in the case of a leader, that he or she likes being adaptable and doing things on the spur of the moment. The perceiving leader is less likely to plan, or make decisions quickly, or follow order. This scale also separates those who value being well organized and structured, from those who thrive on ambiguity. Unsurprisingly, perhaps, many leaders exhibit judging characteristics, especially in situations requiring a great deal of decision-making. However perceiving leaders can be innovative and entrepreneurial, but may need judging supporters to produce results. Combined with E and I approaches this can create a different approach to leadership.

The Myers Briggs exercise tends to emphasize the positive side of a leader's nature and can be very helpful in understanding the strengths and preferences for different styles of operating. One might expect most leaders and managers to be extrovert, sensing, thinking, judging (ESTJ type), i.e. most of their scores are on the extrovert scale, but this is shown to be a stereotyping effect: we ascribe 'leadership' to people who behave the way we think a leader should, and miss the real leadership contribution of people who don't match our expectations.

The MBTI is popular because it gives detailed feedback on each type. For example, a person who is type ESTJ is described as 'practical, realistic, matter of fact, with a natural head for business. Not interested in subjects they see no use for, but can apply themselves when necessary. Like to organize and run activities, may make good administrators especially if they remember to consider others' feelings and points of view.'

By contrast, the opposite of an ESTJ type would be introvert, intuitive, feeling and perceiving (INFP type), who would be described as 'full of enthusiasms and loyalties, but they seldom talk of these until they know you well. They care about learning, ideas, language and independent projects of their own. They tend to undertake too much then somehow get it done. Friendly, but often too absorbed in what they are doing to be sociable. They tend to be little concerned with possessions or physical surroundings.' However, although these types sound completely different, it is possible that various elements might overlap, but the person being tested will have clearer preferences for some dimensions than others.

As the profile of an ESTJ fits a common image of leaders, with the STJ part reinforcing the extrovert style, it is worth explaining this type in more detail. ESTJs tend to be logical, analytical, decisive and tough minded, and are able to organize facts, events and operations well in advance. ESTJs make useful contributions to an organization, in terms of seeing flaws in advance, being able to critique plans in a logical way, being able to organize the processes, products and people, and also being able to monitor to see if the job is done and to follow through in a step-by-step way.

The leadership style of a typical ESTJ is to seek leadership directly and take charge quickly, to apply and adapt past experiences to solve problems, be crisp and direct at getting to the core of the situation, be quick to decide, and act as a traditional leader who respects the hierarchy. ESTJs prefer work environments with hard-working people focused on getting the job done. They are task-oriented, well-organized and structured, and provide stability and predictability. They are focused on efficiency and like to reward the achievement of goals.

The potential pitfalls which face the extrovert, sensing, thinking and judging type include the possibility that they may decide too quickly, they may not see the need for change, they may overlook the niceties involved in working to get the job done, and may be overtaken by their feelings and values if they ignore them for too long. ESTJs should consider all sides before deciding, including the human element, and may need to remind themselves to look at the benefits of change. They may also need to make a special effort to show their appreciation of others, and could need to take the time to reflect on and identify their feelings and values. The same level of detail is available for the remaining 15 of the 16 MBTI types, which can be helpful in leadership development activities (see the related entry Development-oriented Leadership and Job-hopping Leadership). Note that there are over 2,000 other respected and well-researched personality inventories on the market, many of which address issues that are not obvious from an MBTI assessment. Readers are encouraged to seek professional advice if interested.

Here, we look at practical experiences of introvert and extrovert leaders, and the impact on their organizations. This includes a critical view of introversion – but it doesn't need to be the case. These views may be contrasted with the related entry Behind-the-scenes Leadership and Leading from the Front, which includes a discussion of the benefits of quiet leadership.

An ex-CEO/Management Consultant – on extrovert and introvert leadership:

The way I see it is that most extrovert leaders make a big effort to communicate. For introvert leaders it's a bigger challenge, they don't communicate so readily or so easily. The introvert leader may be wise and quiet, be a good listener, and be economical with words rather than garrulous. But the introvert leader has to force him or herself to realize that people need direction, help and appreciation, they need to know what is expected of them, they sometimes need correction, and they want to know about the way the company is going and the vision for the future. The extrovert leader may be better at putting all this across to people inside the company, and outsiders too. Although there are many ways to communicate and many new technologies available, the introvert leader may find it harder to make a big impact and be convincing and, in my experience, may have to work harder to move beyond staff positions to be promoted to a higher level of management responsibility.

A good extrovert leader will not only be a good communicator in most cases, but will find it easier to be clear in delivering a message, even if this message is not all that well thought through. An introvert leader, reticent to engage too much; may come over as uncertain, even if he or she doesn't mean to give this impression this can be a unsettling for some people (especially extrovert subordinates in need of a lot of high-touch communication). The introvert leader may be just as well-informed as the extrovert leader and may have just as good ideas and intentions, but they may not come across as such.

Within business, in my experience, extroversion is highly valued, except in hereditary situations such as family businesses. It isn't that introverts don't make good leaders; rather that they are less likely to compete for leadership positions than extroverts. However, within other arenas – particularly those which highly value specialist leadership contributions – introverts can be more common. A personal example follows.

A leader of an industry association (a form of chamber of commerce) was OK at talking with the external world, but did not know people internally and communicate with them – he saw his job as external communications only. He was basically an introvert and focused all his efforts on this part of his work, as he obviously found it very tiring and was very nervous. It took a lot of effort and energy for him. People who are extroverted see talking to other people – any people – as party time. When I took over this job I talked to all the insiders too, and when I was in industry I would talk with all the workers – I can't really see how you do your job without doing this. From the practical point of view, a leader must be an extrovert, or at least prepared to behave in an extrovert way from time to time, whatever the effort involved.

One problem with extrovert leaders can be that they cover up problems with their flamboyant manner and impression of optimism and confidence, in contrast with introverts, who may appear enigmatic – what are they thinking? Either mode might come over as arrogance. And, as suggested by the MBTI and many others like it, there is much more to a leader's personality type than simple extroversion or introversion. It depends on the remaining dimensions of type – such as sensing and intuition, thinking and feeling, and judging and perceiving. The different combinations can completely moderate an extrovert or introvert leader's behaviour.

FURTHER READING

Abelson, R.P., Gregg, A. and Frey, K.P. (2004) *Experiments with People: revelations from social psychology*. Mahwah, NJ: Lawrence Erlbaum and Associates.

Briggs Myers, Isabel (1987) *Introduction to Type: a description of the theory and application of the Myers-Briggs Type Indicator*. Oxford: Oxford Psychologists' Press.

Bryman, Alan, Collinson, David L., Grint, Keith and Jackson, Brad (2011) *The Sage Handbook of Leadership*. London: Sage.

Conger, Jay Alden and Kanungo, RabindraNath (1998) *Charismatic Leadership in Organizations*. Thousand Oaks, CA: Sage.

Grant, A.M., Gino,F. and Hofmann, D.A. (2011) 'Reversing the extraverted leadership advantage: the role of employee proactivity', *Academy of Management Journal*, 54 (3): 528–550.

Jones, S. (2010) *Psychological Testing*. Petersfield: Harriman House.

Ladkin, D. (2010) *Rethinking Leadership*. Cheltenham: Edward Elgar.

Northouse, Peter Guy (2010) *Leadership: theory and practice*. Thousand Oaks, CA: Sage.

20
Finance-oriented Leadership and Marketing-oriented Leadership

> *Some leaders, especially those who climbed the ladder of leadership through dealing in numbers and focusing on financial control, find it hard to understand those who dream of new possibilities in the marketplace, anticipating customer needs whatever the investment; the misunderstanding is often mutual.*

Focusing on controlling the spending of an organization drives a very different mindset from a focus on new marketing opportunities. Not all finance directors

(FDs) see their job as mainly about control – for some, it is about using capital as a route to new opportunities. Similarly, some marketing professionals focus very clearly on analytic methods driven by marketing research, and are far from flamboyant risk takers. So we should avoid stereotypes if possible, but also recognize that the specific interests and skills of a leader make a real difference to their approach. Financially based leaders are often characterized as task-oriented, analytical, details-obsessed, authoritative and controlling, often introvert and able to operate in a pragmatic and even toxic environment. Marketing leaders like people, can be opportunistic, prefer the sales-driven logic of the private sector, like projects, sometimes behave as celebrities, and are often extroverts. Leaders arising from particular skills and success in either finance or marketing (among other areas) are also part of the expert leader set (see the related entry Expert Leadership and Generalist Leadership). Here we first present issues around finance-oriented leadership before contrasting this with marketing-oriented leadership.

THE FINANCE LEADER

One of the most common organizational specializations from which leaders arise is finance. While many become great leaders, originally having a financial background is characterized by certain behaviours. Relying heavily on an 'expert leadership' style, the financially-oriented leader is likely to be careful, prudent, conservative, reserved, a typical 'monitor-evaluator' (see the related entry Implementer Leadership and Shaper-driver Leadership).

We consider two FDs here – both with a focused attitude to money – but one stuck in an expert role and the other in a leadership position, able to influence the culture of the whole organization. What are their main concerns? How do they impact on their team-members? We then compare these with two more successful examples of finance-oriented leaders who have picked up bigger-picture thinking (see the related entry Broad-based Leadership and Functional Leadership).

An HR/development consultant – on a finance-based functionally dependent leader:

> Our FD – even if he had another job – would probably always be the same. In his work life he tends to lack social skills. For example, he is challenged in terms of communications, he doesn't answer emails, and when he attends staff parties he does so for a short time grumpily complaining about how much they cost. He guards the organization's money as if it was his own. He's reluctant to give any money to anyone, even those working very hard to achieve the goals of the organization. It's like getting water out of a stone. He's controlling, obsessive and sees himself as extremely overworked, but fails to notice these tendencies towards control and obsession – although he can't fail to miss his workaholism. Generally disliked or at best just about tolerated, he delegates only simple, administrative tasks to his immediate staff. Although he likes to regard himself as powerful, all he can really do is advance your expenses if he likes you, and delay them if he doesn't. When confronted with a major issue of policy, he's only an 'implementer' and has no real strategic function. He certainly has no vision.

This example includes many stereotypes of the functional finance leader, summed up in the epithet 'bean counter'. This narrow focus on the bottom financial line can prevent disastrous overspending, but also stifle growth.

A project manager – on working with a finance-oriented leader:

The hospitality sector business – a five-star hotel – where I worked had recently become an independent property, owned by a group of six individual investors, no longer part of a big, famous hotel chain. The FD of this business suddenly felt that he was without any of the props, tools and procedures that he used to have to manage the hotel business before. When he faced difficulties, there was no group structure to fall back on as in the old days. As a financially oriented leader – he made all the big decisions in the hotel – he was very conservative and prudent and most concerned about the costs. This was exacerbated by the point that he was from a 'high uncertainty-avoiding' culture. Basically, he liked lots of rules and guidelines. He kept complaining, 'We now have to make our own decisions, and we have all the more need for structure, as we now have so much more responsibility!

The FD would freak out completely when he thought that costs at the hotel were getting out of control. When the project was nearing completion and the local labourers were working long hours of overtime, their total pay rose dramatically. The FD was shocked. These workers were earning almost as much as he was! As the project manager, I was able to convince him that the overtime work was essential to complete the project on time, and the workers were spending very long hours in the hotel, from 16 to 20 hours a day. In fact, certain rooms in the hotel were then completed ahead of schedule, resulting in increased revenues for the hotel, and the workers were much more motivated than they had ever been before. This income far outweighed the overtime bill – by 600 per cent. Although the FD was, of course, concerned with costs being incurred by the hotel, his sense of order and structure as an FD-type leader was also most alarmed at the high earnings by the workers. As the project manager, I would also take the workers out drinking beer on a Friday afternoon. The FD was initially concerned that he was paying for their time, they weren't working, and for the beer (and he was always far too busy to join them, of course) but he admitted that this loss of time was made up for by enhanced productivity the following week.

It was very important for the FD to 'cross the T's and dot the I's', not just to accept verbal agreements. He wanted everything drawn up systematically on paper. He wanted to see all the design specifications of a supplier before he would commit himself and the hotel. It was very frustrating for him at first, as the new owners were much less interested in paperwork. He thought that eventually they came round to his way of thinking, so that when differences cropped up, he had the paperwork to fall back on. The new owners considered that the conversion was the other way around! 'I like the comfort of falling back on a document. Without a document, you're stuck', insisted the FD, 'you must have a governing piece of paper. If they had not come around to my way of thinking, we would have had disputes with suppliers. These new owners were very difficult. I much prefer working with owners who are much more structured and systematic. Our previous owners went overboard with tons of paperwork, their lawyers have huge contracts and agreements, but these new owners believe that the fewer pieces of paper, the better. This always seems unprofessional to me'.

The FD was particularly concerned that the project manager would not overspend on the two million euros budget. 'In 33 years of working in the hotel industry, this was one of the few projects that didn't go into overspend', the FD agreed. 'But often I didn't know or I didn't agree with how the new owners did it, but they did it. They were incurring costs and not telling me. They seemed to juggle funds around a lot. It caused me a lot of sleepless nights, but the refurbishment project was finished on time and on budget.'

When finance experts become leaders they tend to be task-oriented and directive in style. The danger is they will lack leadership abilities in relation to creativity and innovation, being constantly worried about the costs of investing in the unknown. However, this is not always a negative. In the aforementioned case of David Jones and NEXT plc (see the related entry Behind-the-scenes Leadership and Leading from the Front), the finance leader – who was also open to innovation – saved the company from financial ruin.

David Jones was an accountant by profession, and reached CEO status at NEXT plc – his leadership style was one of careful stewardship, helping the organization to recover after overstretching itself in the George Davis years. This risk-averse style leadership can play a good role in a consolidation mode, but it is mostly internally focused and is cautious about pursuing new opportunities.

A leader without much experience in finance can take big risks without counting the cost. He or she might be effective in a heavily cash-rich business which is on a roll in a bull market, but such scenarios don't always last very long. Finance-oriented leaders might not be colourful or dramatic, but their organizations are usually stable.

Perhaps one exception to the colourless FD image is Michael O'Leary of Ryanair, who is seen as a hugely successful bean-counter leader – 'he should be the poster-boy of the accounting profession', one of O'Leary's competitors reflected. His deliberately offensive advertisements and crude language ('he has the mouth of a drunken sailor') are probably not typical – but his careful husbandry of resources and refusal to pay high costs may be. Also he's arguably anathema to the more marketing-led leader, with his 'no refunds' policy and non-existent attempts at good customer service.

THE MARKETING-ORIENTED LEADER

In contrast to the finance-focused leader, leaders with strong marketing backgrounds are likely to be much more externally focused and opportunistically looking for new areas of market demand, especially if these are high profile and prestigious. This area typically includes all those processes associated with promoting and selling a product or service, and following up on customer relationships. It has been traditionally seen as one of the more glamorous aspects of leadership and management and doing business – but can still be a narrow view of life. Not only is it looking through a specific lens, it can also be a rose-coloured lens. This makes it all the more difficult in the transition to overall, broad-based leadership.

The examples we quote here look at four individual leaders with a strong bias towards the marketing function, and we also look at some more famous cases from the literature. The effectiveness of the leaders in these examples can be seen in some respects, but perhaps this is more short-lived than our finance cases. Marketing guys can be disastrous, but are rarely boring – with finance leaders, it can be the other way around.

An emerging market consultant – on the extreme marketing leader:

Our former CEO came from a marketing background. All he wanted to do was to publish brochures and organize new initiatives with his picture emblazoned all over it. He was good at making speeches and made sure he had a lot of publicity – but it was often about him, not about the organization. If one of the colleagues did something of which he approved, and he could bask in the reflected glory, he could be quite pleasant and friendly. But basically he wasn't a team-player, he was into self-aggrandizement, and could not be bothered with mundane, day-to-day management issues, so most of the time he didn't take calls and didn't answer emails. He was very much a 'resource-investigator' type, liking to start new projects but soon getting bored, and not prepared to do the work involved. He was keen on designing ads and making new marketing initiatives, but many of these were not followed up, and the return on investment was often very low – or we didn't measure it at all. Years after he has gone, his picture is still everywhere. No expense was spared on publicity efforts, but he was very stingy over paying the staff their expenses. He was very flashy in having a big office, always travelling business class and staying in posh hotels, whereas the staff had to operate in a much more frugal style. In some ways he is missed, as he came over well in public events and had a big personality, but that was about all.

An emerging market consultant – on the extreme marketing diplomat:

I was staying in a hotel and the general manager (GM) was extremely marketing and customer service-oriented – but I would not have envied the job of the FD of that property! I met this GM at the hotel bar one night and he bought all the drinks. When my flight was postponed he offered me an extra night in the hotel free of charge – this wasn't entirely necessary, as my employer knew about the delayed flight and it was not a big problem to pay extra. He was a 'diplomat'-style leader – always wanting everyone to be happy – and he avoided confrontation at all costs. There were many problems with his staff which he really should have addressed, but when I mentioned some of these issues – I thought I was doing him a favour, and I tried to make suggestions in a constructive way – he didn't want to know. He would just buy me another drink at the bar! When I lost my receipts to claim back the hotel bill later, I emailed him, and he sent scanned-in copies immediately. He was very popular with all the long-term guests and I'm sure he will remember me when I go back there. But he probably still has the staff problems, and less than optimal profitability – but he doesn't have much competition locally and that's probably how he survives.

An investor in the hospitality industry – on the visionary marketing leader:

I suppose you could call me a marketing-oriented leader – I'm certainly very keen on image – but I'm also concerned about sales and fulfilling market needs in a proactive way. For example, myself and fellow-investors recently invested in acquiring and refurbishing an existing, old, but classic hotel property. I saw it as being in a wonderful location, oozing with character, eclectic style, amazing staff, incredibly loyal guests, with the majority of guests coming so many times and for so long it had become a habit. The hotel for them was a home from home. Guest delight at the refurbishment we were planning was going to be very important for us. Quite frankly, we thought the hotel looked like a nursing home for old people when we arrived. We wanted it to be reborn, but we didn't want the guests to see the changes negatively, we wanted to show respect for heritage. We wanted the 70- and 80-year olds to stay happy, but we didn't want to grow old with the business, so we will keep up the refurbishment process, as there is more to be done. I don't think the finance manager there realized the way we investors saw it, he was just concerned about controlling the expenses of the refurbishment, he couldn't see the overall image in the same way that we did.

A CEO of a management consulting business – on the balanced marketing leader:

In my experience, the guy with the marketing background likes to focus on nice products which appeal to consumers. He likes to find out what the market needs. He doesn't look at earning power so much, but wants to identify a niche in the market. He or she doesn't always make choices which favour value creation for the long-term. He or she might go for market gain and market share more than long-term profit gain for the organization as a whole.

When I was running a packaging business which was bought up by a venture capital firm (see the related entry Coaching and Mentoring-oriented Leadership and Directive, Telling-what-to-do Leadership). I was concerned with the financial soundness of the business, but I saw marketing and sales as the main drivers. In allocating many of the staff members to new positions, marketing and sales made the most gains in terms of head-count, and this helped more than anything to add value for the business. But we also needed efficiency and to improve cash flow. There needs to be a balance, so a company with a leader focused on only one function of business will not be successful. It's no good being sales and marketing-oriented if you don't know the costs involved.

George Davis of NEXT was a typically marketing-oriented leader – and as such was arguably more successful as a consultant in an advisory role (with his subsequent experience with Marks & Spencer) than in a leadership job, where he tended to get carried away by his own marketing hype. Jack Welch was very keen on making GE more market-oriented, but his style of leadership was tempered by his background as a practical chemist. There is a difference between marketing and sales that might also show up in leadership orientation. The marketing leader tends to have more of a vision but less of a bottom-line focus than the sales leader, for whom any product which sells is acceptable. Many large, consumer-product based businesses are led almost exclusively by marketers: focusing on customer perception, building brand image and awareness – and everything else can be happily outsourced, even sales. Coke and Nike may be seen as examples.

While each of these marketing-oriented leaders exhibit positive attributes – the strong personal brand of the extreme market-leader; the care and concern of the marketing diplomat; the innovation of the marketing visionary; the overall outlook of the balanced marketing leader – ideally one would hope to combine aspects of all of these. A leader with a balanced view towards positive brands (for him/herself and the organization), with measured diplomacy and sense of vision, can make for a powerful leadership situation.

Finance-oriented leaders are seen in nearly every organization – and can have a powerful influence. At worst they are the ultimate bean-counters, anti-innovation, humourless, stingy and tight. At best they are careful custodians of their businesses, preserving and strengthening them against the competition with careful steward-ship. But we mustn't expect anything new – for them, making the transition to overall organizational leadership, managing many functions besides finance, is highly problematic, but there are successful examples.

The marketing leader brings a value-added perspective which might then be toned-down by other ways of looking at the business. If left on its own, it can mean all show and no action, being nice but being out of control, an understanding of the appeal of the product or service but not necessarily how to take it forward to the next stage. As with other forms of single-dimensional leadership, it has its problems.

FURTHER READING

Alvesson, M. and Spicer, A. (eds) (2010) *Metaphors We Lead By: understanding leadership in the real world*. Oxford: Routledge.

Bevan, J. (2007) *The Rise and Fall of Marks & Spencer…and How It Rose Again*. London: Profile Books.

Creaton, Siobhan (2007) *Ryanair: the full story of the controversial low-cost airline*. London: Aurum Press.

Jones, David. (2005) *NEXT to Me: luck, leadership and living with Parkinson's*. London: Nicholas Brealey.

Mintzberg, H. (1994) *The Rise and Fall of Strategic Planning: reconceiving roles for planning, plans, planners*. New York: Free Press.

Rooke, D. and Torbert, W. (2005) 'The seven transformations of leadership', *Harvard Business Review*, April, 83(4): 66–76.

21
Global Leadership and Worldly Leadership

> *There are those leaders who see the globe as the same wherever they go, so their leadership style might be 'one size fits all'; others see the world as a patchwork quilt of regional contrasts.*

Today's world is one lived globally by many people – particularly leaders. Individuals in leadership positions, from public to private sector, often travel significantly and lead organizations that are operative in different countries, regions and continents. We all now live in a highly connected world with global issues – economy, climate change, multiculturalism, etc. – facing us every day. What implications does this have for leadership? In this section we compare and contrast 'worldly leadership' – appreciating all the differences - with global leadership – assuming a convergence to common norms.

First some thoughts on worldly vs. global thinking:

- The world is made up of all kinds of worlds. It is not uniform. As international leaders we need to understand its complexity.
- Being worldly is not the same as being global, but it's about relating to different parts of the world as different and unique in a social and environmental as well as an economic way.
- There are clear differences between global and worldly world views – that being a global leader emphasizes commonalities and convergence, and being a worldly leader accepts – even celebrates – differences.
- 'Think global act local' is about being able to relate to different environments as a multinational business.

Following from these points, the global view of leadership is more likely to accept that:

- Generalizations can be made about markets, values, and management practices, and that these are most important.
- Local consequences are of less importance than the overall economic performance of the organization.
- Global companies are not really responsible for local consequences – they just happen for various local cultural reasons which are not our concern.
- Travelling around the world, differences are lost in a blur of similarities.
- The world is converging towards a common culture.

In contrast, a worldly view of leadership is likely to include:

- attention being paid to particular responses to specific conditions, which can be of great importance;
- considering local consequences as a key indicator of performance;
- looking at social as well as economic value in operating in different countries;
- a sense of responsibility for the local consequences of company actions;
- the idea that when landing in different places, we join a plurality of worldviews;
- the view that this is a world made up of edges and boundaries, like a patchwork;
- it's all about being worldly wise – wise to the ways of the world, street-wise, savvy.

Related entries include Eastern-style Leadership and Western-style Leadership – Contrasting and Converging National Cultures, Task-oriented Leadership and People-oriented Leadership (see Chapter 24, HR and Production), Long-term

Leadership and Project Management Leadership, EQ-oriented Leadership and IQ-oriented Leadership, Knee-jerk Leadership and Reflective Leadership. International organizations include multinational companies (which often aim for a cosmopolitan norms); one-nation companies that operate all over the world (which tend to be more quirky); and international governmental and non-governmental organizations. In all of these, countless regional managers and headquarters staff members negotiate tensions between global and worldly mindsets every day.

Here, we look at a variety of worldviews, especially where the study of local conditions revealed the diversity of attitudes of local consumers, which can impact on the success or failure of manufacturing and sales initiatives. Yet, in being worldly we still need to understand the importance of global standards, which cannot be compromised.

As leaders work within different contexts and lead organizations that operate in different cultures they must be open to the different worldviews and actions they encounter. Global companies often seek standardization, assuming that the products and services they provide should be consumed in much the same way regardless of the consumer's context. While this may be very useful in some instances, in others it can mean missing an opportunity. Consider the following anecdote from the manager of the African section of a household products firm.

An ex-CEO focused on emerging markets – on developing a worldly view:

> I was managing the African businesses of a diversified household products firm. We had a massive demand for denture cleaner, when hardly anyone in Africa uses artificial dentures, and I was asked by Head Office to go and check out what was happening. The product was mostly being bought by companies as part of their catering needs in offices. In Africa they like very strong tea, and they keep it stewing in the teapots for hours. The teapots were becoming stained. So they cleaned them with denture cleaner. We would never have thought of this usage, but it actually makes sense. It did a very good job of getting the brown tea stains off the teapot, just as it does off dentures. All the tea boys were buying it. It didn't matter to them what the product was called.

In this example the Western leader-manager was asked to investigate suspicious consumer behaviour. Why would denture cleaner sales be so high in a region where few people wore dentures? What was discovered was a culturally specific behaviour – the enjoyment of strong tea and the requirement to keep it hot in tea pots for long periods of time – leading to a new market opportunity for a product. A worldly leader sees this as an opportunity arising through diversity, embraces it, and can grow the business by re-marketing the product to fit the consumer's need.

Another similar case arose through a Western company selling domestic washing machines in China. An emerging markets consultant – on lacking a worldly view:

> One of our clients in China was a Western company selling washing machines. They wondered why the motors of the machines broke down so quickly, when these motors lasted for years in Western countries. Initially they believed this to be the result of the characteristics of the water or detergent being used. However, the company decided

to organize a focus group of their customers. What they discovered was that some of them were using their washing machines not just for clothes – they were also washing vegetables before cooking them! The washing machines were getting jammed up with mud and small stones and bits of vegetable matter. But it was quite a clever idea, really, from the customer point of view. The company then showed that they could be very worldly, by making the washing machines with much stronger motors, and guaranteeing them for a shorter period, which showed they were willing to adapt to their customers.

Here, the worldly-minded company leaders did not rest on their assumptions that problems were arising from inadequate water or detergent. On further investigation they too found a culturally specific behaviour was the cause of the 'problem' and that in fact the problem was an opportunity. Rather than scaling back sales or simply altering warranty details, the leaders embraced the cultural differences and modified their products (along with the warranties) to better suit the needs of the consumer. As with the denture cleaning product, standardization was not the best solution to this situation, diversification was.

One of the authors – on the lack of a worldly view by a so-called worldly and certainly international organization:

> A company which was rather less than worldly – although they insisted they were both global and local in their advertising – was a very international financial services business. I had accounts with them in Hong Kong and in Dubai. I wanted to make a payment to their branch in Malta – I was buying a house. I dropped into one of their branches in the UK. Plastered all over the walls were pictures of their branches all over the world – from Addis Ababa to Zanzibar with Timbuktu in between. But when I explained what I needed to do, they looked at me as if I had come from another planet. 'You can't possibly do that! They exclaimed. 'But you call yourselves local and global', I retorted. 'Ah, that's just the advertising!', the clerk replied, probably oblivious of the irony here.'

In fact, in many instances like this, standardization just does not work. For example, in terms of leadership training, trainees of a bank in Dubai were being taught using standard training techniques developed in the UK and sold around the world on the assumption that contexts don't matter much. The Western leadership coaches were disappointed by the lack of sustained improvement in their Dubai trainees, which they attributed to 'cultural affiliations'. The training programmes assumed that the trainees could be encouraged to be competitive and problem-solving – but in reality interdependent family, tribe and clan affiliations are far more significant than the training methods recognize. The training company categorized such behaviours as 'compromising and avoiding' – which in most Western meanings have negative connotations. This issue was not taken into account by the providers of Western-style training materials, or by the Western leaders at the bank. These leaders and coaches were thinking globally, being reductionist about their views of the world and its clichéd global community. Leaders have to remember that in any community there are many differences.

However, there are times when leaders do need to be global and standardized, times when leaders should avoid being worldly. There are times when people must be consistent in deliverables to maintain standards. Take, for example, the challenge of running an international business school, with branches in more than 20 countries. The school has international accreditations to maintain, and all the accreditation bodies are most concerned that standards are being kept and the branches or partners are not out of control. This is a very challenging task for a leader, for a variety of reasons. For example, cultures have very different ways of honouring and respecting the authority and contribution of previous generations of scholars. In the West – which has come to dominate global academic standards – there is no crime more heinous than plagiarism, namely quoting someone else's work as one's own. But in some countries – for example China – using another author's words is often seen as a way to honour them. There are many potential responses to this kind of argument, but the point is that the leader of an international university has to determine and enforce common ways of doing things, as these guarantee comparable standards of work, skills and values. There are a whole host of standards issues that arise from beliefs such as 'it is free and easy and available, so it's OK to do it, as long as you are not caught'. For example, the copying of other students' work, the photocopying of books, or Googling for downloadable term papers. The global education leader has to ensure that a degree obtained in one country is worth exactly the same as in another country. If it is obviously easier to get the degree in another country, the currency is being debased.

Thus, being a worldly leader is all about understanding the unique differences about where we work and do business, and it can help us to be more successful managing international enterprises. How do people use our products and services? How can we serve them with items which are more useful to them and designed for their needs? But, being global also has uses for a leader in an international environment – there are times when she or he must insist on maintaining standards and enforcing rules and guidelines in order to protect the quality and integrity of the organization.

FURTHER READING

Andrews, T. (ed.) (2009) *Cross-cultural Management: critical perspectives on business and management*. London: Routledge.

Gosling, J. and Minzberg, H. (2003) 'The five minds of the manager', *Harvard Business Review*, November, 81(11): 54–63.

Iszatt-White, M. (2011) 'Methodological crises and contextual solutions: an ethnomethodologically informed approach to understanding leadership', *Leadership*, 7 (2): 119–135.

Johnson, Craig E. (2011) *Meeting the Ethical Challenge of Leadership*. Thousand Oaks, CA: Sage.

Jones, S. (2008) 'Training and Cultural Context in the Arab Emirates: fighting a losing battle?', *Employment Relations*, January, 30 (1): 48–62.

Trompenaars, F. and Hampden-Turner, C. (1997) *Riding the Waves of Culture: understanding cultural diversity in business*. London: Nicholas Brealey.

Turnbull, S., Case, P., Edwards, G., Schedlitzki, D. and Simpson, P. (eds) (2011) *Worldly Leadership: alternative wisdoms for a complex world*. London: Palgrave Macmillan.

Goal-oriented Leadership and Opportunistic Leadership

> *Many leaders take each opportunity as it comes, always open to a new challenge; others want to achieve a specific purpose throughout their career, and a leadership role is an important step on the way.*

The attitude of a leader who constantly searches for new opportunities, compared with the pursuit of a distinct overall purpose, boils down to an individual's motivations for leadership. For some it is important to have a specific purpose, which could be something they want to become (a CEO, wealthy, a knight of the realm, etc.) or something they want to contribute (a safer society, affordable pensions, a great corporation, etc.). On the way to this goal they might follow planned steps, or be opportunistic, but in either case the goal dominates. Others approach life with an open-minded curiosity about the next turn in the road, taking whatever chances come their way; and in leadership roles, they might make use of strategic plans and goals as helpful tools along the way, but probably remain open to what else might happen! As with all the entries in this book, few people inhabit the extremes, but the distinction is useful, and it is important to note that neither is better or worse. Both kinds of leader may be guided by ethical principles and even spiritual purposes in the here-and-now of their leadership roles.

A goal-oriented leader has high-level or long-term goals which inform his or her leadership practice. The types of high-level, long-term goals vary from person to person. They may include organizationally focused goals such as long-term organizational change to improve operations, profitability and the quality of work life. The goals may be more holistic such as tackling efforts on climate change or fighting world hunger. Often these goals are also career oriented where leaders lay out a long-term career plan to reach a president or CEO position. Whatever the goals, such leaders tend to be driven, focused, almost relentless individuals. It requires a level of commitment, determination, persistence and energy to achieve the intended purpose, including the need to overcome obstacles; many intentionally volunteer for challenging and high-profile assignments in order to test themselves, learn necessary skills, make contacts and display their competence.

Opportunistic leadership, by contrast, is typically not defined by a long-term goal or achievement, though it may be infused with a sense of purpose and inner values. Opportunists may pursue short-term goals; they may even use the rhetoric of higher purposes and great achievements, but they are not wedded to these – in fact, the language and techniques of planning and goal-setting can be used opportunistically to help them lead the kind of life they enjoy, without the necessary commitment.

Opportunistic leaders may be excited (or distracted) by new challenges, making the most of their ability to change direction at short notice; they may also feel themselves to be driven by necessity, responding to emerging customer needs, reacting to higher authorities. Flexibility and curiosity are key characteristics.

Goal-oriented, iconic, visionary leaders with a 24/7 focus seem to speak to a clear purpose and mission. But is it for their fellow human beings, their country or region, the organizations they work for, or for themselves individually? What functions are served by clear-cut purposes that seem to simplify the complexity and uncertainty of life? Does 'increasing shareholder value' really count as a purpose, even if many take it as a goal? In some ways, goals such as this can enable leaders to avoid thinking about higher-order purposes; in fact the idea that life might consist of scoring a series of goals may be a neat way of implying it's just a game. Perhaps this is a rational response to the unknowability of the ultimate purpose of life; or alternatively, an irrational avoidance of the serious and weighty burdens of a purposeful life.

So, goal-orientation as an attitude towards work should not be taken at face value: there are almost always agendas. But in the language of corporate leadership, goal-oriented language often stands in for purposefulness. This makes sense: change initiatives create a lot of disturbance and require special effort, which people will undertake willingly if they can see a reason for it. Leaders are usually required to assert that all the effort is leading somewhere glorious, even if in fact the future is uncertain and the destination not much better than where we are now! Nevertheless, the Jews would not have crossed the Red Sea if they hadn't been convinced of the Promised Land, and NASA would never have taken men to the Moon if the goal had not been set by President Kennedy. Famously, even a sweeper at NASA, asked what he was doing, said, 'I'm putting a man on the Moon'. Would he have replied with such enthusiasm if the goal had been 'increasing returns to shareholders'?

Many famous corporate leaders tell their stories as if they are versions of Exodus (the book in the Bible that described the Jews' exit from Egypt). The tale starts with the recognition that the current business is unsustainable, and the leader's voice – like a prophet – convinces people of the need to change. Leading them through trials and tribulations, they arrive eventually at a new way of doing business, and are rewarded by renewed profitability. Examples include Lou Gerstner of IBM, Jack Welch of GE and Steve Jobs of Apple. John Harvey-Jones, Chairman of Imperial Chemical Industries (ICI) (1982–1987), famously turned around the ailing conglomerate by reminding people of the virtues (and rewards) of paying purposeful attention to their core business. Perhaps the greatest example of all is Nelson Mandela, who held on to his goal for decades, and represented it for millions in Africa and around the world.

However, opportunistic leaders – Michael O'Leary of Ryanair is often cited – do not seem to have a consistent specific personal mission. Opportunistic leaders get their satisfaction from responding to challenges and chances as they come. They tend not to think too much about the future. For example, O'Leary asked staff members at Ryanair to accept lower-than-industry-average salaries on the grounds that the airline was struggling financially. As a private, family-owned business, however, the financial details were kept secret. But when the records went public through an Initial Public Offering the profitability of the airline was revealed and there was an outcry from the poorly paid Ryanair employees. O'Leary's opportunistic strategy of belt-tightening for the good of the company was no longer feasible, nor for that matter honest (Creaton, 2007, and see related entries Change-oriented Leadership and Continuity-based Leadership, Behind-the-scenes Leadership and Leading from the Front, 'Here-and-now' Leadership and Legacy Leadership, Implementer Leadership and Shaper-driver Leadership, Interim Leadership and Tenured Leadership, Long-term Leadership and Project Management Leadership).

In what follows we explore the differences between goal-oriented and opportunistic leaders through the thoughts of two internationally recognized consultants and a teacher/trainer in leadership. We review the behaviours and attitudes of purposive and opportunistic leaders, considering the advantages and disadvantages of both leadership viewpoints in differing contexts.

An ex-CEO/Management Consultant – on opportunistic leadership:

Opportunistic leaders seem to be quite happy most of the time. When they look back over the years they have few regrets. They didn't have high expectations necessarily, and were thus not disappointed. They did many exciting and very real things. Their viewpoint is one of trying something new – let's go for it and make the best of it.

For much of my career I have been opportunistic and I have had a great time, learning new things, meeting new people, learning new techniques, discovering new markets. Opportunists are curious, looking beyond the familiar to new horizons. They jump at the newest opportunity but – ideally – move one step higher, which is something I have tried to do. An opportunistic leader can be multi-experienced, and more qualified to deal with anything that comes along. They see challenges as opportunities to learn, and are happy with change and the need to adapt.

The drawback of being an opportunistic leader is that you might lose sight of your goals and focus – but, on the other hand, these are not always the most important things in life. I like to be challenged and to be inspired, and I get challenges and inspiration from working with different people, in different organizations, with different customers. I've worked in large and small businesses, in different countries, in different sectors, and now I'm semi-retired and working in consulting and advising municipalities. I see the whole experience as a personal enrichment. I was always ambitious and knew I would have an interesting and mostly successful career, but I never planned it exactly. I didn't know what type of career it might be.

By contrast, I knew an executive with a very clear plan of exactly how things would shape up – or he thought he did. He was a very goal-oriented leader. We were both studying textile engineering at college. We had the opportunity to study commerce and also marketing, which was a new subject in Europe in the late 1960s and early 1970s. This particular executive was very keen on becoming a business leader, and took lots of courses to build his capability. However, as a goal-oriented careerist he was always following his plan. Opportunistic leaders like to work with all kinds of people and are interested to learn, but – by contrast – goal-oriented leaders tend to see people through the lens of their plan. Though their goals can be quite lofty or altruistic, they can also be quite manipulative, especially if the goals are more about themselves and their own achieving. Where opportunistic leaders take things as they come, the purposive leader is trying to follow what he or she sees as a very clear plan.

This particular executive with whom I had studied climbed the ladder of the corporate world and eventually reached a point where his ultimate goal was within sight – to be a Board member of a large European commodities company. But when he wasn't chosen to be on the Board, his whole world fell apart. He was desperately disappointed. As a purposive leader he had this very clear, single goal, and when he didn't make it, when he failed, it was a disaster for him, from which he never really recovered. There was nothing left for him. His past experiences, because they were so focused on his singular career goal of reaching the top, didn't help him in looking for another position. He fell into a black hole, from which he lacked the resilience, elasticity and strength to extricate himself.

An opportunistic leader, with the same experience, would not have minded so much, and would have tried to quickly move on. It's hard to de-motivate an opportunistic person. But this particular executive I've described didn't have the character, especially as he was so geared-up for one thing. He was only interested in his own progress, and saw others as getting in the way and being against him. So he was without a job for a long time, and in the end had to accept a job that he didn't think was good enough for him and he didn't like. But he had no choice. An opportunistic leader, on the other hand, finds it easy to make friends and contacts, and is less competitive. He or she likes working with others and likes to learn from others. If the opportunistic leader needs help, there are plenty of people around with ideas and contacts. The purposive leader, however, with the more manipulative view of the world, attracts less sympathy and support.

A teacher/trainer of leadership – on goal-oriented leadership:

The relationship between goals and purposes is well illustrated by those leaders who create organizations with clear missions, often based on something they feel very strongly about. A less well-known but important example is The Aegis Trust, created to raise awareness of genocides around the world, set up by two young British brothers who felt that people were not sufficiently educated about these tragedies, and asked, how could they be prevented in future if people didn't know about them? They helped create a memorial in Kigali, in Rwanda, and raised funds to make an exhibition. They have made a lot of sacrifices on the way as they always suffer from underfunding, when they are well-qualified and could get well-paid jobs as managers in commercial organizations. They have a very strong sense of purpose, which is to raise awareness about genocides so that world leaders and citizens do more to stop them. They set themselves project-related goals along the way, and dedicate their resources to achieving them, but it is the bigger purpose that is the real motive.

An ex-Executive Search Consultant – another perspective on opportunistic and anti-opportunistic leadership:

For many years I was involved in 'headhunting' as it was popularly called, at quite a high level, mostly of functional and general managers, and up to CEOs and non-executive directors. We liked people who were opportunistic – obviously. They were our favourite targets. When we called them up to discuss a new possible role with one of our clients, we especially favoured candidates who responded positively and wanted to know more. The most opportunistic – in a positive sense – were willing to talk and willing to move if the job and the package were right. However, opportunistic individuals were sometimes regarded as risky by organizations. An interview panel or hiring committee may look at the patchwork-quilt CV of an opportunistic leader with great suspicion wondering how long they may actually stay in a new position, debating whether or not it is worth hiring them.

By contrast, some potential candidates pretended to be interested – they wanted to hear more about the opportunity, but mostly because it appealed to their egos ('I was headhunted for this job…'). They also enjoyed the idea of being interviewed to check out their competitors. These 'fake-opportunists' wanted an expenses-paid trip to visit our client, but had no intention of moving, which we regarded as frustrating, unethical and a waste of time and money. We would happily blacklist such candidates from being considered for any future positions.

The third type of candidate was 'anti-opportunistic'. He or she was not necessarily purposive – although this was occasionally explained as a reason, such as pursuing a promised goal of promotion or a development opportunity. These candidates had been given a 'career path' or 'personal development plan' by their company, and really believed in it. We often felt they were too trusting and naïve. A smaller proportion of 'anti-opportunistic' candidates genuinely followed personal career goals they had consciously carved out for themselves and felt that the opportunity we presented to them just didn't fit in. However, the majority of 'anti-opportunists' were just plain unadventurous and conservative. They didn't want to move house, let alone move to another country. They wouldn't move desks, let alone move to a new company. They were buddy–buddy with their staff members and colleagues. Their kids were stable in school. Their spouses had good jobs.

There are, however, times when purposive leaders are the best fit for leadership positions. This occurs in situations where clients have clear missions, which might be a project- or task-based assignment, such as a company turnaround. Organizations want someone who is single-minded and focused, a change agent able to achieve an outcome identified by the Board of Directors or shareholders. We were on the lookout for candidates who were able to combine focus with flexibility.

We came across quite a few leaders who started their careers being opportunistic and then discovered some great purpose to which they then became committed, putting their opportunism behind them as if it was some youthful flirtation. Other leaders we met in our headhunting work began their executive life with a clear mission and strong goals, but then they met a dead end and decided that rather than be disappointed forever, they would accept reality and go with the flow.

This consultant echoes many of the thoughts put forward by our ex-CEO/Management Consultant. Goal-oriented leaders may be great at achieving defined results. Opportunistic leaders can be adaptable and open to new challenges. However, opportunistic leaders can lack focus and this can be risky for an organization seeking dedication and a long-term commitment. We might consider the sub-prime mortgage crisis of recent years: these opportunities turned out to be toxic for many organizations (see the related entry Nurturing Leadership and Toxic Leadership). In these cases the openness to new opportunities, when pursued without a careful level of purpose and reflection, may be the downfall of a leader. At the same time, goal-oriented leaders can be manipulative and difficult to work with. Meanwhile, our headhunter contributor also points out an important reality. Leaders are not necessarily always purposive or opportunistic. They may exhibit characteristics of both throughout their careers or may begin being one and later become the other. Like all leadership theory we must keep in mind that there is a complex continuum of leadership attitudes, styles and behaviours.

FURTHER READING

Bryman, Alan, Collinson, David L., Grint, Keith and Jackson, Brad (2011) *The Sage Handbook of Leadership*. London: Sage.

Champey, J.A. (1993) *Re-engineering the Corporation: a manifesto for business revolution*. New York: Harper Business Books.

Creaton, Siobhan (2007) *Ryanair: the full story of the controversial low-cost airline*. London: Aurum Press.

Gerstner, L. (2002) *Who Says Elephants Can't Dance?* New York: HarperCollins.

Grint, K. (2005) 'Problems, problems, problems: the social construction of "leadership"', *Human Relations*, 58 (11): 1467–1494.

Haslam, S.A., Reicher, S. and Platow, M. (2011) *The New Psychology of Leadership: identity, influence and power*. New York: Psychology Press.

Jones, S. (1989) *The Headhunting Business*. London: Macmillan.

Jones, S. and Gosling, J. (2005) *Nelson's Way: leadership lessons from the great commander*. London: Nicholas Brealey.

Mintzberg, H. (1994) *The Rise and Fall of Strategic Planning: reconceiving roles for planning, plans, planners*. New York: Free Press.

Pfeffer, J. (1994) *Managing with Power: politics and influence in organizations*. Boston, MA: Harvard Business School Press.

Puccio, Gerard J., Mance, Marie and Murdoch, Mary C. (2011) *Creative Leadership: skills that drive change* (2nd edition). Thousand Oaks, CA: Sage.

Snook, Scott A., Nohria, Nitin N., and Khurana, Rakesh (2012) *The Handbook for Teaching Leadership: knowing, doing and being*. Thousand Oaks, CA: Sage.

Welch, J. (2005) *Winning*. New York: HarperCollins.

23

'Here-and-now' Leadership and Legacy Leadership

> *Some leaders are focused on their daily leadership tasks, without an agenda as to how they might be seen by succeeding generations; others are most concerned by what they might leave behind them.*

Legacy is a word often associated with leadership. Though often something discussed when a leader steps down from a position, or dies, there are those who actively plan for their legacy in their day-to-day practice (such as Tony Blair, the UK Prime Minister 1997–2007). Alternatively, there are many who never think about legacy, and never consider what their actions may mean for future generations. This is the contrast between those focused on daily, monthly, year-by-year achievements, keeping the show on the road in a practical way, compared with those trying to make a long-term contribution, whether or not this guarantees their names in the history books.

The idea of making a name for yourself is sometimes seen as looking for glory – but others can share in this too, and it can be inspirational and infectious. It can help others to be over-achievers. The best kind of legacy leader will want to leave the world in a better state than he or she found it. A here-and-now leader may just want to quietly get on with the job, or may flamboyantly display his or her leadership achievements – but neither is concerned about long-term effects beyond their own span of control. Searching for a legacy requires a risky level of commitment. You must nail your colours to a particular mast, and lay the foundations – or plant the seeds – for future developments. This is usually based on expressing a worthy ideal, something that will benefit others after one has gone from this world. But there is a more ancient sense of legacy – to become the stuff of legends, a hero whose exploits will be celebrated for centuries to come. Fame and glory of this kind, far beyond the fleeting celebrity of media stars, always refers to great human virtues – courage, wisdom, justice, generosity and the like. Such is not a legacy of money or institution, but an example of how to live a great life.

A distinction may be drawn between legacy leadership that focuses on the organization or a wider cause, and that which focuses on the individual. Are the policies being designed for the benefit of the leader, the organization, or the country; or are they just for personal advancement? The here-and-now leader doesn't recognize these questions, or is suspicious of their pretensions. Focusing on daily realities and selecting practical options for action, he or she may be deeply concerned about the probity of every action, but know the long-term effects are not so easily determined.

The legacy-oriented leader can also often be purposive, action-oriented, and very much involved in everything. He or she might be inspirational – as suggested above – and might want to lead from the front to be noticed and as part of the legend-building exercise (see the related entries on Change-oriented Leadership, Community-based Leadership, Inspirational Leadership and Low-key Leadership, and Behind-the-scenes Leadership and Leading from the Front). Here-and-now leaders, by contrast, might be more pragmatic, opportunistic and occasionally compromising in the interests of getting things done, without a goal to leave a certain image or reputation behind them (see the related entries Goal-oriented Leadership and Opportunistic Leadership, HR-oriented Leadership and Production-oriented Leadership, Compromising Leadership and Co-operative Leadership).

Here, we look at a legacy-oriented leader who found it difficult to focus on the practicalities of the business world, and who believed his own hype. Then it all went pear-shaped. We also look at another leader who just tried to do his best and had no expectations of being remembered for ever. In contrast with many of his colleagues, he tried to keep out of the limelight – and it paid off in the long term.

An ex-CEO/Management Consultant – on the dangers of legacy leadership practice:

Wanting to be a great person, and do everything according to what people might think – this might be good in politics but I don't think it can be good in business. I knew a business leader who wanted to create a strong legacy behind him in an advertising/promotion business. He wanted to bring in big clients, make fabulous presentations, and expand the company into the big time. But he was so excited about leaving this legacy behind him that he was not careful about money. There were warning signals that the finances were not in good shape, but this didn't impress him. It was just not exciting or memorable to be bothered about all this nit-picking about the budgets and cash-flow. He just went on ahead, building a world-class company, inspiring all those around him.

Unfortunately, this leader was so future-oriented that he never considered the here and now; the business went broke. He was so concerned with the image and exciting brand he was developing, sure that it would last for ever, but he didn't look at the practical issues. It was not going to last, the way it was. Then he tried to merge this business with another to cover up the fact that it went broke, because he thought that if people knew he had led a company to bankruptcy, he would lose credibility. So he tried to avoid losing face by this contrived takeover deal, but he lost both companies in the end.

A real danger with legacy-oriented leaders is they will lead at the cost of others; he or she may be so focused on achieving glory that others may be dragged down in the process. Legacy leadership is often associated with the cult of personality. Sometimes it can be powerful in a positive way. But the trouble with creating hype is that there is a strong tendency for such hype-creating leaders to become their own biggest fans.

A researcher on leadership – on the benefits of here-and-now leadership:

Here-and-now leaders just try to get on with the job. One particular leader I knew didn't seem particularly happy with the type of work he was doing. He wanted to be in a private sector business, in real estate, but ended up in town and country planning in a regional authority in the public sector. But he did a good job, helping to preserve the local character of each local development, and enforced a high degree of fairness despite widespread consultation with all kinds of pressure groups and authorities and coping with many different influences. He had complete integrity and was immune to corruption, despite many temptations. He had no great leadership ambitions and little ego, he just tried to help people and be fair. Some of his bosses became much more high-ranking and earned much more money, but in the end they were investigated by the authorities, and for all their fame and glory, they got greedy and lost it all in the end. My here-and-now leader could always live with himself and didn't ever do anything that might cause controversy, even though he might not have received the promotion that he deserved. He wasn't in it for himself, just to help others, and when there were huge changes in his organization, he quietly retired and looked back – equally quietly – at his former colleagues who came unstuck. He didn't crow over them, but just explained to me why he didn't take that route. In some ways, he left a better legacy than those who hankered after it: he is an example of virtues we all recognize and admire.

Legacy leadership, like purposive leadership, can create a strong vision and mission and can give a goal for others to follow. It presents a focused and united front. But it might be more about individual glory than for the objective of organizational renewal or patriotism. It can look too much to the eulogies at the retirement party (or funeral). Was he or she an example to all, helping others, leaving the organization (or country) diminished as a result of his or her departure? Or clearly just looking after number one?

Here-and-now-leadership can be practical, effective and result in day-by-day progress, especially useful in an organization seeking stability and consolidation after extensive change. But it may not lead to dramatic reformation, and may suffer from constantly changing objectives. Here-and-now leaders however don't rock the boat and can quietly slip away when they want to.

FURTHER READING

Blair, Tony (2010) *A Journey*. London: Hutchinson.

Bryman, Alan, Collinson, David L., Grint, Keith and Jackson, Brad (2011) *The Sage Handbook of Leadership*. London: Sage.

Champey, J.A. (1993) *Re-engineering the Corporation: a manifesto for business revolution*. New York: Harper Business.

Johnson, Craig E. (2011) *Meeting the Ethical Challenge of Leadership*. Thousand Oaks, CA: Sage.

Jones, S. and Gosling, J. (2005) *Nelson's Way: leadership lessons from the great commander*. London: Nicholas Brealey.

Ladkin, D. (2010) *Rethinking Leadership*. Cheltenham: Edward Elgar.

Northouse, Peter Guy (2010) *Leadership: theory and practice*. Thousand Oaks, CA: Sage.

Western, Simon (2008) *Leadership: a critical text*. London: Sage.

24

HR-oriented Leadership and Production-oriented Leadership

Some leaders, by preference or culture, focus on tasks more than people; others seek progress by helping people develop, focused more on a human resource-based approach.

In this entry we contrast leaders who come from a HR career versus those coming from a more production-oriented engineering background. HR professionals develop expertise in assessing talent, working out incentives and rewards, training individuals and optimizing the working relationships of teams. When they come into leadership positions they naturally seek to pursue the organization's goals by mobilizing the people they work with. On the other hand, people who have grown up through operations and production management tend to see people as factors in the process, emphasizing the 'resource' more than the 'human'. This is not just a matter of personal preference, but also the effect of the specific working practices, techniques, priorities and focus that each had become used to. Many companies require talented staff to cross the boundaries between such specialisms, precisely because they want the benefits of both. Nevertheless, the top jobs in organizations have to be filled from somewhere, and the leader's professional background does make a difference. In this section we emphasize the distinction between HR and production 'types'. One way to express this is that one focuses on human resource-fulness, the other on resources, including humans. What are the capabilities and insights that each brings?

THE HR-ORIENTED LEADER

One might expect that a leader coming up through a route involving HR management would tend to be (making use of the Blake and Mouton Managerial Grid (1964)), rather more relationship-oriented than task-oriented. But although they may focus on relationships as the object of their work, they may approach this in a very task-focused and technical way. Conversely, engineers focused on their production processes might ignore the people-dimension, but many are actually acutely aware of the connection between individual, team and task performance, paying great attention to all three aspects (as described by John Adair, 1973). But HR managers are usually responsible for workforce diversity, equal opportunities and avoiding workplace discrimination. It is their job to ensure that everyone is treated fairly, that proper contracts are in place, with job descriptions, and specifications for vacant positions. Paying attention to these things heightens the awareness of personality characteristics, responses to authority and stress, the varieties of ambition and motivations, and so forth.

One of the problems with highly specialized staff – whether from production, HR or any other function – is the tendency to lose sight of business imperatives. HR professionals are confronted with this directly when asked to design and facilitate organizational change, when they become subject to countervailing forces. Change impacts on people, and can be especially troubling when one has little control over it. Anxieties arising from such disempowerment and uncertainty are often expressed as resistance to change, sometimes at an emotional or unconscious level. HR staff members often take the brunt of the anger and frustration as people work out their responses to change – especially if this involves industrial disputes and organized resistance. Reorganizations inevitably also mean more work for HR – new organization charts, job descriptions, performance targets – even salaries and benefits can change too. Experience of all these details can be a formative influence on leaders; for example it is well known that mergers and acquisitions are more likely to be successful if the 'soft' issues of organizational culture and job design are carefully managed. Of course there are benefits to being at the centre of big events: it could be that some HR-oriented leaders create more work for themselves in the process to feel more important! (See the related entries Accommodating Leadership and Competitive Leadership, Change-oriented Leadership and Continuity-based Leadership, Analytical Leadership and an Intuitive, Instant Leadership Approach, Coaching and Mentoring-oriented Leadership and Directive, Telling-what-to-do Leadership.)

Here we look at three examples of HR-oriented leaders and – ironically enough – the one with the HR job is the least HR-oriented. They have their strengths as leaders and people usually like to work with them – but there are some serious drawbacks here, as this can be a limited single dimensional view of leadership, with feet not on the ground.

An emerging market consultant – on an extremely diplomatic HR leader, and a pragmatic HR leader:

> I had a boss once who was very HR-oriented. She was very caring and interested in people, but was rather non-confrontational, so if anyone in her team made a mistake, she couldn't bear to scold them. I messed up one of my assignments by forgetting to get a visa for a business trip, and thought I would be in very big trouble. But I wasn't! She was most concerned that I was worried and would lose sleep over this. I was relieved to be let off lightly, but I thought she should have been much tougher on me. I mentioned this to the Managing Director some time later, and he agreed. But she would never say anything negative about anyone and would never criticize the organization in any way. She was very discreet and diplomatic – or very political.
>
> On another occasion we had a team meeting (this didn't happen very often, as we were located and working in many different places) and this meeting included one of the colleagues who did almost no work, didn't answer emails, refused to contribute to team projects, and was very arrogant and superior in manner. He made an excuse (about his private business) and left the meeting early. On the way back to her office from the meeting, she complained to me that no-one on the team had confronted him about his lack of contribution. I didn't say anything, but I thought to myself, 'That's your job!'
>
> A second example of an HR-oriented leader was actually working in HR, but perhaps he wasn't really human-oriented as there were many aspects of the job he didn't like. He was really just involved in hiring, as the company had a very bad staff turnover problem. He was given targets to improve staff retention but, as he would tell anyone who would listen, he thought this wasn't fair, as the people whom he recruited would then go and work for some awful manager and get fed up and leave. He espoused the duty to be upbeat and positive about the company, pointing out that 'HR is the ambassador of the organization, and the custodian of the culture', but he was more negative and critical than anyone else.

While encouraging good relations within a team is important, leaders need to be able to step up and discipline individuals from time to time. HR leaders are also often a public face of an organization because they are involved in bringing new people to that organization. This gives them a unique perspective on the organization as they see not only the internal workings of the group but also how potential employees perceive the organization from the outside. A good HR leader will be able to draw upon these unique perspectives and rather than just be a good ambassador to the world will also work with the internal culture to improve relations and workplace vitality. This boundary spanning can be a hugely valuable contribution to leadership.

An HR/development consultant – on a nosey HR leader:

> A leader I can think of was fascinated by people, and when a colleague had to deal with a particular group of individuals, she enjoyed giving him or her briefings about them all, trying to be helpful. These briefings were in huge detail, covering several pages of emails, about who had argued and fallen out with whom, about who was having an affair with whom, with all their medical history and family backgrounds, etc. She had a good memory for all of this as she was so interested in gossip. Actually, it wasn't very useful information – it might have been better not to know all this stuff because I for one kept thinking about it when I met these people, but in terms of doing my job it made very little difference.

In any work environment it goes without saying that professionalism is of the utmost importance. While work colleagues and team members often become close and develop an intimate knowledge of each other, respect for people's privacy is always essential. Leaders, particularly those within HR, are often privy to details of people's lives which should not be shared with other colleagues. Leaders need to be able to negotiate personal relationships and censor the information they share with others.

Some apparently HR-oriented leaders focus on role performance, practising the interpersonal styles that are supposed to simulate attentiveness and interest: always with a smile and pleasant manner, asking 'How can we serve you today?' and abiding by performance standards to answer the phone (after three rings) and answer emails (within 24 hours). Common examples here are call-centres where staff are dragooned into behaving politely and sensitively to customers: to paraphrase George Burns, a twentieth-century comedian, 'If you can fake authenticity, you've got it made!'

In an increasingly litigious society, HR professionals are inevitably caught up in more risk-mitigating legal processes. All too often this finds expression in a plethora of forms and audits and the HR department becomes more concerned with compliance than creativity. Standardization can be a sign of this: professional services are expected to adopt global 'best practice', but this is a sham if not directly attuned to the realities of each business.

Another effect of increasing specialization can be a separation between recruitment and retention. Companies hiring staff mid-career are particularly interested in recruiting top talent, and will proudly boast of the star people they have attracted from competitors; but they may not be so strong in managing that talent, or might become totally fixated on accommodating a cast of celebrities (see the entry on leading prima donnas). By contrast, HR specialists from organizations recruiting entry-level talent and growing them to suit the business will have a different perspective. They are likely to have a more developmental attitude, and will adjust the person to the job rather than shaping the company around the people. Like many specialists in support functions, and in spite of their supposed focus on the work that people do, HR specialists don't always make the leap to a general leadership position.

HR-oriented leaders sound like just the kind of boss you would like to have, caring about you as a person, and making sure you're happy in your work. At best, HR-oriented leaders promote people issues, understand people's motivations and fight for a better deal for the staff as a whole. But at worst, they try to make up for their lack of power and the low esteem in which many managers of other disciplines hold the HR function. In many Western organizations, to have come from an HR background can be a negative stigma; in Japan, however, the reverse is the case, with many HR managers stepping up to top executive roles.

THE PRODUCTION LEADER

Leaders with a background in production (often in engineering) are typically focused on efficiency and are in danger of treating organizations and their employees as machines. Reducing defects, smoothing workflows and ensuring quality is the name of the game. Some derive their sense of authority from their technical expertise (see the entry Expert Leadership and Generalist Leadership); others from a record of can-do inventiveness and determination.

Pride in production can be tremendously positive if it drives zealous innovation, continuous improvement and technical excellence. But it becomes negative if production-oriented leaders forget about the other side of the business – delivering what their customers or service users want: 'If the customers don't want what we have made – that's their problem. We make the best products: they should see how excellent these products really are, it's obvious.'

Meanwhile, production-obsessed managers may find themselves wishing people were as malleable as machines: 'We have great technology, well-designed processes, but can't get the staff to make it work properly.' A classic example that gave birth to a whole new field of social science was the introduction of longwall mining in the coal industry in the 1950s. New technology clashed with established working patterns, and it was only when managers were helped to see this as a 'socio-technical system' that they could recognize the productivity gains they had hoped for (Emery and Trist, 1960). In other words, they had to consider the dynamics of group behaviour in the design of their working processes, and that included leadership at all levels, from each mining gang upwards. The same insights have underpinned generations of advice for production managers, including 'business process re-engineering' (Champey, 1993), which was especially concerned with the massive changes brought about by the digitization of business processes. A very important lesson was that often managers are not able to design the perfect process on the drawing board – they have to work it out with staff colleagues, because it is the latter who have to adapt to new challenges and are most likely to discover new uses and opportunities that have been opened up by the connectivity and speed of digitization. This in turn gave rise to new ideas about adaptive leadership (Heifetz, 1994), specifically to provide the conditions in which staff can adapt to rapid changes in competition, consumer behaviour and the turbulence of the global economy. In this context, production managers have also had to become more adaptive and flexible, while at the same time relentlessly striving for consistency and predictability in production processes.

Some of the most useful tools in the production manager's armoury are international standards such as ISO, and those for specific industries (such as IT architectures and platforms). These provide reference points to which they can plan, and also measure progress. Balanced Scorecards are often used to combine measurements of 'hard' and 'soft' factors, usually linked to key performance indicators for managers. Production managers stepping up to generalist leadership roles have become comfortable with assessing such immeasurables as advertising, competitor positioning, innovation strategies and so forth. In this sense, leadership is more about producing the future, by providing the conditions in which an organization or community can innovate and adapt. Managers who remain focused on the dashboard rather than road ahead are ill suited to leadership; it is a truism that most armies spend peace time learning how to perfectly fight the previous war.

There are many qualities that appeal to production-oriented leaders, not least of which is the aesthetic pleasure of a well-run factory or service. A key metric is productivity, defined as the output obtained from inputs of capital, labour and resources such as energy, land and raw materials. Tough as it is to improve productivity, it is seldom enough for the reasons stated above – competition, changes in consumer preferences, economic turbulence. A very significant factor is also the impact of climate change, and the necessity of reducing the impact of human activity on biodiversity, greenhouse gas emissions and ecosystem services. These stand well outside standard productivity measures, but one of the most important challenges facing leaders is to create production processes and techniques that contribute positively to the natural resource base (planet Earth). Production-oriented leaders have a major role to play in this, if they can rise to the challenge.

Promising developments for production-oriented leaders include cradle-to-cradle product cycles (McDonough and Braungart, 2002), and biomimicry (www.biomimicryinstitute.org). Product life cycles are a well-established idea – that products are born, live, and then die, after which they become waste (having most likely also created a lot of waste as side-products in their manufacture and use). Cradle-to-cradle production involves planning the after-use life of products (and all the resources involved in making and using them). The aim is to create 'closed loop' product cycles, with a net impact on the environment of zero or perhaps even a positive effect. Every industry is affected by these requirements, which puts the focus more and more on leaders who are skilled and knowledgeable in production techniques and processes. A key challenge is to shift the focus from product management to life-cycle management, and this almost always involves working with people from outside the traditional boundaries of a single organization. This is because different sub-industries are involved in various parts of the cycle. For example, Tetra Pak, a manufacturer of packaging for liquid foodstuffs, is nurturing entrepreneurial technology companies near its biggest plants in Taiwan and China, encouraging them to find new uses for the waste products. One outcome has already been new materials for outdoor furniture – the benches for the Beijing Olympics were made from re-used Tetra Pak waste. This is an example of production-oriented leadership focusing on producing a cradle-to-cradle cycle, rather than just one product line.

Biomimicry is the idea that we can mimic Nature's solutions, with examples from many different fields. New cement manufacturing processes mimic the way coral reefs are produced; shark skin is the model for work-surfaces that repel micro-organisms; and aircraft designers hope to match the fuel efficiency of migratory birds. Organization specialists are also seeking ways to design companies and public services that mimic the production processes of natural systems, which are wonderfully generative, in which the waste from one process is the fuel for others.

Biomimicry and cradle-to-cradle processes call for a new generation of production-oriented leaders, especially those who are able to develop the strengths of an HR-orientation as well.

Here we look at three cases of production-oriented leaders, which exemplify these characteristics – of excellence in structure and presentation, but leaving important issues to do with people and culture unresolved.

An emerging market consultant – on the extreme production-oriented leader. Example 1:

A close colleague of mine, a leader in the oil business, had a strong engineering-based mentality. He was very good at his job and extremely precise and efficient, but he was weak at relationships, except with other engineers at his senior level. He had little ability at empathy and was very conservative. The idea of changing his job or doing something a bit daring was quite shocking to him. Anything out of control was scary. And it was difficult for him to work in the Middle East, because many of the staff there were relationship-oriented, and liked to build close friendships as a way of doing their jobs; he found this difficult and time-consuming. But give him an oil-rig shutdown to manage and he was in his element, organized efficiently down to the second. His personal relationships were very fraught, and he himself admitted he never had an original idea in his life.

Example 2:

I spent some time as a quality auditor and assessor and met many production-oriented leaders in the course of doing quality inspections with my team. But when we were assessing the progress of different organizations with people-development, achieving localization, and setting-up HR systems, it was difficult for these production-oriented leaders because they tried to reduce everything to numbers and engineering-speak. And if they had very good product-style manuals, with everything described and listed and documented, they thought this was great and all they needed to win a quality award. These companies would hire people simply to make impressive reports. So we would meet this product-oriented leader with his complete quality manual of which he was very proud. It gave the impression that everything ran like clockwork in the company – which was obviously his intention.

Then we would wander all over the organization, even chatting to people in the toilet (this would drive him crazy as he could not control it, especially in the ladies' toilet) and we would discover that most of their quality submission was made up, it wasn't real at all. All the calculations and percentages were there and looked very convincing, but in reality the data were exaggerated, and most of their beautiful, nicely illustrated manuals were a work of fiction. When it came to assessing people rather than things, it was especially hard for these production-oriented leaders.

Example 3:

> I worked with a very smart senior engineer in Kuwait who had designed a fantastic system for running a training function, with an analysis of competencies, analysing where people had to improve, scheduling them for training, assessing the training result – it was a complete system, like a machine. However, this system was worrisome for the managers, whose lack of competencies would soon be revealed to all. There was no hiding place in this system – so culturally it was too efficient and transparent; no senior person would allow it to be implemented, although it was a product-oriented leader's dream – it just didn't connect with culture and people. These product-oriented leaders couldn't understand cultural sensitivities.

Product-oriented leaders will have to overcome tendencies to be precise and nit-picking, to bring a system-wide perspective to production as well as strategy. They will have to find ways to maintain their focus on achieving high quality and reliability, being very organized and structured, while at the same time being inventive and open to new ideas from beyond their own sphere of influence. But for many this will be a struggle, as the qualities that made them successful as engineers (for example) may be a hindrance in leadership roles. This style of leader – who often trained as an engineer and understands accuracy and maintenance – can struggle with softer issues such as people management, and the uncertainty and ambiguous shades of meaning inherent in the emerging globalized economy.

FURTHER READING

Alvesson, M. and Spicer, A. (eds) (2010) *Metaphors We Lead By: understanding leadership in the real world*. Oxford: Routledge.

Colvin, Geoff (2009) 'How to build great leaders', *Fortune*, 4 December, 160 (10), http://money.cnn.com/magazines/fortune/fortune_archive/2009

Copeland, Michael V. (2010) 'Google: the search party is over', *Fortune*, 16 August, 162 (3): 42–49.

de Bono, S., Jones, S. and van der Heijden, B. (2008) *Managing Cultural Diversity*. Oxford: Meyer & Meyer.

Hirst, G., Knippenberg, D.V., Chen, C.-H. and Sacramento, C.A. (2011) 'How does bureaucracy impact individual creativity? A cross-level investigation of team contextual influences on goal orientation-creativity relationships', *Academy of Management Journal*, 54 (3): 624–641.

Jones, S. (2009) 'Implementing software for managing organizational training and development: an example of consulting to a large public sector organization in the State of Kuwait', *International Journal of Commerce and Management*, 19 (4): 260–277.

Mintzberg, H. (1994) *The Rise and Fall of Strategic Planning: reconceiving roles for planning, plans, planners.* New York: Free Press.

Ulrich, Dave (1997) *Human Resource Champions.* Boston, MA: Harvard University Press.

Valcea, S., Hamdani, M.R., Buckley, M.R. and Novicevic, M.M. (2011) 'Exploring the developmental potential of leader–follower interactions: a constructive-developmental approach', *The Leadership Quarterly*, 22: 604–615.

25

Implementer Leadership and Shaper-driver Leadership

Some like to do it themselves, while some provide the conditions for others.

Perhaps we can tell most about a leader by the way he or she interacts with teams – after all, most leadership is actually accomplished through teamwork. Some psychologists have focused on team behaviours, rather than individual characteristics, and have defined assessments of the various roles that people play in a team. This can be helpful in developing a broader understanding of leader behaviours.

Meredith Belbin (1993, 2000, 2004), an influential British psychologist, developed a classification of nine 'team roles', and an instrument to enable all those working in teams to assess their 'tendency to behave, contribute and interrelate with others in a particular way'. They are: Plant, Resource-Investigator, Monitor-Evaluator, Shaper, Co-ordinator, Teamworker, Implementer, Completer-Finisher and Specialist. For each of these, Belbin lists desirable characteristics labelled 'contributions' and 'allowable weaknesses' – the latter including some of the behaviours we have to put up with to get the contributions we want. What are these desirable contributions and the less desirable weaknesses? What does this tell us about leader behaviour? Does this really help us in understanding leadership styles and competencies more effectively?

In this section we will introduce all nine team roles, and then focus especially on two extremes: the Shaper leader, whose team role is predominantly that of the Shaper, the dynamic but easily irritated driver of others, and the Implementer, who can also be a leader but is known especially for being a follower, dedicated to hard work, conservative and reliable. Although we do not discuss the other team roles in such detail in this volume, there are similarities between analytical leaders and Monitor-Evaluators, participative leaders and Teamworkers, expert leaders and

key concepts in leadership

Specialists, marketing-oriented leaders and Resource-Investigators, goal-oriented leaders and Completer-Finishers, etc.

The first team role to be identified was the 'Plant'. The role was so-called because one such individual was 'planted' in each team. They tended to be highly creative and good at solving problems in unconventional ways. If they were missing, the team would get stuck solving problems. One by one, the other team roles began to emerge. The Monitor-Evaluator was needed to provide a logical eye, make impartial judgements where required and weigh up the team's options in a dispassionate way. Co-ordinators were needed to focus on the team's objectives, draw out team members and delegate work appropriately. When the team was at risk of becoming isolated and inwardly focused, Resource-Investigators provided inside knowledge on the opposition and made sure that the team's idea would carry to the world outside the team. Implementers were needed to plan a practical, workable strategy and carry it out as efficiently as possible. Completer-Finishers were most effectively used at the end of a task, to 'polish' and scrutinize the work for errors, subjecting it to the highest standards of quality control. Teamworkers helped the team to gel, using their versatility to identify the work required and complete it on behalf of the team. Challenging individuals, known as Shapers, provided the necessary drive to ensure that the team kept moving and did not lose focus or momentum. It was only after the initial research had been completed that the ninth team role, Specialist, emerged. The simulated management exercises had been deliberately set up to require no previous knowledge. In the real world, however, the value of an individual with in-depth knowledge of a key area came to be recognized as yet another essential team contribution or team role. Just like the other team roles, the Specialist also had a weakness: a tendency to focus narrowly on their own subject of choice, and to prioritize this over the team's progress.

According to Belbin's research – and the many thousands who have used this framework in further research – team performance is predicated on having people able to contribute to each of these role functions. Most people can take up several roles, but will have preferences for just one or two, and the Belbin team types assessment instruments (self test and observer test) help identify these preferences. Note that the test works best with mature, experienced people who have figured out, more or less consciously, the part they play in collective efforts. One of the strengths of this approach is that it avoids a simple list of traits, good and bad, but accepts that characteristics that might be dysfunctional for one role could be acceptable in another. For example, someone with a low attention span but an excitable imagination could be a great Resource-Investigator, but would need a lot of self-discipline to contribute as a Completer-Finisher (although the two roles can be preferences for the same person). Another contrasting pair of roles are those of Shaper and Implementer, discussed below.

Shaper roles – pushing people to action and keeping them moving – are typical of many leaders. A Shaper needs to be good at challenging others, keeping the pressure up and overcoming barriers. Because they are strongly task-oriented leader, Shapers cooperate with others to get things done, and can complement the role of the Coordinator, if they respect each other (often leadership in a team defaults to Co-coordinators, in the absence of a Shaper).

A researcher on leadership – looking at a practical application of these team roles:

I know a ship's captain, managing a super-yacht in the worldwide charter business, whose job requires managing a crew of frequently changing and highly mobile individuals. Many of them are specialists, all working to the highest level of service for big-spending super-yacht guests, and sometimes in a risky environment at sea. This is a classic Shaper role, and a perfect fit for someone with these characteristics: dynamic, outgoing, dominant, extroverted, excitable, short-tempered, nervous and anxious. He has a great need for achievement, wants to put his name to things, and is very impatient. Sometimes he can be paranoid, and is certainly assertive, showing emotional responses and outbursts of anger. He is obsessed with authorship and doesn't want anyone to take over what he thinks is his. He thrives under pressure and happily takes unpopular decisions, moving forward urgently to take action and wants to gain results. He often sees others as an extension of his ego, and often comes over as arrogant and abrasive. He gives clear orders and everyone knows what needs to be done – there is no ambiguity on this ship. But the collective responsibility on board is limited because others know that the captain will want to sort everything out in his own way, and they risk more by getting involved than staying quiet. This is a team with room for only one person with Shaper preferences: others on board have to fill other roles – or jump ship, which many do.

One example of another possible Shaper in the team is the Chief Engineer – who sometimes acts as second in command on the same ship, in the absence of the First Mate. He may well have the capacity to lead his own team, but in this circumstance he successfully mobilizes his preference as an Implementer. He is generally disciplined and reliable in his work, fairly stable and controlled emotionally (but with the occasional ant-Shaper outburst), conservative and efficient: a practical organizer, turning ideas into actions. He is concerned with what is feasible and operates in a logical manner with a high degree of commitment and stability. But he can come across as inflexible and slow to respond to new possibilities, and can be upset by a sudden change of plan, and gets annoyed when things go wrong. He likes structures and systems, and tries to build these when they don't exist. He is not keen on speculative ideas that can't be pinned down (not one for 'brainstorming' exercises). But he can be counted upon to do reliably what needs to be done, even if no one else wants to do it; in fact he can over do this: like most implementers, he is reluctant to delegate because he would rather 'do it right' himself. In the case of this particular individual, he prefers solving big, occasional problems rather than routine work, but he's still predominantly an Implementer.

The characteristics ascribed here to Shapers (using Belbin's framework) are similar to those described in other entries in this volume, such as authoritarian leaders, competitive leaders, leadaholics, generalist leaders, knee-jerk leaders and involved leaders. Implementers can be seen as similar to accommodating leaders, behind-the-scenes leaders, continuity-based leaders, co-operative leaders, expert leaders and low-key leaders.

It is important to note that Belbin approaches character traits not as good or bad in themselves; he is interested in how they contribute to team roles. For example, if a team is deviating from goals or timelines, then an inflexible, controlling leader – such as a Shaper – might be able to put them back on track. The key point here is that leadership is often a subtle, dynamic activity requiring a complex balancing act, one which is situationally dependent. From one situation to the next, the same leader may need to change from being courageous and inspiring to being provocative and inflexible. An Implementer can be counted on to get the work done, but may be most appropriate for a situation of continuity rather than change.

It is important to note that Belbin did not intend this tool for analysing individual leadership styles, but to focus on team-specific behaviour and the type of contribution these make to team performance. Most people have two or three of these team roles as dominant preferences, which they mobilize interchangeably. Also, the adoption of a particular team role is not only impacted by circumstances and the situation, but also by the organizational culture. So it's only useful in a cross-sectional study of leaders at work, because one leader could adopt many different team roles during a long working career. A longitudinal study would show most people able to take up a variety of team roles over time, but rarely adopting their lowest preference. A Shaper can become an Implementer if his or her job changes so that overall responsibility is denied and the Shaper's job is confined to just a small or limited element of the work. An Implementer could become a Shaper if suddenly given a challenging task and more responsibility, but it is likely that he or she would still be a 'super-doer' and would focus on task execution and completion.

In the process of identifying the team role of an individual, it also depends on the care taken in completing the assessment test itself, and if the subject deliberately wanted to appear in a different light. For example, a subject wanting to come over as a strong leader might want to skew the outcome of the test to appear as a Shaper or Co-ordinator, with some Implementer to show a willingness to work hard.

These team roles, looking at ways of leading in a team-based context, are based on sound research and can be especially useful in looking at leadership styles, leadership potential and motivation for leadership. It has often been thought that respondents with a strong emphasis on the roles of Implementer, Completer-Finisher and Specialist would seem to be focused on the daily job in hand rather than looking at strategic issues and thinking ahead – and this might also apply to Teamworker and Plant. Thus it might be more challenging and difficult for them to aspire to a senior leadership role – which is very often occupied by Shapers, who do not welcome competition in their role.

FURTHER READING

Alvesson, M. and Spicer, A. (eds) (2010) *Metaphors We Lead By: understanding leadership in the real world*. Oxford: Routledge.

Belbin, R.M. (1993) *Team Roles at Work*. Oxford: Butterworth Heinemann.

Belbin, R.M. (2000) *Beyond the Team*. Oxford: Butterworth Heinemann.

Belbin, R.M. (2004) *Management Teams: why they succeed or fail*. Oxford: Elsevier/Butterworth Heinemann.

Jones, S. (2010) *Psychological Testing*. Petersfield: Harriman House.

Katzenbach J. and Smith, D. (1994) *The Wisdom of Teams*. New York: Harper Business.

Northouse, Peter Guy (2010) *Leadership: theory and practice*. Thousand Oaks, CA: Sage.

Western, Simon (2008) *Leadership: A critical text*. London: Sage.

26

Individualistic and Relationship-Oriented Leadership

> *Many leaders seek to get the best out of their people by a partnership approach; others see themselves as the keystone, on whom everything depends, often clamouring for the credit and wanting to be seen to be in charge.*

Relationship-oriented leadership, built on win/win relationships, is closely related to 'engaging management' (Gosling and Mintzberg, 2003). Having a collaborative mind-set, being on the inside, being involved, managing throughout an organization, getting things done through other people: all these tend to show that the leader appreciates value-added relationships with people. It's not just being a boss and a subordinate, but being a colleague and a partner. It's not about seeing people as resources or assets which can be moved around, bought and sold or even downsized, in a manipulative or selfish way. It's all about the attitude of the leader to the other staff members of an organization. These people are valuable partners, valued individuals and important to the maintenance and growth of the community – a non-mechanistic metaphor for the organization.

By contrast, individualistic leadership, by a sole leader at the top, is likely to be more manipulative, closely related to 'heroic management' which separates the leader from the organization through a strict hierarchical structure. Manipulative leaders, working for their own individual goals and not necessarily focused on achieving things through other people, tend to see their followers as simply cogs in the organization to be moved around and/or dismissed as deemed necessary through human resource data sheets and reports. Individual or manipulative leaders, or heroic managers, tend to impose strategy from on high, value only what can be quantitatively measured, and to enforce their will with little regard for the viewpoints of others. Its effectiveness depends on the culture of the organization and what is expected by the followers (see the discussion on transactional and transformational leadership in the Introduction).

We can see Individualistic Leadership as including:

- the leader being separated from the rest of the organization;
- the existence of a hierarchical structure;
- the leader imposing a strategy from on-high;
- the allocation of resources, including HR, based on facts from reports;
- rewarding leaders based on their individual performance;
- what matters is what can be measured;
- the leader thrusting his will on others.

This is a very familiar approach to leadership, common in large organizations and those in the public sector. By contrast, we can see relationship-oriented leadership (related to participative leadership and developmental leadership – see the entries Authoritarian Leadership and Participative Leadership, and Developmental Leadership and Job-hopping Leadership) as including:

- integrated styles;
- networked approaches;
- nurturing change from the inside;
- inspiring people to engage;
- rewarding everyone who improves the organization through their own efforts;
- the leader earning the respect of others.

Leaders who are keen on developing relationships with their staff, who are willing to identify and understand their full range of potential in interacting with an organization, may be seen as collaborative or relationship-building leaders. This kind of leader sees staff members – from high to low – as members of the community (not mere assets) who can make a unique and probably hard to quantify contribution to the company. There may also be an appreciation of their individual brands as people, rather than their need to conform to the company brand (see the related entry 'Company-Branded' and 'Individual-Branded' Leadership). The work of the company – in an organization focusing on collaborative and relationship-oriented leadership – can only really be achieved through the staff members' willing efforts.

This kind of leader sees his or her job as needing to create opportunities for each staff member to exercise their talents and skills. The same goes not just for staff members, but also for business partners, suppliers, and even competitors. Building relationships is the way that these leaders operate. They often have a high degree of what Charles Handy (2000) calls 'referent power', where due to their ability to make friends and get on with people, others gladly want to help them. Even if they do not occupy a very high position of power, these leaders can be very influential, because they are so relationship-oriented, and people want to help them.

Other leaders – more focused on what they can gain personally from the transactions – may see their staff members as not much more than indentured labour. This can be an issue in some developing economies where there is a large cultural and power divide between the senior staff (who may be locals of the country) and expatriate labour, often third-country nationals, who are seen as a possession or chattel of the organization (see the related entries Eastern-style Leadership and Western-style Leadership – Contrasting and Converging National Cultures , and Global Leadership and Worldly Leadership). It is possible that the leaders of this kind of company are actually suffering a sense of insecurity and self-doubt in a context that seems to require certainty and self-confidence. One outcome of such insecurity can be an authoritative style (see the related entry Authoritarian Leadership and Participative Leadership). The reasoning of these leaders is something like this: 'Staff members can earn a lot more money here than they can at home. We have brought them in here, and they are on our work permits. They must work for us and only for us. They want the money, we want the labour, there is no point building a relationship here, it is a simple business transaction. They are low-skilled and temporary staff with low expectations, so why waste time on consultations when straightforward commands can be effective in this kind of environment.'

The distinction we draw here between individualistic 'heroic' and community 'relationship' oriented leadership is akin to the classic distinction between task-orientation and relationship orientation (as represented in the Blake and Mouton managerial grid discussed in 'Leadership Definition, Theory and Practice'). (See the related entry HR-oriented Leadership and Production-oriented Leadership.) Relationship-oriented leaders get to know people; task-oriented leaders use people. The people play a key role in making business happen; or the business needs people from time to time to fulfil certain functions.

Here, we look at the power of relationship-oriented leaders – but it is power with responsibility. Individualistic leaders have a limited connection with their colleagues, and find no need to build relationships with them. The impact of these different styles of leader varies a great deal. It's all about the difference between being close or distant, and how people feel as a result. It's also about getting things done through people, or trying to do everything on your own.

The following example is a reflection on one individual's experience in a new job, a university academic appointment, and his experiences with a relational leader as Dean, who was highly effective at achieving a collaborative environment of teamwork.

A junior academic – on showing relational leadership:

> During my first full-time academic appointment I had the pleasure of working under a Dean who was very people oriented – a truly relational leader. He was very collaborative, encouraging others to work together. As a result, the achievements of the university were shared by many people, who felt empowered. This individual had a very strong academic background in research and teaching and had been involved in senior university administration in several different institutions. Under his leadership the faculty grew significantly with new programmes, more students and more staff. But he didn't do everything himself. He encouraged others to work together.
>
> When this leader was coming toward the end of his last term as Dean I asked him about his accomplishments and how he had been so successful. Always a humble individual, he said the success was not his but that of the wider faculty. As I pressed him about this he eventually said, 'What I do is see potential, potential for growth and the potential in others, and then help realize that potential'. When I thought about this I realized that his leadership was all about nurturing relationships and inspiring people.
>
> This leader encouraged people to do what they wanted to do, but were perhaps hesitant about, but the university as a whole benefited. From my own experience he had always been supporting and encouraging with me, and I could see him doing this with others. This Dean was a very visible presence in the faculty, the wider university and the community in general. He sought out and nurtured professional relationships and friendships. From time to time he would just drop by a colleague's office for a chat. He always made you feel welcome, valued and important. He was always

open to the ideas of others and encouraged them to develop those ideas into new research projects, courses, articles, books, etc. But it wasn't just him as an individual leader which was the important thing. It was the way he encouraged others to get on with helping the organization to grow and develop, in a way they might not have done before.

He was, at the same time, a highly respected leader. Though he was an approachable, friendly and collegial boss we all knew that in the end he was in charge (and he sometimes 'ruffled feathers'), and we respected that. As a leader he earned followership through his dedication, inclusive nature and affable personality, which was highly motivational in producing results in others.

In this example, the relational leader is successful because he respects his colleagues and in turn they respect him. He offers them something they value, an amalgam of support, advice, encouragement, and organizational headroom, which he does by virtue of his position and his personality (there are plenty of deans who don't do this!). We refer to this as 'relational leadership' because the leadership emerges from the special qualities of the relationship between dean and colleagues. Both leadership and followership are created by the way they work together; and because the faculty and administrative staff value the leadership he offers, they are able to improve and grow. A relational leader may not be especially visionary, because this kind of work focuses on what is near at hand, sees the potential for growth and opportunities for innovation, and finds ways to grow that potential into a reality. A very important aspect is the leader's understanding of the wider context, its opportunities and constraints. In the case described above, the Dean is able to guide his colleagues such that their ambitions benefit from the university environment – and if their projects are contentious and a bit counter-cultural, he might be able to provide 'cover'. Successful relational leaders are great at managing upwards and laterally, as well as in relation to subordinates, because this is how they create the space for growth.

An ex-CEO/Management Consultant – on the danger of overly individual or manipulative leadership:

An organization to which I consult has a very powerful Chairman of the Board, who is also a senior politician, and is certainly a highly individual and manipulative leader. He is selfish and egocentric. He doesn't even know some of the most important people in this organization, because he hasn't bothered to ask who they are. He is a leader by appointment and by his position only. He wants to see himself as responsible for the achievements of the organization. If he mentions others, it might belittle his perceived 'contribution'. He has pushed himself up into a high-status leadership job by using others just to help him look good – in his political party and in the organization which he chairs. He wants to be associated with these organizations for the power and prestige they might bring to him – he actually doesn't care that much about them and the people in them. He's not a leader of people, he just occupies a position. He likes being around other top people, he likes to be seen at national level but he doesn't have followers – just people who tolerate him or who have benefited from hanging out with him, like parasites.

This leader comes over as very impressive, especially at meetings or big events – he loves a large audience – but if you listen carefully to what he says, it amounts to not a lot. He does not express an exciting vision of the future, or if he tries to, it's not convincing. He's not inspirational or visionary. He's a top civil servant, a kind of stuffed suit, looking good in an annual report. He knows how to behave at social functions and in front of the press and the public, and he has in fact put the organization on the map, or at least this is the perception of many outsiders. He has a very famous, prestigious position in the national government. But actually he is contributing more or less nothing, and manages to get praise for achievements which he hardly even knows about, let alone helped to make happen. He takes himself very seriously, and basks in the reflected glory of others, without realizing it's all them and not him.

When our individual/heroic/manipulative leader talks about strategy, he is often just going on about strategic plans developed by others. But he's actually very powerful. He can get rid of someone if he doesn't like them, and he has done this a number of times, so no-one dares to stand up to him. Although he's a figurehead, he likes to be dominant. He has actually hired a manager in the organization he chairs to spy on the other managers and employees and report back to him. The effect is rather unsettling for the organization, and has led to reduced morale, uncertainty and conservatism. No-one will stick their neck out as he obviously will not tolerate any threat to his position.

In this example we have a leader who is the absolute opposite of relationship-oriented. He is not interested in making things happen in the organization through the willing collaboration of others, as he's not interested in these 'others'. This particular Chairman does not even know all the senior executives in the organization, let alone individuals further down the hierarchical ladder. He has risen to a leadership position, at least in name, by using others to further his career with little concern for the consequences of his actions, other than their effect on his reputation. As a leader he uses his position to maintain and grow his public persona but gives no consideration to how he is affecting the organization which he is supposed to be leading. Those that follow him do so out of fear or because they have benefited from his connections (in a sense they are manipulating him!). As is so common with situations like this, the manipulative leader creates a culture of fear where no one is willing to suggest change, discuss new ideas, or be creative. What results is organizational stagnation which may eventually lead to organizational collapse. When a leader practises leadership with only the self in mind, the leadership fails, collaboration does not happen and the organization may well go down with it.

This inevitably begs the question as to whether or not collaborative or relationship-oriented leaders are always better than individual or heroic leaders. Certainly, most work environments benefit from leadership which is accessible, inclusive and encouraging, and more is achieved by the people in the organization. However, there are many dangers with collaborative leadership, including becoming so caught up with building relationships that the leader never gets round to facing important decisions. In the minefield of organizational politics, a leader who has great relationships with colleagues might be seen as having 'gone native' by upper management (the board, council or shareholders) who will want someone to do their bidding, and mistrust a leader who is too close to the people. But this is really just a warning to look in all directions at once – perhaps the greatest talent of leaders with longevity!

The collaborative or relational leader can be very effective as a manager and a good team-player, but he or she should maintain the commitment of purpose to get things done. Beware spending too much time trying to work through others and encouraging their contribution, when they might want more direction and less collaboration. Collaboration is a two-way thing: if the leader concentrates on building relationships because they are very collaborative by nature, but if the other person is not matching this, it's not going to work, and the achievement of organizational goals through collaboration may not be effective. The individualistic or heroic manager may be very personally driven, which could translate into a strong task orientation (but doesn't always), and will thrive in environments with a surplus of talent which can be easily hired and fired, and where there is less need to build collaborative relationships in order to grow new opportunities and to get things done. Things do get done, but through coercion or reward – and not through the use of referent power and collaboration. It's hard to say which is more or less successful – it all depends!

FURTHER READING

Bryman, Alan, Collinson, David L., Grint, Keith and Jackson, Brad (2011) *The Sage Handbook of Leadership*. London: Sage.

Gosling, J. and Minzberg, H. (2003) 'The five minds of the manager', *Harvard Business Review*, November, 81(11): 54–63.

Grint, K. (2005) 'Problems, problems, problems: the social construction of "leadership"', *Human Relations*, 58 (11): 1467–1494.

Handy, C. (1992) *Understanding Organizations*. Harmondsworth: Penguin.

Iszatt-White, M. (2011) 'Methodological crises and contextual solutions: an ethnomethodologically informed approach to understanding leadership', *Leadership*, 7 (2): 119–135.

Jones, S. (2009) 'Implementing software for managing organizational training and development: an example of consulting to a large public sector organization in the State of Kuwait', *International Journal of Commerce and Management*, 19 (4): 260–277.

Katzenbach J., and Smith, D. (1994) *The Wisdom of Teams*. New York: Harper Business.

Kets de Vries, Manfred (2009) *Reflections on Character and Leadership: on the couch with Manfred Kets de Vries*. San Francisco, CA: Jossey-Bass.

Leithwood, Kenneth A., Muscall, Blair and Strauss, Tiiu (2009) *Distributed Leadership According to the Evidence*. New York: Routledge.

Snook, Scott A., Nohria, Nitin N. and Khurana, Rakesh (2012) *The Handbook for Teaching Leadership: knowing, doing and being*. Thousand Oaks, CA: Sage.

Trompenaars, F. and Hampden-Turner, C. (1997) *Riding the Waves of Culture: understanding cultural diversity in business*. London: Nicholas Brealey.

Inspirational Leadership and Low-key Leadership

Some leaders have the flair and charisma to excite their followers; but this is not the only way of leading, and a more modest and even pedestrian approach can be just as effective.

Here we are talking about the colourful and attractive leader who paints a picture of an appealing future, compared with the leader who is much more low-key. Is leadership about winning hearts and minds or just getting the job done? Leadership is ideally both being inspirational and getting results – and there can be low-key ways of getting results, too. Inspiration makes people come to life and works best when the leader is enthused about a cause or goal: 'you can't inspire others if you are not inspired yourself' (Jones and Gosling, 2005: 177). But a lack of inspiration doesn't necessarily mean that the people being led are not engaged, or are simply going through the motions. A low-key leader can help his or her team members to find inspiration among themselves, and free them up to do their jobs in the way they think best (see the related entries Behind-the-scenes Leadership and Leading from the Front, Coaching and Mentoring-oriented Leadership and Directive, Telling-what-to-do Leadership).

In this entry, we focus on the differences between the inspirational leader – who lights fire in the hearts and minds of followers – and the low-key or pedestrian leader – who focuses on the task without instilling passion. In the latter case, such a person might be more meticulous, prudent and capable of careful judgement, playing a role like the Monitor-Evaluator in Belbin's team roles (see the discussion of team roles in the related entry Implementer Leadership and Shaper-driver Leadership).

First, let's consider what makes a group or large organization susceptible to inspiration? If there is a clear necessity to act in concert – for example, if under attack from a common enemy – why would a community need to be inspired? One answer could be that there is always an incipient level of anxiety in any group, to which people will respond with a few well-worn patterns of behaviour. Often they will behave as if they believed that 'fight or flight' will relieve the anxiety, and any leader who seems to personify (for example) the fight response will seem to be 'inspirational'. The leader is really just picking up the vibes of the group, and representing an the hoped-for salvation. The group's success in repelling an attack might be successful, in which case they are likely to ascribe the cause at least partly to the leader.

So, inspirational leadership might be developed mostly to serve follower needs – so do followers ever need low-key leadership? Yes – at times when the organization is more in consolidation mode and is not necessarily driven towards great change. And when followers are more self-contained and self-motivated, and are not used to hands-on leadership, but in getting on with their own work.

So, what makes an inspirational leader? He or she has to communicate well, simplify and clarify, be animated, and the people in the organization must be convinced enough to believe in him or her. He or she may be charismatic – this helps, but it's possible to be inspirational even without the charisma. The successful inspirational leader needs to create legends, and make gestures of caring for people. He or she needs to earn respect, make an effort to understand individual problems, be sincere and honest, and create teams. The inspirational leader has no problems with the question, 'Why should others follow you?' Ideally he or she shows dedication to the purpose, appeals to the highest aspirations of people working in the organization, promotes their values and emphasizes the importance of values-based operating approaches. The inspirational leader with problems with his or her team members can appeal to their pride and sense of achievement, and then celebrate joint success together (Jones and Gosling, 2005: 178–180).

But there are many dangers associated with inspirational leaders; part of their attractiveness is often the huge confidence that comes with successful narcissism, projected into the conviction that what the world needs most is 'more of me'. The desire to leave a legacy is just one (usually positive) example. Followers can be willingly inspired to take a direction that turns out to be inappropriate in the long term. They get wrapped up in inspirational leadership and stop thinking about what they are doing – such as the traders working for Jeffery Skilling at Enron (see the related entries Here-and-now Leadership and Legacy Leadership, Authoritarian Leadership and Participative Leadership, Extrovert Leadership and Introvert Leadership, Nurturing Leadership and Toxic Leadership).

Low-key leaders can still gain respect – by quietly responding to follower needs, quietly creating goals for people and doing everything the inspirational leader does – but in a less animated, obvious fashion. The low-key leader can be accommodating, more participative, more collaborative, and more developmental in approach – and might be more authentic to him- or herself and to individual personal values and beliefs (see the related entries Accommodating Leadership and Competitive Leadership, Authoritarian Leadership and Participative Leadership, and Coaching and Mentoring-oriented Leadership and Directive, Telling-what-to-do Leadership).

Here, we discuss an example of a low-key leader and we consider the possible drawbacks of his lack of ability to connect with others in an inspirational way. And in another example, we see a leader with problems to overcome, and show how, when he first started to handle the problems, he gained the ability to inspire others. Sometimes pedestrian behaviours reflect inexperience and a lack of self-confidence. A final example discusses the attempts of a pedestrian leader to transform himself into what he thought would be more inspirational, but found that his low-key approach was actually more authentic for him and was respected as such by his followers.

An ex-CEO/Management Consultant – on the impact of a low-key style of leadership:

I think that if you are not an inspirational leader you are lacking a very important leadership competency; however, I have seen examples of successful low-key/pedestrian leaders, but it depends on the personality of the leader and the needs of the situation. Many leaders are obviously not open to feedback and don't realize how they are perceived. They may think they inspire others but they don't, and perhaps they don't realize that their lack of ability in this area can be damaging. Not always, but sometimes.

I was helping a start-up family business and the father was suggesting how it should work. He was bossy, arrogant, seeing everything from his point of view and made no attempt to engage the others. His daughter was clearly embarrassed about how awful he was but he couldn't see it at all. He was unexciting and not at all able to encourage others, just seeing things from his own, narrow perspective and with no sense of values or mission which might be seen as attractive by others. His daughter tried to give him feedback about the need to have everyone on his side and to be excited about the project but he didn't see the point of this. Although if you had asked him 'Are you inspirational?' he would probably have said 'Yes'!

To be an inspirational leader does not mean you have to be an innately charismatic person (though it helps to be narcissistic!). To be inspiring involves skill: it is a leadership competency that requires work, thought and dedication on the part of the leader. All leaders must ask themselves, 'Am I encouraging my followers?' Anyone wanting to improve in this respect must be sensitive to feedback.

It is in any case hard to inspire others if not enthused oneself. In the following example an initially low-key or pedestrian leader was able to move towards inspirational leadership after addressing his own lack of inspiration, much of it caused by an unfamiliarity with the organization.

A Management Consultant – on a former pedestrian leader gaining the confidence to be able to inspire others:

There was a leader I know trying to introduce a new strategy. Initially he came over as very uninspiring, announcing the strategy in a vague way and failing to engage employees. Staff assumed he was going to be a very pedestrian leader.

However, when analysing the situation we (the consultants) realized there were two problems: first, that it was not him calling the shots – he was being told what to do by the Chairman behind the scenes. He lacked inspiration because he was not empowered. He couldn't be inspirational because he himself did not buy into the vision he was trying to present. The second problem issued from his newness, that he didn't know the people in the organization, and he wasn't sure if they were on his side, and to compound it all, he was lacking in self-confidence generally.

However, the story changed after six months. He had gained more experience with the organization and more familiarity with the staff. With experience came a clearer understanding of the strategy, which he now believed in fully and had the authority to introduce, and he had developed good relationships with his team, particularly the small group of committee members whom he had come to trust. Now the leader talked values, listened to ideas from others, was creative in problem-solving and showed a sense of humour. This formerly pedestrian leader had become inspirational and developed warm and friendly personal interactions with followers.

Sometimes the leaders who inspire can become overwhelming; their personalities seem to take up more space than the mission. Some might think a case in point is the endless media coverage of Richard Branson of the Virgin Group. This can be an issue with inspirational leadership – you may be seen to be a 'person with a mission', but let the person outshine the mission, and it becomes a turn-off.

An HR/development consultant – on an ineffective inspirational leader, and on a low-key leader trying to 'reform' himself, but realizing that his authentic, more pedestrian style was acceptable in its own way:

> I had an inspirational leader once – but he was a disaster. He was great fun, very entertaining, and painted a picture of an exciting future where we would all be successful and make loads of money. But the firm went bust and we all lost money. He didn't even tell us about the bankruptcy of the firm – we just had phone calls from the finance guy, who told us – the partners – in a very matter-of-fact way without any emotions. No-one had the heart to criticize this poor finance guy, who was doing his best and had tried to warn us before, and probably lost as much personally as we did.
>
> Another leader I knew was extremely reticent and shy and asked for help. I advised him to join a class of similar executives who wanted to learn how to be leaders but he preferred to learn on his own. I tried everything I could think of – exercises, activities, case studies, examples – and after each topic, he would say, 'OK, what's next?' He kept saying he wanted to be inspirational, as if to wave a magic wand he could suddenly become a completely different person. This went on for four days of one-on-one training classes, and I had to have dinner with him every night, too. I felt I had made no impact on him at all, and had completely exhausted my portfolio of leadership training offerings. However, I met his colleagues a few months later and they said that after my course he had changed dramatically. Although shy and quiet still, he was more interested in people, expressed the importance of values, looked for buy-ins, and tried to build a clear role for himself – as a father-figure leader building a caring and inclusive culture, based around a powerful vision of the future. He gave up on trying to be extroverted and found his own way to inspire others – still pedestrian but personal and authentic. People grew to respect him for his efforts, as they knew his shy, introverted personality prevented him from being overtly inspirational on a grand scale. His company has now gone from strength to strength.

Inspirational leadership can be fabulous – but on its own it can bring calamity because of the lack of a daily focus and implementation, which though pedestrian is necessary. On the other hand, purely pedestrian leadership can be stiflingly mundane. It is challenging to be competent in both areas, but possible. Inspirational leadership drives people to a new dream, but if the dream never becomes a reality it can fall flat. Even if you want to fly, you still have to walk. Pedestrian leadership can sound negative, but it has its place, especially if it authentically reflects the personality of a leader doing his or her best. It can be an element of 'soft' leadership, as opposed to 'tough' leadership – where 'soft' doesn't mean 'weak' (Peace, 1991).

FURTHER READING

Conger, Jay Alden and Kanungo, RabindraNath (1998) *Charismatic Leadership in Organizations.* Thousand Oaks, CA: Sage.

Grint, K. (2010) 'The sacred in leadership: separation, sacrifice and silence', *Organization Studies,* 31 (1): 89–107.

Hackman, Michael Z. and Johnson, Craig E. (2008) *Leadership: a communications perspective.* San Francisco, CA: Jossey-Bass.

Haslam, S.A., Reicher, S. and Platow, M. (2011) *The New Psychology of Leadership: identity, influence and power.* New York: Psychology Press.

Jones, S. and Gosling, J. (2005) *Nelson's Way: leadership lessons from the great commander.* London: Nicholas Brealey.

Ladkin, D. (2006) 'The enchantment of the charismatic leader: charisma reconsidered as aesthetic encounter', *Leadership,* 2 (2): 165–179.

Ladkin, D. (2008) 'Leading beautifully: how mastery, congruence and purpose create the aesthetic of embodied leadership practice', *The Leadership Quarterly,* 19: 31–41.

Ladkin, D., and Taylor, S. (2010) 'Enacting the true self: towards a theory of embodied authentic leadership', *Leadership Quarterly,* 21 (1): 64–74.

Mintzberg, H. (1973) *The Nature of Managerial Work.* New York: Harper & Row.

Northouse, Peter Guy (2010) *Leadership: theory and practice.* Thousand Oaks, CA: Sage.

Western, Simon (2008) *Leadership: a critical text.* London: Sage.

28
Interim Leadership and Tenured Leadership

> *Many leaders, especially after a long corporate career, like short-term leadership assignments; others would much prefer to be permanently engaged in one job in one company.*

Interim managers or 'executive temps' are leaders brought in by organizations to solve particular problems or issues, usually for six months or a year at a time. They are not permanent employees but work full-time for the company, probably paid on a daily rate, contracted independently or through an executive temping agency or interim management services provider. Such appointments are made by a parent company to help a subsidiary in distress, often by private equity investors for a specific purpose, such as change management, mergers and acquisitions, redundancies, start-ups and new branch-openings.

When is it better to hire these highly paid, focused and roving trouble-shooters than more permanent leaders, recruited for the long term and whose jobs don't necessarily have a specific time-frame?

As a career choice, is it more fun and more remunerative to be a 'temp' leader or to work for a company on a steady, permanent basis? If you like a lot of variety, it might be preferable to be a 'temp' even though your CV will look like a laundry list. Conversely, if you find yourself moving from job to job, it could be that you are becoming an interim leader without intending it!

Some leaders are less likely to be recruited permanently because of their preferences for specific stages of a company life-cycle. Long-term leaders need to be able to handle the evolution of an organization, constantly adapting to changing scenarios as the fortunes of the company ebb and flow; others thrive in bull or bear markets, but not both. To put it baldly, some hire and others fire!

Interim leaders are often highly competitive, as they have to live off their wits and keep looking for new positions. They tend to be action-oriented and pragmatic, working in any sector of industry from any functional background. Some are celebrities in their own specialization, such as in turning companies around. Leaders in more permanent positions might be more concerned with continuity, with collaborative and developmental styles of leadership, with a long-term view and implementation focus (see the related entries Accommodating Leadership and Competitive Leadership, Change-oriented Leadership and Continuity-based Leadership, Implementer Leadership and Shaper-driver Leadership, Long-term Leadership and Project-based Leadership, Goal-oriented Leadership and Opportunistic Leadership). Our examples here focus on the challenges of interim, task-based work, as many of our other examples throughout this volume focus on leaders in tenured positions as a norm.

Here, we look at a leader who made a career of being an executive 'temp'. There are issues with the personal handling of these kinds of jobs, and working with others. Then we look at an executive who was able to thrive in handling whatever happened in organizations, in a more timeless and permanent way. But leaders who can react quickly to changing circumstances need to be good at both situational or 'temp' leadership, as well as the more long-term way of operating.

The client of an executive search consultant – on being an 'executive temp':

I was working as a contractor through an agency which matched executives looking for short-term assignments with opportunities in the manufacturing sector, mostly in China and other parts of Asia. We received a very attractive daily rate, even after the agency had taken their cut. It was a bit of a risky life, as you were never quite sure if you would be able to pick up a new job when you finished the current one, and we were expected to provide our own healthcare and insurance cover. We had to stay for a while wherever we were sent, to live in hotel rooms or rented furnished apartments, and to organize ourselves. I didn't often take my family with me, but tried to visit them as much as possible. I was given a lot of autonomy in my work, to make changes in the organization to which I was sent. It would depend on the objectives, which were always very clear – to set up a new operation, to close one down, to launch new products, to carry out import/export in a new area, in my case mostly in manufacturing. I didn't have baggage from being in one place for many years – I kept moving. I would hire consultants and recruit people and I had instant access to the boss, who was usually a long way away and trusted me to get on with it, based on my objectives.

I quite enjoy life as a 'temp', as I have a lot of freedom and I learn a lot. I don't like getting bogged down in office politics but this is never a problem as a 'temp'. Sometimes it was hard when I had to fire people and make unpopular decisions, but it was easier for me, as a temporary trouble-shooter. I could come in and be a hit man. I have done 'temp' work since my late 30s, because as soon as I felt I had the talent, I wanted to do this kind of work. I have now built-up specialist knowledge and can easily get enough work, and I will carry on as long as I have the energy and desire to zip around all over the place.

An emerging market consultant – on taking advantage of a temporary situation as a leader:

I recently met a leader who made his greatest achievements during the 2010 Eyjafjallajökull volcanic ash cloud disaster. He was head of sales in a logistics and distribution company. They, and all their competitors, could not move courier packages as the hub airport was closed. Urgent packages were backed up in huge piles and nothing was moving for days. The customers were screaming and the volcano was still spewing out dangerous ash clouds and didn't seem to be stopping. Then this young man decided to offer his sea-based service to the air freight and express courier customers. It might take four days, but it would get there. A few desperate customers put aside their suspicions and tried the service, and it worked. So the young sales rep went back to his sales prospect list of the potential clients who had stayed loyal to his competitors. His phone calls came like manna from heaven: we are still moving our shipments! But he would not ship on behalf of his competitors; only directly on behalf of their customers. And once these customers had seen the proactive lengths the sales rep would go to, they stayed. The ability of this young man to be inventive and adaptive in this new environment showed that he had the potential to be a good trouble-shooter: the sort of person who might enjoy being stretched by an interim position.

'Temp' leaders should be flexible, responsive, and able to move with changing needs in a highly proactive and hands-on way, and also be able to cope with constant change and a lack of permanence in their jobs. Their way of operating will be quite different from that of the guys with permanent positions in the organization, whom they may work beside for the time they are employed.

FURTHER READING

Alvesson, M. and Spicer, A. (eds) (2010) *Metaphors We Lead By: understanding leadership in the real world*. Oxford: Routledge.

Golzen, Godfrey (1992) *Interim Management: a new dimension in corporate performance*. London: Kogan Page.

Groysberg, Boris, Nanda, Ashish and Nohria, Nitin (2004) 'The risky business of hiring stars', *Harvard Business Review*, May, 82(5): 92–100.

Jones, S. (1989) *The Headhunting Business*. London: Macmillan.

McGovern, Marion and Russell, Dennis (2001) *A New Brand of Expertise: how independent consultants and free agents are transforming the world of work*. Woburn, MA: Butterworth-Heinemann.

Northouse, Peter Guy (2010) *Leadership: theory and practice*. Thousand Oaks, CA: Sage.

29
Knee-jerk Leadership
and Reflective Leadership

> *Getting on with the job with 'no time to stand and stare' is favoured by many leaders, especially in a fast-paced environment; others prefer to take time out and assess what is happening to themselves and those around them – on a regular basis.*

Here we contrast an approach that is dominated by immediate reactions to events with a more mindful approach, aware of the choices one is making and thinking about the implications and what can be learned from these. First of all, we ask what reflective leadership is all about, and then consider the diametrically opposite style. Reflective leadership is:

- attending to and noticing differences to identify subtle issues and communicate them clearly to others;
- reflecting on experiences, clarifying learning points, considering explanations;
- values, attitudes, and beliefs, which will influence whether you can differentiate between certain events.

Reflective leadership is all about thinking through the impact and ramifications of your own actions and achievements; reflection slows things down (racing-car drivers are trained to see the world in slow-motion). But it is possible to reflect too much, to over-analyse, and to avoid making decisions and moving to action.

Knee-jerk reactions are spontaneous, fresh and intuitive, and are often based on tacit knowledge. Malcolm Gladwell's recent study *Blink* (2005) makes the case for knee-jerk action. What do you understand in the blink of an eye? Sometimes you can make very accurate judgements, based on the tacit knowledge derived from experience, without any conscious deliberation.

But knee-jerk leadership can be a way to avoid noticing subtle differences and not taking time to think about what they mean – it is about pressing on regardless. It's not about thinking what might go wrong and trying to prevent it, it's about bravado and being thankful when things go smoothly – this time. Don't worry about problems until they happen! It's also not much about differentiating between events, but responding in real time, letting everything roll in together. (Related entries include Analytical Leadership and an Intuitive, Instant Leadership Approach, Change-oriented Leadership and Continuity-based Leadership, Compromising Leadership and Co-operative Leadership, Developmental-oriented Leadership and Job-hopping Leadership, and Goal-oriented Leadership and Opportunistic Leadership).

Here, we look at a case of a series of reflective leaders – one in Northern Europe, one in Egypt, and one in Southern Europe. Knee-jerk leaders abound in many examples in the business press and literature – perhaps because action makes for better stories than reflection!

An ex-CEO/Management Consultant – on reflective leadership, a view from Northern Europe:

I am very much a reflective leader. A company is a set of processes and it's important to know and understand how these processes all work together. I would look in the mirror to find out where I failed, and how I can improve the results I need to get. I do this very often. I sit at home, with a glass of wine and a notepad, and I write down the things I've learned and the things I'm succeeding at, and what went well in the company in the recent past. And then – which is sometimes more difficult – I think carefully and I write down what I still need to do, such as persuade one of our stakeholders, listen more carefully to our sales reps, and so on – all things that easily get forgotten in the hurly burly of the day job. I also think about what went wrong over recent months and how can I learn from this? Which particular relationships are problematic? It is a constant process of reflection. I do this very often, and regularly.

A leader based in Egypt – on reflective leadership:

I have set up my own business here in Egypt recently, and it's growing. I must admit that I'm a beginner in being a leader, and I have probably made many mistakes. I have tried to think about why I make these mistakes and what I need to do to be more effective. In some ways I think I'm quite a 'soft' manager – not 'weak' I hope, but not that 'tough' either.

One ongoing problem in particular is with two women who work for me – and I don't know what to do about it. One of them is an old family retainer who has worked for my father and now for me for many years. I know she is very fond of me, and is quite possessive. She has never married and has few interests outside work. I dare not fire her because she might go into a huge decline and become very depressed. I know I feel a great obligation to keep employing her. But this might be a big mistake. I hired a consultant to work with her and she advised me to help her find other interests and gradually let her go. But somehow I haven't been able to follow this advice, although rationally I know it is right.

The negative implications of her continued employment with me are several and serious. She acts as a gatekeeper and won't let anyone come and see me unless she approves them first. Worst of all, she is obsessively jealous of another, younger woman who heads up my sales team, who is one of my star employees. When we go on a business trip, she keeps this younger woman away from me by booking her on another flight! She tries to stop information going to the younger woman and to make her look incompetent whenever possible. I know it makes me look bad in front of my staff – that I cannot manage this situation – but I really don't know what to do. I want to keep both these women, but at the moment their combative relationship (the younger woman is also beginning to obsess against the older one) is causing stress and reduced productivity in the office. I know I need to be more decisive and sometimes make tough decisions, but my personality is stopping me, and I am suffering the consequences.

On the other hand, my thoughtful and quiet approach to leadership and lack of leadership experience – I bought a company fairly late in life and I'm learning to manage and lead the people I've hired – can be an advantage. I have a less domineering attitude to the people, which is a pleasant contrast, I'm told, with the average manager in Egypt, who is bossy and demanding. It's a 'high power-distant' country, so people accept leaders who are unapproachable and expect instant obedience, and I'm not like that.

A finance leader based in Southern Europe – on reflective leadership:

I'm in charge of a leading hotel in our city and, even though I hate to admit it because I'm very patriotic – outsiders can be more effective in the project management of change initiatives at our property. If we had used a local guy he would have come up with lots of excuses about why the project was running late, why it was costing more, and why it wasn't quite what we wanted. But, thinking about it, having a foreigner in charge meant we had more action on the spot. There were no special relationships with suppliers. He was always in charge. He could get a more sustained performance out of local staff. He wouldn't allow them to cut corners and not do their work properly. In over thirty years in this job, I've never had a project completed on time and on budget in this way before, so I've thought about what was different this time. It was this foreign project manager who was very driven to sticking to the deadline. I wonder how I can change my local project managers and make them more effective? I could send them on courses but really we're looking here at a need for culture change. So I would have to change the performance measures, the rewarded behaviours, the incentives. Make it difficult to cut corners, and crack down hard on petty corruption. I would need to institute penalties for late completion, as I know is done in other places. I would be very unpopular and it would take time, but it would make a big difference.

In each of these three examples the personal reflections of each of the leaders have different results. In the first, the leader uses reflection in a very positive way. Reflective space and time are resources for him to consider the processes of his business and to analyse his own performance. The reflective space is not only used to reflect and analyse but is also used to draw up solutions to the problems of laying out plans for improvement. Additionally, the reflective space is a way for this leader to document success and failure and keep a record of what he still needs to do and what he still wants to accomplish.

In the second example, the reflective leader is using the reflective space positively to identify and understand the complexities of a human-resource problem. However, he is failing to act, and is finding excuses to justify the way he operates. The reflective space and time is being used to identify and analyse, but not to generate solutions. Reflection can be an excuse to procrastinate.

Finally, in the third example we see a leader analysing a very specific situation, the engagement of a foreign project manager for a hotel renovation. While it seems the leader in question initially had reservations about bringing in a non-local project manager, upon reflection he sees the benefits this has brought about. By analysing this situation with an open mind the leader discovered that this was a particularly good decision, and perhaps has identified this as a solution to streamlining future building projects, as he has started to think about what could be done to bring such objectivity to all his projects.

What happens if a leader does things without thinking and reflection? There are many examples in the business literature. Michael O'Leary of Ryanair banned unions from recruiting members amongst his staff, and his staff from joining a union – but he didn't think through the implications of all his staff negotiating individually with the airline, which became very time-consuming. Another knee-jerk reaction was trying to save money by buying less ice for the in-flight services, but he then discovered that many passengers didn't want to buy drinks any more – especially at the high prices charged by Ryanair – if they couldn't have ice with them.

The Enron bankruptcy case of the early years of this century also includes many examples of a lack of reflection by the executives. Think about the implications of the California power scandal, whereby Enron traded in local electric power, forcing the prices up by rolling black-outs which systematically closed down part of the grid. Enron made lots of money in the short term but the great energy-trading rip-off in California effectively killed the company.

Reflective leadership is helpful to leaders who want to think about how they can improve, how they can solve problems, and how and why they are successful in certain circumstances but not in others. But it takes time and a certain interest in intellectual pursuits to be reflective. Many leaders haven't the patience for it – action is more important than thinking! But a drawback of knee-jerk leadership is a failure to learn from mistakes. Tacit knowledge can lead to good instincts, but these can be more powerful if they are thought through. It's a trade-off – speed and instinct versus time and intellectualizing.

FURTHER READING

Bryman, Alan, Collinson, David L., Grint, Keith and Jackson, Brad (2011) *The Sage Handbook of Leadership*. London: Sage.

Colvin, Geoff (2009) 'How to build great leaders', *Fortune*, 4 December, 160 (10), http://money.cnn.com/magazines/fortune/fortune_archive/2009

Creaton, Siobhan (2007) *Ryanair: the full story of the controversial low-cost airline*. London: Aurum Press.

Gladwell, M. (2005) *Blink: the power of thinking without thinking*. New York: Time Warner.

Gosling, J. and Minzberg, H. (2003) 'The five minds of the manager', *Harvard Business Review*, November, 81(11): 54–63.

Grint, K. (2010) 'The sacred in leadership: separation, sacrifice and silence', *Organization Studies*, 31 (1): 89–107.

Johnson, Craig E. (2011) *Meeting the Ethical Challenge of Leadership*. Thousand Oaks, CA: Sage.

Kets de Vries, Manfred (2009) *Reflections on Character and Leadership: on the couch with Manfred Kets de Vries*. San Francisco, CA: Jossey-Bass.

Ladkin, D. (2010) *Rethinking Leadership*. Cheltenham: Edward Elgar.

McLean, B. and Elkind, P. (2003) *The Smartest Guys in the Room: the amazing rise and scandalous fall of Enron*. New York: Penguin.

Mintzberg, H. (1994). *The Rise and Fall of Strategic Planning: reconceiving roles for planning, plans, planners*. New York: Free Press.

30

Long-term Leadership and Project Management Leadership

> *Some leaders thrive on leading specific, discrete projects which each have a beginning, middle and end; others see organizational life as a continuous process, like an endless soap opera, albeit punctuated by short-term projects and other episodes.*

Long-term leadership can also be seen as programme leadership, which encapsulates a long-term intention, with many complex interdependent aspects, many of which can be parcelled up as discrete, finite projects. Coping with the pressures of project management is particularly challenging and difficult for leaders of long-term programmes, who have the responsibility for a whole system. In previous entries we have focused on Continuity-based Leadership, Developmental-oriented Leadership, Legacy Leadership, and Tenured Leadership. Here we contrast these long-term foci with leaders who prefer contained project management, related to Change-oriented Leadership, Job-hopping Leadership, Opportunistic Leadership, etc.

One area of challenge for the project manager is to sustain his or her own 'will and skill' to do the job. What does this mean? On the 'will' side, projects tend to be short, so the leader must be self-motivated, time and time again. Just as the team members become familiar and the leader enjoys working with them, one project finishes and a new project starts. Just as the leader is enjoying the accolades of doing a good job, he or she is back to square one, with no work and looking for the next project. This type of leadership has none of the permanence and routine of a regular job, and needs the ability to create and bond with a new team each time. No wonder many leaders and managers are more comfortable with a steady-state situation, especially in terms of the reduced need to be constantly motivated to take on a new challenge every time.

Programme-oriented positions enable the leader to gradually accumulate competencies, whereas project management keeps demanding the same ones over and over again. On the 'skill' side, being a project manager is far from easy to do well – especially compared with less urgent, less task-oriented ways of working. It requires working to tight deadlines, within a specific budget, having to meet the quality definitions and expectations of the client or principal stakeholder, and to manage the relationships involved in the project as a whole. Successful project managers are able to find interest and excitement in the unique challenges of each new project. They approach it as a constant learning curve.

Programme-oriented, long-term leaders may be more suited to permanent leadership roles. Project managers are usually action-oriented, highly involved, living in the here-and-now – and can be pragmatic and opportunistic: the project must be completed! Although some are highly analytical, there are also successful project managers who are quite unstructured and free-flowing in their approach (see the related entries Change-Oriented Leadership and Continuity-based Leadership, Developmental-oriented Leadership and Job-hopping Leadership, 'Here-and-now' Leadership and Legacy Leadership, Interim and Tenured Leadership).

Here, an experienced project manager shares his views on the pressures faced by this type of leader, and suggests competencies that are needed to survive in the world of projects – a vastly different environment from the regular, permanent position enjoyed by stable, salaried staff.

A project manager – on the extreme challenges of project management leadership:

Time Management is especially important in projects. The project leader must provide accurate information to suppliers, to ensure that there are no delays in producing the materials and other items needed. If any relevant information is missing, it can take time trying to find out the details. All this 'to-ing' and 'fro-ing' takes time and leads to delays. Everything must be specified to an exact standard, otherwise suppliers will keep coming back asking more questions. What colour? What size? Which material? To keep everyone involved in the project on time, the project leader has to keep monitoring the main contractor, the sub-contractor – all of them – and making inspections of sites to see how the work is progressing, even wandering around factories to inspect the progress of an order, identifying potential delays before they happen. Anticipating problems with staff members also saves time – who is happily getting on with the job and can be left with minimal supervision? Who is lagging behind and getting stuck? Time management is one of the hardest jobs in being a successful project leader, when most projects are highly perishable, and on-time delivery is one of the most critical components of success.

Cost management is another vital element in project leadership. Anyone can spend a lot of money; the challenge is to manage resources to achieve the goals which have been set. Careful project managers build in contingency funds, but the leadership is more than this. They know that clearly defining the scope of work at the beginning is crucial. Leaders must work closely with the rest of the management team: the FD, the design team, and the project client. Any new ideas which cost money may have to be nipped in the bud, unless additional budgets are available. The leader may end up saying 'no' more than 'yes', and will not be popular in the process. Yet time and cost constraints are a given for all projects, and project leaders are called on to be forthright and clear in defending their positions and championing their projects. They are also required to be transparent, honest and ethical when it comes to money matters – control of time and cost means being in control of suppliers at all times. Control can be lost if relationships with suppliers become too close. What if a special deal is struck with a supplier and then he doesn't perform? The project manager is in no position to exert control, and things start getting out of control.

Managing expectations is a third task of the project leader, in terms of the need to achieve client satisfaction in terms of his or her quality expectations. On time and on budget is one thing, but if the client doesn't like the project, the project leader is in trouble. Again, there is a need for a clear definition of scope from the outset. What do the principal stakeholders want? This is especially difficult if they don't know what they want. Part of the project leader's job helps them to know, in such a way that they don't feel pressurized. He or she may not prevent disappointment, and some clients are never happy, but leaders need to champion each project in a highly committed way, gaining approval for each step, refusing to tolerate negativity and doom-saying, but will turn these people around, so that everyone expects the project outcome to be successful, and thereby increasing the chances that it will be.

Managing relationships is a fourth task, managing all the different stakeholders in a project especially challenging because it will have so many unknowns. Arranging that all the stakeholders have signed off on the project from the beginning is one of the most difficult tasks. There will be a need for a high level of exact specifications, according to the requirements of all the stakeholders, bearing in mind that they are biased to their own needs at the cost of those of others. Stakeholders will include people who will have to live and work with the project long after the designers and builders have left. Project managers must think beyond the here and now, but of the impact of their projects is in years to come. Consulting all stakeholders and taking all their needs into account is difficult and time-consuming but must be done to ensure the successful management of all these different relationships. Gaining the support of all the stakeholders early on also wins allies against potential critics as the project progresses.

The competencies of a project leader include being diligent, adaptable and able to handle project variances all the time. He or she has to foresee potential risks, making careful risk analysis, but not allowing this to prevent the important task of seeing and taking advantage of opportunities. The people working on the project must be encouraged to carry through the necessary changes. It won't work if the team can see the problems but won't do anything about them, lack initiative and wait to be told what to do next. As the project progresses, the leader will often get more and more involved and occupied, anticipating and dealing with problems, not as a 'super-doer' but as a team leader.

The less-than-perfect project leader may be paying attention to certain aspects of the project but not to others. He or she must look at everything. The need for health and safety requirements is often seen as boring and far from glamorous, but cannot be ignored. The project manager has to juggle all these different balls in the air. He or she has to keep seeing the big picture, obtaining a first-hand view of the progress of the project, not staying in the office all day.

Successful project leaders tend to conceive of their careers as a series of projects, like stepping-stones to nowhere in particular. For many it is a deliberate choice to steer clear of the compromises of corporate careers. Project leadership requires a liking for variety and constant change, and the need to keep starting again. The job of project management needs not just expertise, but also general management ability, flexibility and the drive to learn new things. In these situations leadership requires being action-oriented and leading from the front, especially as a project nears completion and the pressure is mounting.

Project leadership requires tight control of resources and people, but with an ability to inspire people with a sense of urgency. In project leadership the task of building a willing followership can mean talking with and consulting the most junior people, seeking their support and help, winning them over from the very beginning. At the same time, all the inputs must be closely monitored. At the end of the day, the project manager/leader is only as good as his or her most recent project, and this defines his or her reputation. Consistency and staying-power can be the most challenging requirement. More long-term positions might not experience such pressures!

FURTHER READING

Figenti, E. and Comninos, D. (2002) *The Practice of Project Management*. London: Kogan Page.

Jones, S. and Duffy, P. (2009a) 'Staying on top in project management', *The Effective Executive*, September.

Jones, S. and Duffy, P. (2009b) 'Twelve reasons for project management failure', *The Global CEO*, October, pp. 11–15.

Northouse, Peter Guy (2010) *Leadership: theory and practice*. Thousand Oaks, CA: Sage.

Project Management Institute (2008) *The Project Management Body of Knowledge*, 4th edition. Pennsylvania, PN: PMI.

31
Macro-leadership and Micro-leadership

> *Visionary, big-picture and strategic leadership styles may be contrasted with a more day-to-day and tactical approach.*

Macro-leadership and micro-leadership are different levels of focus. The macro-level is more about vision, strategy and future planning whereas the micro-level is more about management of an organization's day-to-day activities. Should either focus predominate, or does excellent leadership depend on both functions being carried out simultaneously or at least sequentially? The debate is explored in many discussions, including in *The Five Minds of the Manager* (Gosling and Mintzberg, 2003). Management without leadership can be humdrum and boring, whilst leadership without management can be exciting but out of control.

Consider the following commonly cited characteristics of leading and managing. Leading involves:

- creating a clear and compelling vision;
- making major change happen;
- achieving breakthroughs in performance;
- taking big risks and innovating;
- developing and implementing strategy.

Managing means:

- facing the current reality, and taking action;
- controlling and keeping things in a state of balance;
- achieving incremental improvements in performance;
- staying loyal to the mission;
- managing or mitigating risk;
- managing tactics.

Clearly, any organization needs both leadership and management, but it has been fashionable to draw a clear distinction, suggesting that some people are leaders, whilst others are managers, who fail to focus their attention above anything but day-to-day affairs, and are slow to step up to the challenge of defining and articulating a vision and purpose for their organization. But actually most managerial jobs involve quite a lot of leadership and vice-versa; indeed, the distinction works better in theory than in practice.

However, this does not mean that leaders have to personally attend to all leading and managing responsibilities. In many organizations this would be practically impossible. Leaders need to be aware of their leadership and managerial requirements, but be able to trust, work with and benefit from the abilities of others. Those with a stronger tendency to be inspirational, visionary, big-picture thinkers, action-oriented, risk-taking – will need people who can manage – in terms of the day-to-day concerns, having an eye for detail, being focused on implementation, and able to keep a handle on what may be happening on the ground, ideally with inventiveness and cunning, because local solutions to humdrum problems can sometimes turn out to be the foundations of new directions. Leadership sometimes comes from managers.

If one person can do all of this – vision, problem-solving and administration – the results can be fabulous (Admiral Lord Nelson was a prime example). In most cases a leadership team can achieve the same results. Leaders who have a handle on the big picture, an understanding of the details, and who can bring all the parts together in a compelling way, are a very powerful resource for a top team.

Ideally, as we have suggested, the leader and manager roles would be combined in the same person. But if they have to be brought together in a team of two or more, we suggest there are four key elements in the relationship between leaders and managers. To begin with, there has to be trust, first that things can quickly get back on track if they go wrong, and that there will be no blame; second, that there are clear intentions, so managers can be left to get on with it, with no micro-management – or 'long screwdriver' – from the centre; third, that responsibility is felt on both sides. There is a need to take on responsibility as a leader, whilst knowing how the system works as a manager. Finally, both sides must appreciate the risks involved (Jones and Gosling, 2005: 146–8).

Macro-oriented leaders belong in the same categories as those described elsewhere in this volume as action-oriented and leading from the front; they might be celebrities, they might be heroic, they could be extrovert generalists favouring broad-based leadership, and could be purposive with shaper tendencies (see related entries). Micro-oriented leaders may well be more continuity-based, collaborative introverts who operate behind the scenes and may also be expert in a sector or function (see related entries).

Here, we look at examples of an extreme macro-leader and an extreme micro-manager, neither being really satisfactory as they are. We then consider an example of a combination of these approaches.

An HR/development consultant – on the extreme macro-leader:

Imagine an infectiously inspirational individual, with all the outrageous behaviour of an extroverted personality, overseeing a globally active consulting firm. This particular leader was very sociable, and was well remembered for his antics in bars and restaurants around the world. The leader had a certain joie de vivre. He was wild and uncontrollable, but had the most amazing ideas. His employees were highly motivated to achieve targets and would go the extra mile to help achieve his vision for the consulting firm. The people he recruited were quite adventurous and had something unusual to offer, such as specific expertise, language skills, qualifications, contacts in certain high places and a desire for travel and taking on challenging tasks.

Though his colleagues were all fired up, the firm was mismanaged. There were conflicts in the firm between the crazy, visionary leadership side and the careful, prudent, administrative side. This extreme macro-leader drove the firm's 'bean-counters' crazy. It was enormous fun but a complete disaster. Eventually the leader's focus on visionary ideas to the exclusion of all practicalities and without any prudent financial management led the firm to bankruptcy. Despite their adoration and commitment to the leader and the mission of the firm, the employees found themselves unemployed, and missing an entire year's salary and bonuses.

This was a charismatic leader. Through his vision, drive, energy and larger-than-life personality, he inspired followership. His employees loved him and worked hard for him. However, his lack of managerial skills, knowledge of management or even respect for some people desperately trying to manage resources led to the demise of the firm. This leader was so caught up with the macro-focus that he neglected the micro-focus practical realities of managing a business. He was so busy leading he ignored the mechanisms that supported his ability to lead and in the end his leadership failed. It was quite a fun ride while it lasted, but none of his team could sustain it for long.

An emerging market consultant – on the extreme micro-leader:

The extreme micro-focused leader is obsessed with managing every detail of an operation to the point of disempowering and intimidating employees so the work environment itself becomes unhealthy or even unbearable. In this example of an extreme manager, an expatriate Westerner was running a business in the Middle East, which was referred to by her employees as the Gulag, Stalag or Colditz. You may be getting the message…

The manager was obsessively controlling, looming over every matter of expenditure to the point where the tiniest order of paper clips or ball-point pens had to be approved by her personally. When she was away from the office, nothing happened. If she suspected that an employee might not turn up for work, she would send someone around to his or her apartment to see where he or she was, especially if this employee ignored phone calls. When staff returned from leave, they were required to sign a form saying they were back and were returning to work. For a time, the manager even kept all staff passports locked in her safe to prevent anyone from leaving the country without permission. She wanted to have access to everyone's bank account details to check that they were not earning more money by moonlighting. There was no sense of purpose, no value-system beyond control, no plan for the future, just day-to-day grind, hard labour in the prison yard. Many employees quit as soon as possible.

This extreme micro-manager is no leader at all, despite having a job title usually associated with leadership. Such individuals are so preoccupied with minutiae that they cannot provide the vision and strategy required in leadership. In extreme management situations the development and maintenance of followership is very difficult, if not impossible. Extreme managers are often deluded into thinking they are leading. But as indicated in the above situation, followers only follow out of intimidation and will do so only as long as there is no other option. When they can leave, they will do so as soon as possible.

A researcher on leadership – on the ideal leader–manager mix, quoting from a biographer of Admiral Lord Nelson, speaking in almost hagiographic terms:

> Nelson was amazing. He had true clarity of vision, of what had to be done and how it was to be achieved. He was in command at a time when a real emergency was facing the navy and the country, yet had a chance to be more successful than ever before. By 1805, with an invasion army ready on the Normandy coast, the navy stood for the survival of the British nation; and at the same time was the guarantee of the vast and rapidly spreading commercial empire that fuelled the agricultural and industrial revolution. To be a leader in the navy at that time carried far more weight than simply being the top sailor! In the view of the country as a whole (and Napoleon's assessment), it was one of the world's most powerful and prestigious organizations of the time. Nelson made the vision of dealing with this emergency the most important thing for his sailors. They readily understood it and believed in it. It was risky and action-oriented, and they bought into the heroic idiom it represented. The narrative of patriotism was used to tremendous effect, notwithstanding the active critique of terms and conditions, of poor management, expressed in large-scale mutinies by sailors at the Nore and Spithead, naval ports in Britain.
>
> But although he had these strong inspirational attributes, he was dedicated and meticulous about small, day-to-day things. He was diligent in helping others. He was a bit of an insomniac, and often wrote more than 20 memos before breakfast, many to help people get new jobs and get resources they needed. He never forgot someone who had done something he admired, and was full of praise and support for his immediate subordinates, who worshipped the ground he walked on. He had an amazing memory for people and remembered names and faces and things they had done for him. When he met someone – and he came in contact with hundreds of people – he would speak to them in an intimate, friendly, individual way, even though he was in a

very senior military rank and was something of a celebrity. He had this fantastic ability to see the big picture of what everyone was working towards, yet to appreciate the finer details of what was needed to keep a very big organization operational in difficult circumstances. He literally combined this focus on long-term, visionary leadership with day-to-day administration in a very supportive way.

Macro-leadership, with great vision and inspiration, is exciting and attractive, and many people will be attracted by it. But will it really happen the way the leader has described it? Or will it be an empty dream? This is the big question with a leader who sees the future, but not necessarily how to get there. It all sounds great, but will it actually work out? A management-oriented leader can be so practical and nit-picking that it puts people off. They can't see a future plan, just a daily grind. It's tedious and settles into a repetitive routine very quickly. There's no time to think about where things are going and people feel like cogs in a machine.

What the best leadership requires is both leadership and management. When they come together – whether in one individual or through a leadership team – things get done and positive results can emerge and grow.

FURTHER READING

Alvesson, M. and Sveningsson, S. (2003) 'Managers doing leadership: the extra-ordinarization of the mundane', University of Lund Institute of Economic Research Working Paper.

Bryman, Alan, Collinson, David L., Grint, Keith and Jackson, Brad (2011) *The Sage Handbook of Leadership*. London: Sage.

Conger, Jay Alden and Kanungo, RabindraNath (1998) *Charismatic Leadership in Organizations*. Thousand Oaks, CA: Sage.

Fryer, B. (2004) 'The micromanager', *Harvard Business Review*, September, 82(9): 31–40.

Gosling, J. and Mintzberg, H. (2003) 'The five minds of the manager', *Harvard Business Review*, September, 81(11): 54–63.

Grint, K. (2010) 'The sacred in leadership: separation, sacrifice and silence', *Organization Studies*, 31 (1): 89–107.

Haslam, S.A., Reicher, S. and Platow, M. (2011) *The New Psychology of Leadership: identity, influence and power*. New York: Psychology Press.

Jones, S. and Gosling, J. (2005) *Nelson's Way: leadership lessons from the great commander*. London: Nicholas Brealey.

Katzenbach J. and Smith, D. (1994) *The Wisdom of Teams*. New York: Harper Business.

Leithwood, Kenneth A., Muscall, Blair and Strauss, Tiiu (2009) *Distributed Leadership According to the Evidence*. New York: Routledge.

Mintzberg, H. (1973) *The Nature of Managerial Work*. New York: Harper & Row.

Northouse, Peter Guy (2010) *Leadership: theory and practice*. Thousand Oaks, CA: Sage.

Pfeffer, J. (1994) *Managing with Power: politics and influence in organizations*. Boston, MA: Harvard Business School Press.

Snook, Scott A., Nohria, Nitin N. and Khurana, Rakesh (2012) *The Handbook for Teaching Leadership: knowing, doing and being*. Thousand Oaks, CA: Sage.

key concepts in leadership

32
Nurturing Leadership and Toxic Leadership

> *Some leaders create toxic environments, poisoning relationships and destroying motivation; others foster a constructive and development-oriented culture.*

Some leaders are lucky enough to operate in mostly constructive and positive organizational environments – and they may also have a tendency to encourage this state in the way they operate. By contrast, the term 'toxic leadership' generally refers to the idea that an environment for leadership, a specific leader, and even leadership as an activity, can act like a poison, weakening and even destroying an otherwise healthy organization. A certain style of leadership can be actively healthy and growing and – conversely – damaging and destructive. The leader can have a positive, nurturing influence – or a negative, debilitating influence. An organization can be healthy and help other organizations to improve, and it can be toxic too, and infect others in a long-term damaging way. Toxicity in organizations can be the result of constant change and an authoritative, directive, task-oriented and micro-managing approach, but not necessarily. It can result from an excessively knee-jerk rather than a reflective approach – but it represents an extreme (see the related entries Change-oriented Leadership and Continuity-based Leadership, Authoritarian Leadership and Participative Leadership, Coaching and Mentoring-oriented Leadership and Directive, Telling-what-to-do Leadership, Knee-jerk Leadership and Reflective Leadership). Toxicity can emerge in both private- and public-sector organizations, and even in not-for-profits and among volunteers. It can evolve quickly or slowly, and it can take an organization a long time to recover from toxicity, rather like a person suffering from a long-term illness.

Here we look at an example of a toxic leader, and the negative impact which he brought to his organization. We then consider toxic organizations, how they get this way, and how we can possibly deal with it. There are many reasons for the development of toxicity, especially insecurity, hanging-on to power, suspicion and mistrust. Even positive leadership can become toxic over time.

An HR/development consultant – on an extreme toxic leader:

Our Managing Director was appointed by the Board to keep an eye on what we are doing in the organization. He certainly does that, but in a way that is making everyone retreat into self-preserving behaviours. Many of the staff members say they don't want to come to work because of him. He is critical in non-constructive ways. He has created his own power base, and anxiously protects it. If anyone threatens him, he tries to move them into another position out of his way. I applied for a job reporting to him, temporarily replacing a colleague away for a year. The colleague agreed that I was perfect for the job, and encouraged me to apply. But he saw me as a threat, so he changed the location, pay and tax implications of the job, which left me no alternative but to withdraw my application.

When colleagues ask him for an appointment, he agrees and sets the time and date for a meeting, but then cancels it five minutes before the meeting, even when the person has flown in from overseas at considerable expense to the organization. He has moved his favourite departments of the organization under his area of responsibility, even if they do not logically work together and the organization chart looks really stupid. He became 50 this year and was obviously looking for somewhere to make his mark. He made a new strategic plan which was so ridiculously flawed it was a joke. He could not counter the arguments of those who attacked it, so he just cancelled any meetings scheduled with them, in order to defend himself in the only way he could.

He never thanks anyone for their help nor offers praise or encouragement. The atmosphere of the organization has become totally toxic. The employees protect their own domains, seeing any offers of help as encroachment rather than assistance. When I joined the organization, I was told to 'keep my head down, do my job, never answer emails, and certainly never send emails'. He's really practising leadership by exception in the active mode, as he knows what everyone has done wrong, but not anything about what they have done well, and nothing about their personal issues, such as bereavement or other family matters.

He would conduct performance appraisals with his staff and leave them depressed and de-motivated for weeks. He was getting worse. Then suddenly he was sacked. The burden lifted from the organization was immense. To a certain extent the business is still toxic, it will take a while to recover, and the good people he sacked are still missing and the bad systems he introduced are still there, but the overall feeling is more positive. He was allowed to get away with his toxicity for too long, and was unmanaged, and was really in the wrong job, because he became toxic out of defensiveness, because he was out of his depth and did not understand the business environment in which he was operating. So in some ways it wasn't completely his fault.

An alternative use of the term implies that taking on a leadership role can have toxic effects on the person who becomes a leader. It is this latter meaning that has most prominence in the world of executive coaching, because it is often convenient for coaches to assure their clients who are leaders that their problems arise from the harmful effects of the job they do and the organization for which they work, not themselves. The job itself is inherently toxic because the organization encourages negative behaviours. Conversely, other organizations can be positive and encourage constructive behaviours, even in those leaders who are not disposed towards this way of operating.

The toxic organization concept is exemplified by the case of Enron (in addition to the many financial institutions embroiled in the sub-prime market crisis), which ultimately dissolved into bankruptcy. The traders, excited by the pressure of making deals and carried away by the thrill of making millions, behaved like gamblers in a casino. Observers related the phenomenon to the 'Milgram Experiments' of the 1960s and 1970s, which asked if there was such a thing as an inherently evil person, or if ordinary people were capable of evil acts when encouraged by persons in authority willing to sanction such acts (see Abelson et al., 2004). When Enron was broking electric power in California, forcing the prices up to make greater profits, even with the result of power outages causing personal hardships for the inhabitants, the traders found themselves sucked into the game. The organization was itself toxic.

An author and researcher on leadership – on organizational toxicity:

In the first meaning – that leadership can poison an organization, or in the context of 'a fish rots from the head' as Sun Tzu says – we are assuming that organizations are like organic substances, living beings or even complex ecosystems that can be harmed by the impact of toxins. The metaphor of a living system implies a high degree of interdependency, functions reliant on each other, and also an ability to adapt and evolve, but all within a certain degree of constancy and continuity.

Bad or negative leadership, as we have seen in the case above, might have a subtle and slow-acting effect on the life of the system of an organization in any number of ways, and is likely to be through a demoralizing effect on working relationships. These might be the effect of the personality of the leader (as in the example above) and through the making of poor strategic choices. In fact, if we think that leadership is only 'direction setting', we are thinking of the leader more like the driver of a car, making a defined set of mechanical processes, rather than as part of a living system. This can easily be 'toxic', which affects every other part.

So by using the term 'toxic leadership' we are approaching an organization as if we are medics rather than mechanics. Why would we want to do that? First, if we are members of the organization in question, it's not much fun to think of ourselves as cogs in a machine; far better to be self-willed humans in a living environment, even if it is a bit polluted by the leadership. Second, if we are consultants, students or analysts looking at the organization as if it were suffering from an illness, we can begin to think about a route back to health, and can consider a wide range of treatments, from radical surgery (remove the leader, for example) to an exercise regime (quality improvement programmes, for example), and many others besides. Third, as organizational researchers we can study the epidemiology of leadership: in what circumstances does it turn sour, which varieties are most virulent and resistant to treatment, how does it adapt to new environments and is there a certain amount of toxic leadership below the surface in every population?

The toxic effects of leadership can be mistrust, disengagement, cynicism, sabotage, low morale, despair. Leadership is likely to be a part of the rot if it is exploitative, abusive, bullying, self-absorbed, selfish, dishonest or malicious. It can be caused by a leader with a dysfunctional personality, or by the effects of destructive team dynamics especially in senior management.

It is usually manifest as sustained misuse of power; an organization with a healthy system of checks and balances can survive a toxic leader for a while, or even adapt to make use of that person's particular strengths. But very often those adaptations become compromises that simply spread the rot of cynicism and dishonesty.

An academic – on a positive environment turned toxic:

I was working for a university which was a branch campus of an Australian university, and the branch was located in the Middle East. The Australians working there were fun-loving and almost permanently in a holiday mood. They did their work competently, but they knew how to enjoy themselves, and had fantastic parties and outings and a way of making laid-back jokes about everything. The students picked up the mood to a certain extent, and there was a highly positive culture, reinforced by good HR systems which ensured that everyone was looked after. Then things changed. The university was facing profitability challenges – not because of a lack of students – but because of rising costs imposed by the management company which ran the campus facilities, owned by the local authorities who thought they had a captive market and pushed the prices up. Then the Australians and other Western expatriates were sent home, as they were too expensive. The university was then dominated by staff members with fewer alternative career options (from North Africa and South Asia), whose main priority was job security, and worked out ways to live with the increasingly toxic leadership of the institution.

Dealing with toxic leadership is difficult because it is caused by deeply pathological behaviours. These are not easily identified by popular categories of leadership styles. It is not enough to say that 'authoritarian leaders are toxic', because this is obviously not always the case. But underlying some authoritarian behaviours, and some chronically consultative dithering, are pathological problems that will spread rapidly throughout an organization. It is not quite right to say that some people are toxic: rather, some people have toxic effects in certain circumstances, and this might be because of changes in their own inner life, or undeclared toxicity in the relationships among senior staff. It is very hard to pin down and, like most poisonings, by the time one knows it's happening it is too late to stop it. A perfectly decent person can become poisoned by pride and hubris if over-egged by a recruitment process, and this rapidly ruins a team's sense of collective achievement. Ambition, drive, competitiveness and passion can lead to successful leadership outcomes, but can also deteriorate into negativity. Curing a toxic environment is not easy, and leaders who are capable of nurturing an organization back to health are hugely valuable. It's a complex picture, and seldom the work of just one person.

FURTHER READING

Case, Peter and Gosling, Jonathan (2007) 'Wisdom of the moment: pre-modern perspectives on organizational action', *Social Epistemology*, special issue on Wisdom and Stupidity in Management, 22 (4).

Colvin, Geoff (2009) 'How to build great leaders', *Fortune*, 4 December, 160 (10), http://money.cnn.com/magazines/fortune/fortune_archive/2009

Creaton, Siobhan (2007) *Ryanair: the full story of the controversial low-cost airline.* London: Aurum Press.

Goldman, Alan (2009) *Transforming Toxic Leaders.* Stanford, CA: Stanford University Press.

Johnson, Craig E. (2011) *Meeting the Ethical Challenge of Leadership.* Thousand Oaks, CA: Sage.

Jones, David. (2005) *NEXT to Me: luck, leadership and living with Parkinson's.* London: Nicholas Brealey.

Kets de Vries, Manfred (2009) *Reflections on Character and Leadership: on the couch with Manfred Kets de Vries.* San Francisco, CA: Jossey-Bass.

key concepts in leadership

Kusy, Mitchell and Holloway, Elizabeth (2009) *Toxic Workplace: managing toxic personalities and their systems of power.* San Francisco, CA: John Wiley.

Lipman-Blumen, Jean (2005) *The Allure of Toxic Leaders: why we follow destructive bosses and corrupt politicians – and how we can survive them.* New York: Oxford University Press.

McLean, B. and Elkind, P. (2003) *The Smartest Guys in the Room: the amazing rise and scandalous fall of Enron.* New York: Penguin.

Pfeffer, J. (1994) *Managing with Power: politics and influence in organizations.* Boston, MA: Harvard Business School Press.

Rooke, D. and Torbert, W. (2005) 'The seven transformations of leadership', *Harvard Business Review*, April: 66–76.

Shaw, J.B., Erickson, A. and Harvey, M. (2011) 'A method for measuring destructive leadership and identifying types of destructive leaders in organizations', *The Leadership Quarterly*, 22: 575–590.

Snook, Scott A., Nohria, Nitin N. and Khurana, Rakesh (2012) *The Handbook for Teaching Leadership: knowing, doing and being.* Thousand Oaks, CA: Sage.

33
Pragmatic Leadership and Principles-driven Leadership

> *Leading for the betterment of others has become a mission for many contemporary leaders; others consider that 'the business of business is business'.*

The future for leadership and leadership development arguably now lies as much in valuing and developing ethical, moral and socially responsible leadership as in meeting narrow project objectives and maximizing profit margins. Leaders are challenged to respond to pressures to be green and sustainable in the midst of an economic recession. Following a strict ethical code in leading an organization has become more and more of an active, explicit requirement since the business world has been rocked by massive corporate scandals, such as Enron, WorldCom and the sub-prime mortgage crisis. 'Corporate governance' and 'corporate social responsibility' are popular terms in everyday business-speak. But many business leaders are more impressed by Milton Friedman's assertion that 'the social responsibility of business is to increase its profits' (1970). This is not to suggest that business people behave unethically – far from it. Rather, that the ethics appropriate to business are encompassed in the logics of free enterprise; as a citizen and community member, business people have other responsibilities, nothing to do with profit.

The point is that all social activity, and especially leadership, is the expression of beliefs and customs about what is right, what is valued and what is appropriate. The argument, if there is one to be had, is not whether leadership is ethical, but which particular ethics are in use, and whether they are adequate to the needs of the situation. The call for leaders to behave ethically is usually better understood as a call to understand the situation in an expanded context – to consider the welfare of a larger set of stakeholders, for example, even 'future generations' or vast general categories such as 'the environment'. If this is understood as merely adherence to a code of conduct or set of rules, it can be experienced as a straitjacket, restricting a leader's way of operating, and putting him or her under a constant need to justify each decision. So the issue in this section is not so much between ethical and unethical leaders; rather it is between those who consciously focus on aims and methods that are informed by a moral position, and those who consider that the pragmatic needs of the situation speak for themselves.

On the other hand, can a pragmatic leader carry on in his or her pragmatic way indefinitely, or will he or she inevitably have to make a choice about the rights and wrongs of an action, and thus risk unethical behaviour? Is this kind of moral jeopardy an inevitable cost of doing business, or the essential nature of leadership itself?

It would be a mistake to equate principle-driven leadership with charity work, and pragmatic leadership with hard-nosed business. Many businesses are led and staffed by people with a passionate belief in the good their industry can do for the world – in energy, food, hygiene, defence, banking, and so forth – while charities are often led by intensely pragmatic people with a narrow focus on their own cause and a narrow constituency. Similarly, principle-driven leaders can be so driven by their long-term vision that they become quite authoritarian, and overlook the niceties of participation, inclusiveness and coaching. On the other hand, treating people well might be a core leadership principle, and override short-term objectives. As with many dichotomies that appear to make sense at first glance, the reality is more complex. (In relation to pragmatic leadership, see the related entries Authoritarian Leadership and Participative Leadership, Directive Leadership (Chapter 9) and Compromising Leadership and Co-operative Leadership; in relation to principles-driven leadership, see Individualistic Leadership and Relationship-oriented Leadership, Knee-jerk Leadership and Reflective Leadership, Goal-oriented Leadership and Opportunistic Leadership, and the 'Servant Leadership' section in 'Leadership Definition, Theory and Practice'.)

Here, we review the practical reflection of a business leader who appreciates the dilemma of trying to run an ethical business, whilst being pragmatic too; the challenges of training business ethics to practical business students; and the response of an industry sector as a whole to this issue. Overall, there is a widespread feeling that operating ethically is very important – but the business world puts significant pressures on a business leader, which may derail leadership activity into unethical and immoral behaviour. This is further problematized by the changing nature of ethics and morality, particularly in our twenty-first-century globalized world.

An ex-CEO/Management Consultant – on the business ethics dilemma:

A company needs to make money but it can still do this in an ethical way. Each business certainly needs to obey the law, be conscious of its environment, must not be exploitative, and must try to give back what it takes out. I think the typical business leader should be ethically sensitive, but with a balanced view of productivity. Debating these issues can put a brake on the company and slow decision-making. Making profits is important – but an overwhelming emphasis on profit can lead to short-term decision-making. Businesses have to make decisions, on investments, product developments and markets often in conditions of great uncertainty, so it is not surprising that they prefer options with fairly immediate returns. Ethical considerations are sometimes pretty clear-cut; and you at least know what you ought to do. But more often you can't be sure of the outcomes of whichever course of action you choose: there are just too many other factors outside your own control. So selecting what is right for the company, for the investors, for customers, for community members…it is always a matter of judgement. That is what leaders are expected to do, of course; people are far more likely to follow if they know what you stand for, what you value. Your values will inform every judgement you make, and every decision you take in any case; you can't just leave them behind, even if sometimes you feel you are compromising one set of values in the interests of another – there are always trade-offs, such as cutting down on an employee benefits programme in favour of improved bonuses for sales staff. But if agonizing over ethical considerations takes up too much of your energy, you should probably talk it through with someone impartial. Being stuck on the horns of a dilemma is uncomfortable if it goes on for too long!

What you decide today says something about your attitude towards the future. Perhaps this is more of a concern of leaders who are parents, and see the future through the eyes of their children and grandchildren. (Some people say wise judgement requires us to think of the next seven generations – Seventh Generation Inc, for example.) But notions of what counts as 'good' seldom stay fixed for long. Not long ago all hunting of animals was considered negatively. Now some targeted hunting of species (those becoming too dominant and threatening urban areas, or where hunting brings in tourist dollars to needy communities) is being advocated. Meanwhile, some principles-driven pressure groups are using unethical means to get their views across, such as making exaggerated accusations and interrupting normal business practice. Leaders have to be increasingly savvy about this, and know when to take these groups seriously or not. Leaders also have to be very sensitive to the views of their staff members to these ethical issues, to not alienate them when they have strong views, but be mindful of the overall business objectives too.

Some businesses discover an ethical way of operating almost by accident and then justify doing this, using the environmentally friendly image they have accidentally created as a valuable positioning tool, even pretending that this was their motivation all along.

For example, a packaging company I managed uses recyclable brown paper for business-to-business packaging. It didn't start off using paper rather than plastics for ethical reasons, but now that this is the practice, it can be justified on ethical grounds. Paper packaging can be recycled more easily and cheaply, and by planting trees, raw materials are sustainable. The company's focus on paper can be effective at the point of sale, as a strong differentiator. The salesmen tell customers that they don't sell plastic packaging – all the more reason to focus on paper as it makes the company sound ethically more convincing and consistent. If the company offered plastic packaging too it would undermine its own mission. It has also become of added-value to the clients, because they can say that their use of paper only in packaging makes them more CSR-compliant. So it helps to sell more products too.

This is an example of a company discovering a happy coincidence between economy and ethics – where pragmatic business decisions turn out to fit socially valued principles. Savvy leaders can sometimes find synergies between ethical concerns and business practices. Increasingly, particularly in relation to environmental and sustainability issues, as regulation and best practice norms develop, companies can actually improve their business long term by investing in more sustainable practices. With a more ethically concerned consumer market the value added through ethical business practices is increasingly more attractive in the marketplace (see, e.g., Laszlo and Zhexembayeva, 2011).

Ideas of what is right or wrong in business often have a cultural dimension. People within the same cultural setting often also share ethical assumptions – for example, about the rights of individuals, the morality of 'interest' and usury, giving and receiving gifts or 'baksheesh'. These hardly rank as ethical dilemmas for them because the choices are so obvious, but to outsiders – foreigners – these appear to be ethically-driven choices. But not all differences of this nature can be ascribed to culture: experience has a lot to do with it. The following example highlights some of the different opinions held by current and future managers. We see that it is quite a different matter to take an ethical position on something about which one does not have to act; and that those with experience of taking action – practising managers – are less likely to seek a moral high ground.

An MBA teacher – on the perception of business ethics:

> In Dubai I was trying to teach a business ethics class to a student group including UAE nationals, Iranians and expatriates from all over the Middle East and the Indian sub-continent. The students who were more academic, with less business experience, who were more reflective and philosophical, were fascinated by the ethical dilemmas and were heavily geared towards taking an ethical stance. Many of the younger ones, who came from rich families and had never been exposed to hardships or making difficult decisions, thought there was no argument – they would take the ethical choice each time.
>
> But many of the other students were totally pragmatic and business-oriented. If you could get away with being a bit unethical but make loads of money, good for you! If you got caught out by some ethics watch-dog or do-gooder whistle-blower, this was tough and unfortunate. Ethics were a luxury for the future, but business was practical here-and-now. These students were mostly less academic, with more business experience, and came from hard-working entrepreneurial families.
>
> We invited the Ethics Manager of a multinational electronics firm to the class to discuss ethics issues with the students. He explained that when he arrived at the firm and was given this appointment, he discovered that the brother of the Marketing Manager was running the firm's advertising agency, and had been paid practically all of the firm's PR and advertising budget. The 'ethical' students were shocked, pointing to the conflict of interest issues and how this was not right, fair, etc. The 'pragmatic'

students, on the other hand, could not see a problem with it. The ad agency boss was giving his brother a good price. Keeping it all in the family is the best idea – an outside firm might be a rip-off. The Marketing Manager would explain the firm's needs very clearly to his brother, because they were family and would have lunch at weekends, etc. There were definitely two sides to this issue!

This example contrasts the responses of two groups of relatively young people. Over time, and with the benefit (and costs!) of more experience, seeing the results of their decision, one would expect more changes in individual choices. But even the best-intentioned leaders can struggle to make their organizations reflect the values they would like to see: the logic of costs and benefits is such a powerful norm that individual managers are left to seek marginal opportunities for discretionary ethical practices. In the following example one researcher's work on multinational hotel chains showed that in many cases ethical practices were not standardized, as one might expect of such high-profile companies, but were developed on an ad hoc basis, and almost always justified in terms of the bottom line.

An emerging markets researcher – on the ethics of the bottom line:

I made a study of the multinational hotel sector, of several different hotels operating all over the world. These were nearly all big, five-star hotels, and I focused on the way they operated in developing countries. It was widely agreed by most observers of this industry in these countries that the hotel sector had a chance to really help regions in these countries to develop, based on encouraging sustainable tourism. I analysed and compared their ethics and CSR policies, especially in terms of the employment of local staff, the use of local suppliers, the encouragement of recycling, making donations to local charities, etc. Did these hotels give surplus food, furniture and equipment to the local communities? Did they ever help with supplying water and electricity to the surrounding village when they set up in remote areas? Did they give back to the community, or were they just alien enterprises, built and managed by foreigners, staffed and supplied by foreigners, offering holidays to foreign customers who would just come and go?

I must say, I expected these big hotel groups to have strong ethics and CSR policies at least, even if they didn't do much in reality (that was another question I didn't try to answer). But they didn't necessarily have this focus, and many ethics and CSR initiatives were the result of the interest and conscience of individuals working in the hotels. The management were only interested in ethics and CSR if it directly led to increased profits for shareholders. For example, they would hire locals if they were good, and cheaper than expatriates. They would source local goods and services only if they were cheap and easy to obtain and high quality. They wouldn't do much for the local community unless it cost very little and had a direct business benefit, such as cleaning their own hotel beach. All this stuff about not washing towels and sheets every day for a guest staying for several days, in order to protect the environment by using less detergent…they would do it because it saved time and money!

This commentator was frustrated that companies say they value environmental protection, but actually never put it at the forefront of their policies. The underlying values, the ones that are most important, are those of 'time and money', and it is these that underpin their ethics. Does this mean that statements about environmental and social concern are mere hypocrisy? Or is there a hierarchy of values, in which profits come first, because the firm can't survive without them, but then come other social and environmental concerns? This is an ethical landscape that is not divided into black and white, self-interest or social responsibility, but a complex and dynamic balance of profits, people and planet. The researcher quoted above seems appalled by the cynicism of the hotel firms, but perhaps fails to notice the debate and challenge that go on inside most companies, and increasingly with NGOs and local civil organizations. Ethics are the expression of this debate and contest – outcomes of real-time decision-making in real-place contexts. Abstract principles are just one of the inputs to ethical business, not the sum total.

In this section we have concentrated mainly on profit-oriented companies, and framed the dichotomy between principles and pragmatism in terms of values versus profits. But a similar dichotomy can also bedevil public organizations, especially in a political domain: it can be hard to distinguish a clear line between personal gain and public good. Ethical leadership is seldom a zero-sum game – an either/or possibility. Although many leaders would like to think of themselves as primarily driven by principles, or by pragmatism, neither is exclusive of the other.

FURTHER READING

Creaton, Siobhan (2007) *Ryanair: the full story of the controversial low-cost airline*. London: Aurum Press.

Friedman, M. (1970) 'The social responsibility of business is to increase its profits', *New York Times Magazine*, September 13.

Haslam, S.A., Reicher, S. and Platow, M. (2011) *The New Psychology of Leadership: identity, influence and power*. New York: Psychology Press.

Johnson, Craig E. (2011) *Meeting the Ethical Challenge of Leadership*. Thousand Oaks, CA: Sage.

Kakabadse, Andrew and Kakabadse, Nada (2007) *Corporate Social Responsibility in Practice: delving deep*. London: Palgrave Macmillan.

Ladkin, D. (2010) *Rethinking Leadership*. Cheltenham: Edward Elgar.

Laszlo, Chris and Zhexembayeva, Nadya (2011). *Embedded Sustainability: the next big competitive advantage*. Stanford, CA: Stanford University Press.

McLean, B. and Elkind, P. (2003) *The Smartest Guys in the Room: the amazing rise and scandalous fall of Enron*. New York: Penguin.

Northouse, Peter Guy (2010) *Leadership: theory and practice*. Thousand Oaks, CA: Sage.

Porter, Michael E. and Prahalad, C.K. (2003) *Harvard Business Review on CSR*. Boston, MA: Harvard Business School Press.

Remme, J., Jones, S., van der Heijden, B. and de Bono, S. (2007) *Leadership, Change and Responsibility*. Oxford: Meyer & Meyer.

Rok, B. (2009) 'Ethical context of the participative leadership model: taking people into account', *Corporate Governance*, 9 (4): 461–472.

Vogel, David (2005) *The Market for Virtue: the potential and limits of Corporate Social Responsibility*. Washington, DC: The Brookings Institution.

in this book we have presented 'concepts of leadership' as a series of dichotomies: is leadership like this, or like that (and should it be one or the other)? These dichotomies are constructs – artificially created intellectual structures on which to hang the evidence, which is leadership as observed in practice. Each construct gives a specific shape to our enquiry – a construct that stretches between EQ and IQ will show up different aspects of leadership from one that compares East and West. We have selected 33 constructs that we believe expose as much as possible of leadership. Some of our constructs are designed to provide better descriptions of leadership – what to look for and how to understand it. Some aim to guide a more normative approach – what leadership should be like. Some express commonly held prejudices, and we hope our discussions and examples provoke a greater nuance and tolerance of differences.

Overall our aim has been to inform talk and study about leadership by bringing to the surface the key concepts that are mobilized in leadership studies – concepts such as authority, transformation, intelligence, trust and so forth. These are abstractions, and we have chosen to show how they are used in the 33 constructed dichotomies that (we suggest) characterize leadership studies. Readers who would like to pursue abstract concepts through the text will find many listed in the Index, with references to the pages and entries in which they are applied.

There is one big dichotomy we have not included in our 33 topics: are leaders born or made? Our answer has to be, as with all the preceding topics, both – and it depends what you want to do with this question. People who become leaders were born, like anyone else, with some physical and emotional characteristics inherited from relatives, and like anyone else they have been through experiences that shaped them. This is not so interesting; more the point – why are you asking? What do you hope to gain, in terms of understanding, by framing the question like this? Is it because you want to argue that anyone can learn how to lead? Or that you would like to express your admiration for someone who always takes charge of the situation? As we have shown, the most fruitful approach to apparently simple 'either–or' questions (born or made) is to look for ways in which both might be true. Then, the even more interesting stage is to follow the trails that are exposed by posing this question. To the extent that leaders are 'made', how are they made, by which processes and at what costs? In this book we have tried to establish a rhythm alternating between concept and example, asking, 'What does this look like in practice?' So, to stick with the born-or-made theme, let's think of some leaders who have been made, people put into situations in which they have had to lead, and as we tell their story, let's work out which theories and models are useful – perhaps theories of learning, teamwork, psychological types, and so forth. In this way the construct of 'born-or-made' becomes clear: an architecture consisting of concepts, models, theories, examples and perspectives.

The 33 constructs in this book are set up as dichotomies, two options in tension, as if one must be torn between them. None are outright contradictions – if one extreme is true, the other must be false. Most are juxtapositions, in which one proposition is put alongside another, not as a direct opposite, rather because they throw light on each other. For example, Goal-oriented Leadership and Opportunistic Leadership juxtaposes concepts that are not really opposites to each other (a goal-oriented person can be opportunistic, and an opportunist can focus on goals); but the point is that by constructing our enquiry in these terms we are able to discover something about the relationships between the two, and to understand varieties of leadership practice (and theories) in terms of the assumptions they make about opportunism and goal-orientation. An analogy for the way we have used juxtaposition is that we have laid the concepts out like a railway track, side by side, held together and also held apart, not destined to blend into one, but useful precisely because they are laid out like this. And proceeding along one rail means one is also proceeding along the other. So to pick up the same example, as we looked more deeply at goal-orientation, we also came to appreciate the nuances about opportunism. This structure has been important for the book, setting it apart from traditional encyclopaedias that seek to find definitions of concepts like these in abstraction from each other.

In some of our topics the concepts are more loosely contrasted; that is, there is no inherent or necessary opposition, but by examining them together each is brought into clearer focus – like switching perspective between foreground and background, as a means to bring greater and clarity and depth to each. Leading volunteers and leading employees, for example, involves no fundamentally different issues, techniques or dilemmas. But by contrasting them we are able to expose questions of motivation and authority that are pertinent to both, but which might have remained hidden if we hadn't asked, 'What is the difference between leading volunteers and paid employees?'

So in conclusion we hope that this book provides keys to understanding concepts of leadership – where these concepts come from, how they are constructed, their uses and misuses. We believe that having these keys to concepts, readers will be better able to appreciate what we are calling the 'key concepts in leadership studies'.

Bibliography

Abelson, R.P., Gregg, A. and Frey, K.P. (2004) *Experiments With People: revelations from social psychology*. Mahwah, NY: Lawrence Erlbaum.

Adair, J. (1973) *Action-Centred Leadership*. New York: McGraw-Hill.

Andrews, T. (ed.) (2009) *Cross-cultural Management: critical perspectives on business and management*. London: Routledge.

Badaracco, Joseph L. Jr. (2002a) *Leading Quietly: an unorthodox guide to doing the right thing*. Boston: Harvard Business School Publishing.

Badaracco, Joseph L. Jr. (2002b) 'A lesson for the times: learning from quiet leaders', *Ivey Business Journal*, January/February, 1–6.

Bass, B.M. (1985) *Leadership and Performance Beyond Expectations*. New York: Free Press.

Bass, B.M. (1998) *Transformational Leadership: industrial, military and educational impact*. Mahwah, NJ: Lawrence Erlbaum.

Bass, B. M. and Riggio, R. E. (2006) *Transformational Leadership*, 2nd edition. Mahwah, NJ: Lawrence Erlbaum.

Belbin, R.M. (1993) *Team Roles at Work*. Oxford: Butterworth Heinemann.

Belbin, R.M. (2000) *Beyond the Team*. Oxford: Butterworth Heinemann.

Belbin, R.M. (2004) *Management Teams: why they succeed or fail*. Oxford: Elsevier/Butterworth Heinemann.

Bevan, J. (2007) *The Rise and Fall of Marks & Spencer…and How It Rose Again*. London: Profile Books.

Birkenshaw, J. and Crainer, S. (2004) *Leadership the Sven-Göran Erikson Way*. London: Capstone.

Bion, W.R. (1963) *Learning from Experience*. London: Heinemann.

Blair, Tony (2010) *A Journey*. London: Hutchinson.

Blake, R.R. and Mouton, J.S. (1964) *The Managerial Grid*. Houston, TX: Gulf Publications.

Blanchard, K. (2007) *The Secret*. San Francisco, CA: Berrett-Koehler.

Bolden, R. (2011) 'Distributed leadership in organizations: a review of theory and research', *International Journal of Management Reviews*, 13(3).

Bolden, R., Hawkins, B., Gosling, J. and Taylor, S. (2011) *Exploring Leadership: individual, organizational and societal perspectives*. Oxford: Oxford University Press.

Borton, Lady and Ryder, P. R. (2000) 'Working in a Vietnamese voice', *Academy of Management Executive*, 14(4): 20–31.

Burns, James MacGregor (1978) *Leadership*. New York: Harper & Row.

Case, Peter and Gosling, Jonathan (2007) 'Wisdom of the moment: premodern perspectives on organizational action', *Social Epistemology*, special issue on Wisdom and Stupidity in Management, 22 (4).

Casey, Susan (2007) 'Patagonia – the coolest company on the planet', *Fortune*, 12 April, 155 (6) .

Champey, J.A. (1993) *Re-engineering the Corporation: a manifesto for business revolution*. New York: Harper Business Books.

Colvin, Geoff (2009) 'How to Build Great Leaders', *Fortune*, 4 December, 160 (10), http://money.cnn.com/magazines/fortune/fortune_archive/2009

Conger, Jay Alden and Kanungo, RabindraNath (1998) *Charismatic Leadership in Organizations*. Thousand Oaks, CA: Sage.

Copeland, Michael V. (2010) 'Google: the search party is over', *Fortune*, August, 162 (3), http://money.cnn.com/magazines/fortune/fortune_archive/2010.

Cotter, David A., Hermsen, Joan M., Ovadia, Seth and Vanneman, Reece (2001) 'The glass ceiling effect', *Social Forces*, 80 (2): 655–81.

Creaton, Siobhan (2007) *Ryanair: the full story of the controversial low-cost airline*. London: Aurum Press.

Dawkins, R. (1976) *The Selfish Gene*. Oxford: Oxford University Press.

de Bono, S., Jones, S. and van der Heijden, B. (2008) *Managing Cultural Diversity*. Oxford: Meyer & Meyer.

Dowd, Maureen (2005) *Are Men Necessary? When sexes collide*. London: Headline Book Publishing.

Drucker, P., guru interview, Part One, page 3, http://www.emeraldinsight.com/drucker.pdf

Dyer, F. (2005) *Why Do I Do This Every Day? Finding meaning in your work*. Oxford: Lion Hudson.

Emery, F. and Trist, E. (1960) 'Socio-technical systems', in C.W.Churchman and M. Verhulst (eds), *Management Sciences*. London: Pergamon.

Fiedler, F.E. (1964) 'A contingency model of leadership effectiveness', in L. Berkowitz (ed.), *Advances in Experimental Social Psychology*. New York: Academic Press.

Fiedler, F.E. (1967) *A Theory of Leadership Effectiveness*. New York: McGraw-Hill.

Fleishman, E.A. and Harris, E.F (1962) 'Patterns of leadership behavior related to employee grievances and turnover', *Personnel Psychology*, 15: 43–56.

French, R. and Simpson, P. (2010) 'The Work Group: redressing the balance in Bion's Experiences in Groups', *Human Relations* 63(12): 1859–1878.

Friedman, M. (1970) 'The social responsibility of business is to increase its profits', *New York Times Magazine*, 13 September.

Fryer, B. (2004) 'The micromanager', *Harvard Business Review*, September, 31–40.

George, J.M. and Jones, G.R. (2002) *Organizational Behaviour*. Upper Saddle River, NJ: Prentice-Hall.

Gerstner, L. (2002) *Who Says Elephants Can't Dance?* New York: HarperCollins.

Gladwell, M. (2008) *Blink: the power of thinking without thinking*. New York: Time Warner.

Goleman, D. (1998) 'What makes a leader?', *Harvard Business Review*, November–December, 94–102.

Greenleaf, Robert K. (2002) *The Servant Leader Within: a transformative path*, ed. Hamilton Beazley, Julie Begg and Larry C. Spears. Mahwah, NJ: Paulist Press.

Greenleaf, Robert K. and Spears, Larry C. (1977). *Servant Leadership: a journey into the nature of legitimate power and greatness*. Mahwah, NJ: Paulist Press.

Gronn, Peter (2002) 'Distributed leadership as a unit of analysis', *Leadership Quarterly*, 13 (4): 423–451.

Gronn, Peter (2008) 'The future of distributed leadership', *Journal of Educational Administration*, 46 (2): 141–158.

Groysberg, Boris, Nanda, Ashish and Nohria, Nitin (2004) 'The risky business of hiring stars', *Harvard Business Review*, May, 92–100.

Handy, C. (1984) *The Future of Work: a guide to a changing society*. New York: Blackwell.

Handy, C. (1992) *Understanding Organizations*. Harmondsworth: Penguin.

Handy, C. (1995) *Gods of Management: the changing work of organizations*. Oxford: Oxford University Press.

Handy, C. (1996) *Beyond Certainty: the changing worlds of organizations*. Boston: Harvard Business School Press.

Handy, C. (2000) *21 Ideas for Managers: Practical Wisdom for Managing Your Company and Yourself*. San Francisco, CA: Jossey-Bass.

Haslam, S.A., Reicher, S. and Platow, M. (2011) *The New Psychology of Leadership: identity, influence and power*. Hove and New York: Psychology Press.

Heifetz, R. (1994) *Leadership Without Easy Answers*. Cambridge, MA: Harvard University Press.

Hersey, P. and Blanchard, K. (1988) *The Management of Organizational Behavior*. Upper Saddle River, NJ: Prentice-Hall.

Hofstede, G. (1980) 'Motivating, leadership and organization: do American theories apply abroad?', *Organizational Dynamics*, 9(1): 42–63.

Hofstede, G. (1991) *Cultures and Organizations: software of the mind*. London: McGraw-Hill.

Hofstede, G. (1993) 'Cultural constraints in management theories', *Academy of Management Executive*, 7 (1): 81–94.

Hofstede, G. (2001) *Culture's Consequences: comparing values, behaviors, institutions and organizations across nations* (2nd edition). Thousand Oaks, CA: Sage.

House, R.J. and Baetz, M.L. (1979) 'Leadership: some empirical generalizations and new research directions', in B.M. Straw and L.L. Cummings (eds), *Research in Organizational Behaviour*. Greenwich, CT: JAI Press.

Hyatt, Josh (2010) 'Building Your Brand (and keeping your job)' *Fortune*, 16 August, 162 (3): 50–55.

Jones, David (2005) *NEXT to Me: luck, leadership and living with Parkinson's*. London: Nicholas Brealey.

Jones, S. (1989) *The Headhunting Business*. London: Macmillan.

Jones, S. (1991) *Working for the Japanese*. London: Macmillan.

Jones, S. (1999) 'Managing people in China', unpublished manuscript.

Jones, S. (2000) 'Beyond the stereotypes: the changing face of China's workplace', *China Staff*, VI (9): 19–24.

Jones, S. (2008) 'Training and cultural context in the Arab Emirates: fighting a losing battle?', *Employment Relations*, 30 (1): 48–62.

Jones, S. (2009) 'Implementing software for managing organizational training and development: an example of consulting to a large public sector organization in the State of Kuwait', *International Journal of Commerce and Management*, 19 (4): 260–277.

Jones, S. (2010) *Psychological Testing*. Petersfield: Harriman House.

Jones, S. and Duffy, P. (2009a) 'Staying on top in project management', *The Effective Executive*, October, 12(10): 34–39.

Jones, S. and Duffy, P. (2009b) 'Twelve reasons for project management failure', *The Global CEO*, October: 11–15.

Jones, S. and Gosling, J. (2005) *Nelson's Way: leadership lessons from the great commander*. London: Nicholas Brealey.

Katzenbach, J. and Smith, D. (1994) *The Wisdom of Teams*. New York: Harper Business.

Kowitt, B, and Thai, K. (2009) '25 top companies for leaders, *Fortune*: http://money.cnn.com/2009/11/19/news/companies/top_leadership_companies.fortune/

Ladkin, Donna (2006) 'The enchantment of the charismatic leader: charisma reconsidered as aesthetic encounter', *Leadership*, 2 (2): 165–179.

Ladkin, Donna (2010) *Rethinking Leadership: a new look at old questions*. Cheltenham: Edward Elgar.

Langley, Ann (1995) 'Between "paralysis by analysis" and "extinction by instinct"', *MIT Sloan Management Review*, Spring: 63–76.

Laszlo, Chris and Zhexembayeva, Nadya (2011) *Embedded Sustainability: the next big competitive advantage*. Stanford, CA: Stanford University Press.

Leithwood, Kenneth A., Muscall, Blair and Strauss, Tiiu (2009) *Distributed Leadership According to the Evidence*. New York: Routledge.

Lukes, S. (1974) *Power: A radical view*. London: Macmillan.

McDonough, W. and Braungart, M. (2002) *Cradle to Cradle: remaking the way we make things*. New York: North Point Press.

Maslow, Abraham (1954) *Motivation and Personality*. London: Harper & Row

McGregor, D. (1960) *The Human Side of Enterprise*. New York: McGraw-Hill.

McLean, B. and Elkind, P. (2003) *The Smartest Guys in the Room: the amazing rise and scandalous fall of Enron*. New York: Penguin Books.

Mintzberg, H. (1973) *The Nature of Managerial Work*. New York: Harper & Row.

Mintzberg, H. (1983) *Structure in Fives: designing effective organizations*. Englewood Cliffs, NJ: Prentice-Hall.

Mintzberg, H. (1994) *The Rise and Fall of Strategic Planning: reconceiving roles for planning, plans, planners*. New York: Free Press.

Moodian, M. (ed.) (2009) *Contemporary Leadership and Intercultural Competence: exploring the cross-cultural dynamics within organizations.* London: Sage.

Moran, R., Harris, P. and Moran, S. (2010) *Managing Cultural Differences: global leadership strategies for cross-cultural business success.* Oxford: Butterworth-Heinemann.

More Torres, D.A. and Jones, S. (2010) 'A changing scene: comparing business cultures in Peru and the Netherlands', *Global Business and Organisational Excellence*, May/June: 53–66.

Morrison, A., White, R. and Van Velsor, E. (1987) *Breaking the Glass Ceiling: can women reach the top of America's largest corporations?* Cambridge, MA: Perseus Books.

Peace, William H. (1991) 'The hard work of the soft manager', *Harvard Business Review* (reprinted December 2001), 79(11): 99–105.

Pfeffer, J. (1994) *Managing With Power: politics and influence in organizations.* Boston: Harvard Business School Press.

Prahalad, C.K. (2006) *The Fortune at the Bottom of the Pyramid: eradicating poverty through profits.* Upper Saddle River, NJ: Wharton School Publishing.

Raelin, J. (2011) From leadership-as-practice to leaderful practice, *Leadership*, 7(2): 195–211.

Remme, J., Jones, S., van der Heijden, B. and de Bono, S. (2008) *Leadership, Change and Responsibility.* Oxford: Meyer & Meyer.

Rock, David (2009) *Quiet Leadership.* London: HarperCollins.

Rooke, D. and Torbert, W. (2005) 'The seven transformations of leadership', *Harvard Business Review*, April: 66–76.

Ryan, M.K. and Haslam, S. A. (2005) 'The glass cliff: evidence that women are over-represented in precarious leadership positions', *British Journal of Management*, 16: 81–90.

Salovey, P. and Mayer, J.D. (1990) 'Emotional intelligence', *Imagination, Cognition, and Personality*, 9: 185–211.

Sforza, L. and Perret, J.-D. (2011) *6th European HR Barometer: trends and perspectives on the human resources function in Europe.* London: AON Hewitt.

Spillane, James P. (2006) *Distributed Leadership.* San Francisco, CA: Jossey-Bass.

Stidl, D. and Bradach, J. (2009) 'How visionary nonprofits leaders are learning to enhance management capabilities', *Strategy and Leadership*, 37 (1): 35–40.

Stogdill, R.M. (1974) *Handbook of Leadership: a survey of the literature.* New York: Free Press.

Trach, E. and Thompson, K.J. (2007) 'Trading places: examining leadership competencies between for-profits vs. public and no-profit leaders', *Leadership and Organizational Development Journal*, 28 (4): 356–375.

Thomas, K.W. and Kilmann, R.H. (1974) *The Thomas Kilmann Mode of Conflict Inventory.* New York: Xicom.

Trompenaars, F. and Hampden-Turner, C. (1997) *Riding the Waves of Culture: understanding cultural diversity in business.* London: Nicholas Brealey.

Ulrich, Dave (1997) *HR Champions.* Boston: Harvard University Press.

Watson, T.J. (2002) *Organising and Managing Work: organisational, managerial and strategic behaviour in theory and practice.* London: Prentice-Hall.

Welch, J. (2005) *Winning.* New York: HarperCollins.

Western, S. (2008) *Leadership: a critical text.* London: Sage.

Whittington, J. Lee, Coker, Renee H., Goodwin, Vicki L., Ickies, William and Murry, Brian (2009) 'Transactional leadership revisited: self-other agreement and its consequences', *Journal of Applied Social Psychology*, 39 (8): 1860–1886.

key concepts in leadership

concept index

concept index

163

name index